Angel on My Shoulder

Remembrances at Eighty

Christopher G. Janus

West Virginia Library Commission Foundation
Charleston, W. Va.

Copyright © 1993 by Christopher G. Janus and
West Virginia Library
Commission Foundation

All rights reserved. No part of this book may be used or reproduced in any form by any means, or stored in a database or retrieval system, without prior written permission of Christopher G. Janus or the West Virginia Library Commission Foundation except in the case of brief quotations embodied in critical articles and reviews. Making copies of any part of this publication for any other purposes other than personal use is a violation of United States copyright laws.

International Standard Book Number: 0-87012-501-X

Library of Congress Catalog Card Number: 93-091421

Printed and bound in the United States of America by McClain Printing Co., Parsons, W. Va.

Distributed by Sheffield Books, P.O. Box 10334, Chicago, IL 60610.

For my loving and strong family, and my loyal and joyful friends—this book is for you. Enjoy and share!

BOOKS AND PUBLISHING PROJECTS

By CHRISTOPHER G. JANUS

ONLY FOR YOUR EYES   First Printing 1961
Quadrangle Press, Chicago
West Virginia Library Commission   Second Printing 1992
Charleston, W. Va.

GREEK HERITAGE QUARTERLY   1963-1964
Kimon Friar, Editor
Athens, Greece

EIGHTEEN TEXTS   (U.S. Edition) 1972
Willis Barnstone, Editor
Harvard University Press
Cambridge, Mass.

SEARCH FOR PEKING MAN   First Printing 1975
(with William Brashler)
Macmillan Publishing Co., Inc.
New York

SEARCH FOR PEKING MAN DOCUMENTARY   1977
Canadian Broadcasting Corp.
Christopher Plummer, Narrator

MISS 4TH OF JULY, GOODBYE   First Printing 1985
Sheffield Books
Lakeview Press   Second Printing 1989
Chicago
(made into *A DISNEY PREMIERE MOVIE* 1988)

WHAT THEY ALWAYS WANTED   First Printing 1988
Sheffield Books
R. R. Donnelley & Sons Company
Chicago

ANGEL ON MY SHOULDER   First Printing 1993
West Virginia Library
    Commission Foundation
Charleston, W. Va.

Contents

Foreword	vii
Preface	xi
Acknowledgments	xiii
West Virginia, Goodbye	3
Harvard Years	24
An Interlude with Santayana	36
On the Wadham Crew	51
Decisions, Decisions, Decisions	65
Greek War Relief	82
I Enter the War	89
The Greek Civil War	102
On Tour with Hitler's Car	114
Dancing Girls in Winnetka?	127
Goldmining at Maravilla	136
Bache and Company	155
Greek Heritage	175
President Johnson Meets Prime Minister Papandreou	186
Intervals in a Life	195
Greatest Event since Creation	214
A Birthday Party for Persepolis	222

The Search for Peking Man	235
Poets at the White House	247
No Sale at the Taj Mahal	258
An Irresistible Prank in Bali	268
Cricket's Love Song	276
Beatrice	284
Big Bash at Eighty	288
In the Offing	299
Epilogue: Great Grandfather George	304

Foreword

At long last we have Christopher Janus's memoirs—a cause for celebration! Not only are they vastly entertaining, as expected, but they remain always light-hearted. Through subtle example, they show a way of life characterized by courage, humor, success against great odds, great creativity, and, above all, tolerance, warm understanding, and a generosity, in many instances totally undeserved, toward his fellow men and women. Chris Janus offers us a world and a man seldom seen today. His way of life will appeal to all but the faint-hearted.

Because of his stories—and he is above all else a great storyteller—he has been called a "Greek Somerset Maugham," but the ancestry of his race goes beyond that: to Aesop, Homer, and all the ancient and modern Greeks who either in song, poetry or prose, or just conversation over an ouzo in a taverna have a special God-given calling for storytelling. Janus shares in that calling today.

Even though his early years as the son of Greek immigrants in West Virginia suggest a humble background, his parents raised him with love and pride for his heritage. They recognized his early bent for literature and the arts, and although they felt that being a writer or a teacher was not the best way to earn a living (and as much as they may have needed his support) they encouraged him to pursue a literary life; what they called a "nonbusiness" life.

His early scholastic achievements made it possible for him to go to Harvard, where he was a student of Alfred North Whitehead, and to pursue further studies at Oxford. (And during the reading period at Oxford, he studied with George Santayana in Rome.) At this time, he was also writing not only short stories but a weekly column, "Inside Out," for the Montclair, New Jersey, *Times* and the "Student Vagabond" column for the *Harvard Crimson*.

Throughout his life he has met and in many instances formed friendships with some of the prominent personalities of his era. Among them are Sir Maurice Bowra, Somerset Maugham, Winston Churchill, Robert Hutchins, Mortimer Adler, James Bryant Conant, Aristotle Onassis, King Constantine of Greece, Margaret Thatcher, George Seferis, George Papandreou, the Shah of Iran, Haile Selassie, Bernard Baruch, King Farouk (they played poker together), Lord Keith Joseph, Harry Mark Petrakis, Robert Frost, T. S. Eliot, Carl Sandburg, Franklin D. Roosevelt, Gerald Ford, Jimmy Carter, Adlai Stevenson, Henry Kissinger, Charles Percy, David and Jay Rockefeller, Robert Moses, Otto Kerner, Jay Pritzker, Huntington Hartford, John Swearingen, Spyros Skouras, and Art Nielsen. In the sports world he numbers Jack Dempsey, whom he met as a boy in West Virginia, as a friend, as well as Red Grange ("the galloping ghost"), Jack Brickhouse, a fellow member of The Tavern Club, and Mohammed Ali, who read Janus his poetry and wanted his help in getting it published in *Poetry Magazine*.

These memoirs also tell tales of a lifetime of entrepreneuring activities: from investment banking with Bache & Co., to publishing the highly praised *Greek Heritage Quarterly*; from owning and managing a gold mine in Brazil to acquiring Hitler's armored parade car to conducting the widely publicized search for the Peking Man fossils and most recently to having Disney make an award-winning movie based on his book *Miss 4th of July, Goodbye*.

Constantly observing and always creative, Christopher Janus makes new friends and enjoys life wherever he goes and whatever he does, keeping a diary in Samuel Pepys fashion. His memoirs will captivate you, and be on your guard: they could influence your own style of life! Finally, as you read these memoirs you get the feeling Chris Janus at eighty has just begun!

David Grafton

Preface

Shortly before my eightieth birthday, author Harry Mark Petrakis and I had lunch at Chicago's Tavern Club, where he urged me to write my autobiography. "There is a valuable and interesting story here," he said, "but you must not leave out anything, and above all, tell all, tell the truth." Actually, one of my publishers had also asked me to write my memoirs and urged the same thing: "Above all, tell all. Tell the truth."

I hope they didn't bring up this business about telling the truth because they thought I had some great, dark, mysterious secret to share (I don't), but rather because they believe that an autobiography is more interesting, perhaps more saleable, and certainly more valuable as literature if it is complete and is completely truthful. The demand of completeness may seem a fair one, but can I honestly convince myself to tell the whole truth and nothing but, if the truth could be hurtful to someone? Not necessarily to me (which I can handle) but hurtful to someone else?

When I started these memoirs, I still had not decided which way to go, but now my feeling is that there is already so much malice and sorrow and unhappiness in the world, I don't want this book to add to it. Truth must always be the goal of science—and in science there can be no exceptions for holding it back—but the importance of "the whole truth" at all times in our relationships with each other remains, in my opinion, greatly overvalued.

Some examples. A once good friend, a Greek general during the 1967 dictatorship, was the mastermind of the most grievous and cruel tortures ever inflicted on innocent people in Greek history. He has since reformed and is now perfectly respectable, with an innocent wife and lovely young daughters. Do I owe it to "truth" to expose him when I shall at the same time be exposing them to the shame they haven't deserved? On a humorous but nevertheless tragic note, I once played an elaborate practical joke on a dear friend, and he died (not from the prank!) believing that a beautiful, socially prominent Philadelphian wanted to marry him (actually she was an actress we hired to play the part). My friend died happy but believing a lie. Should I have told him the truth? No, truth and completeness may be important, but so are privacy, loyalty, and compassion. In this book, I tell the truth about myself. But not the whole truth.

Christopher Janus

Acknowledgments

I thank Susan Laity, who edited and restructured the memoirs. I've worked with many editors on my books. She is the most enthusiastic. It is doubtful if the memoirs would have ever been written without the prodding, encouragement, and all around expert help of Valerie Valentine. Through thick and thin she is always on my side. I thank author David Grafton, one of our most gifted writers today, for his most generous introduction. I am grateful to Frederic Glazer, Director of the West Virginia Library Commission, for his warm friendship and exceedingly valuable suggestions and for being most instrumental in bringing my books and other writings to more readers in West Virginia. Finally, I'm deeply indebted to and thank artist David Martin for reading the memoirs in manuscript form and doing the beautiful jacket for *Angel on My Shoulder*.

Angel on My Shoulder

Remembrances at Eighty

West Virginia, Goodbye

I'm not writing the history of my life which, as history, is hardly of any great importance. I'm writing of things I remember best (not necessarily in chronological order), and which I think can be of general interest.

I am writing this autobiography in Belgrade, Maine, where my daughter, Niki, and her husband, David Davis, have a beautiful modern house on the lake. My whole family is together: Niki and Dave, my son Chris, his wife, Thea, and their daughter, Olivia, and my son Lincoln and his wife, Myra, and their children, Alexander, Elizabeth, and Nicholas (born March 25, which also happens to be my birthday). Niki is very calm and hospitable in the face of this invasion. After I read part of my notes to the assembled group, Olivia, who is nine, asked what the title *Angel on My Shoulder* meant, and why did I choose it. I'm not sure how to explain this without sounding too mysterious or pompous—and of course, just because I believe in it doesn't mean it's true.

As I look back on my life, I've always felt that some force was motivating and guiding me, a force that had nothing to do with particular circumstances of place, time, or action. For example, there was nothing about my life or family in Montgomery, West Virginia, where I grew up, that was likely to inspire anyone to be a teacher of philosophy and a writer. Yet that is what I wished to do. At the age of thirteen, when I mentioned my ambitions to my mother, she, a very loving but practical person, objected, "And how will you earn a living? We are starting a new life in this country (my family had recently emigrated from Greece), and thanks to your father we are surviving, but he is not well." I could not fault my mother for her advice, but on the other hand, I felt driven to study philosophy (of course, at that age, I knew little about what such study entailed, nor even whether I had a talent for scholarship). Where did my ambition come from? Not from books—there wasn't a library in Montgomery at the time—not from friends or teachers, and certainly not from my surroundings, which were beautiful to look at, but dominated by the figures of moonshiners, coal miners, and the Ku Klux Klan. And I cannot believe that the feelings arose simply from my being Greek—Plato and Socrates calling to me through my genes. What drove me? To me it is clear only that something did, and that something has continued to drive and protect me in various ways throughout my life.

Symbolically, call that force an angel. Maybe everyone has one, I don't know. But I know that there have been so many adverse occurrences in my life that could have caused others to fail, or give up, or just plain die. But as I tell my story, the reader may see how the angel and I have prevailed—for the most part, I hope, with dignity and joy. Over the years, my angel has taken me far from Montgomery, but I'd like to start my memoirs with the time it brought me back, in 1991, at the age of eighty, when I was invited as an honored guest to attend the centennial celebration of the founding of the town.

In 1985 I wrote an epistolary novel called *Miss 4th of July, Goodbye*. Disney Productions liked the book and made it into an excellent movie, which was nominated for four Emmy Awards. The book and the movie tell the story of my family, who came from Greece in 1910 and eventually settled in Montgomery, West Virginia, twenty-seven miles east of Charleston, the capital. Montgomery had a population then of some 2,000 people (it's only about 2,200 today), and like so much of the rest of the state, it was economically dependent on the coal industry. It was a nice enough little town, situated on the Kanawha River, nestled among the beautiful Appalachian Hills. Why and how my family—my father, George, my mother, Olympia, my brothers, Trefon and Alexander, and my fifteen-year-old sister, Androniki (Niki)—ended up in West Virginia while most immigrant families during that time stayed in New York and Boston is a mystery to me, but they did, and my father eventually found a job with a chemical company near Montgomery and also had an interest in a restaurant (what else?) in Montgomery. Apparently he got along fairly well, with one ugly exception.

Montgomery at that time was dominated by the notorious Ku Klux Klan. Your specific race, nationality, or religion, whether black, Catholic, Jewish, or Greek made little difference: unless you were a white Protestant, you were not a first-class citizen. You did not fit in with the Klan's white-supremacist philosophy. Nearly every Saturday night in Montgomery the Klan, wearing their white masks and gowns, would march down Main Street and then, at about 9 o'clock at night, they would burn a cross on a nearby hill or in front of some particular family's house. During the fifteen years that the Janus family lived in Montgomery several crosses were burnt in our front yard, but for some reason my father, who was a strong and jovial man, told us not to be afraid and not to take the burning cross in our front yard too personally. "It is a gesture that the Klan makes against all foreigners and blacks—not necessarily just against us," he claimed. Even at the age of seven or so, when I saw my first cross burning in our yard, I did not find my father's assessment of the situation very convincing. Later I discovered that on many occasions after the Klan had burnt the cross on the hill or in our front yard, some of its members would come over to the house (I was made to go to bed) and kill a couple of bottles of moonshine liquor with "good old George." "We don't mean you no harm," they assured him. I once heard one of the Klansmen say that my father was a survivor. He seemed to agree with this. "We survived the Turks," he would say, "and the Klan's cruelty is nothing compared to the Turks."

My sister, Niki, would not tolerate this behavior, however, and she, not my father, is the central character of *Miss 4th of July, Goodbye*. She was about fifteen when we arrived in Montgomery, and in Greece she had received an excellent education. She knew seven different languages and she had a rebel's spirit. She strongly disapproved of my father's having anything to do with the Klan and once during one of the Klan's Saturday-night drinking sessions at our home she ordered them all out of the house. I believe my father and most of his Klan buddies were too intoxicated at the time to do anything but leave. Niki was so angry that she yelled at them in both Greek and English, which awakened me, so I saw the whole thing. Before my father passed out, he weakly reprimanded Niki for violating the Greek's code of hospitality. Niki was never afraid of the Klan—nor do I believe my father feared them—but Niki was angry. The Klan violated every sense of what America stood for in her mind. And she fought the Klan by writing articles in the newspaper, petitioning the governor, and organizing a little march in Montgomery against it. Essentially, the book *Miss 4th of July, Goodbye* is about Niki's confrontation with the Klan: her success and her tragedy.

The book and later the Disney movie (which they entitled *Goodbye, Miss 4th of July*) were the chief reasons, I believe, for my being invited to Montgomery in celebration of their centennial. They also invited my daughter, Niki Janus, who bears the same name as the heroine of the book. We had a wonderful time and the people of Montgomery could not have been more kind, warm, and hospitable. The prime movers of our involvement in the centennial were Melba Lou White and her husband, Bill. Melba had read my book several times, had arranged for it to be read in several of the classes in the Montgomery grade school, and later had showed it to many of her friends in Montgomery.

I decided to return to Montgomery the way my family first arrived in West Virginia in 1910—by train. When I called Metro in Chicago to make the reservations they could not be very accommodating. They could offer only a lounge seat, not a sleeping room. I took it, consoling myself that when my family made the trip from New York, they had probably had to sit up all night too, probably not by choice but because they couldn't afford a stateroom.

I boarded the Metro train, the *Cardinal*, at the Union Station in Chicago, with the help of an obliging porter who directed me to my reclining seat in coach. We were about a half hour late in leaving (the electrical system malfunctioned in one of the cars) and I was contemplating the prospect of spending the night out of a comfortable bed (ever since I was a child I have always needed eight hours of good sleep). Just as I was getting used to my situation, however, the genial conductor approached me and asked if I were Christopher Janus. (My first thought was, Am I on the wrong train? or in the wrong seat? Nothing good went through my weary mind.) But to my great and pleasant surprise he said that a message had gotten through to him that I was a guest of honor at the Montgomery centennial and that he had a stateroom up front for me. I offered him a twenty-dollar tip, which he refused. Then he said, "Have a good night, Senator (I don't know where he got that from), and let me know if I can be of any service."

What a relief, and what a way to start my memorable trip back in time and back to Montgomery!

I arrived about two hours late in Charleston, West Virginia, the following morning, and to my great surprise I was met by Doctor Joseph Skaggs, direct from the Charleston Medical Clinic, and son of the doctor who had been our family doctor when we lived in Montgomery. He was accompanied by Helen Lodge, sister of Melba Lou White and looking very beautiful, and by reporters from two TV stations in Charleston and a reporter from the *Charleston Daily Mail*. After the interviews and pictures I was driven to the Marriott Hotel, where I was given an elegant suite, with flowers from the management welcoming me, along with a note from Senator Jay Rockefeller.

I unpacked my bag, showered, and shaved, and then met Helen Lodge and a friend she brought with her, Sophia Pappas, who apparently knew of some members of my family and is in touch with cousins of mine who now live in California and Texas. Sophia, who is regional manager of the prestigious Stone & Thomas chain of department stores in West Virginia, took us to lunch at the Edgewood Country Club, a charming club nestled in a beautiful hilly countryside. I had a delicious Monte Cristo sandwich. Several friends of Helen and Sophia came over to our table and I was introduced. Apparently all of them knew why I had come back to West Virginia. One gentleman was a black guest (or member) and I could not help thinking to myself: "Charleston, you have come a long way." It was unthinkable back in 1910 when the Janus family first arrived in West Virginia for a black to be a member of a country club, and I'm sure that applied to most foreigners as well. As a matter of fact, I'm not sure Charleston had any country clubs at that time. The town has changed, and in this way for the better, but the Klan is still very visible in West Virginia. They even advertise in the *Charleston Gazette*, the daily newspaper, inviting people to join the Klan, and they have added a "Ladies' Auxiliary." I don't believe they burn crosses the way they used to, and they try to present a more charitable view of their activities—but the purpose of the Klan in West Virginia, Alabama, Mississippi, and elsewhere remains the promotion of white supremacy.

My daughter, Niki, was scheduled to fly in from Washington, D. C., to meet me in Charleston the same morning I arrived, but her plane was delayed and we didn't meet until late in the afternoon. Helen Lodge drove us to Montgomery, where for the first time I met Melba Lou White—and what a wonderful and hospitable lady she is. She and her husband, Bill, cooked a superb dinner for us and at Niki's request gave us a bottle of the moonshine liquor for which West Virginia is well known. But nowadays it isn't necessarily moonshine. You can buy West Virginia moonshine in liquor stores in Montgomery.

Melba Lou arranged for a special showing of *Goodbye, Miss 4th of July* at the West Virginia Institute of Technology auditorium, which, much to our delight, was packed, even though many of the people who attended had already seen the movie on the Disney Channel. Afterward, I was asked to say a few words, and I was moved almost to tears when the audience of over four hundred people gave Niki and me a standing ovation. In my excitement, I forgot to introduce Niki! But the mayor of Montgomery, James Higgins, Jr., saved me, saying, "Now let us hear from Niki Janus, the namesake of the Niki in the movie."

Niki spoke eloquently of how glad she was to be in Montgomery and for the first time come in contact with her family's roots. A small reception followed the showing, where I was asked to sign copies of my book, and where I met not my boyhood friends, like Meredith Arbaugh, Henderson Kelly, Jimmy DuPey, Tommy Robinson, and Doyle Wyckline—they are now all deceased—but their relatives, and friends who knew them.

The following day, Saturday, was the big day of the Montgomery centennial celebration, and the main event was the parade. Niki and I were asked to ride in an open car, sitting on the top of the back seat. Melba Lou and the driver were in the front. Niki turned out to have her own way of waving in a parade. Before coming to Montgomery, she and her husband, Dave, had attended a reception for the queen of England at the British Embassy in Washington, and it seems that Niki had had a conversation with the queen about her royal manner of greeting people and waving in parades. Queen Elizabeth confided that at times during the parade she would use a mechanical waving, gloved arm. She would just sit back, press a button, and smile, while the arm did the waving. So I was very amused to watch Niki wave in our parade. She lacked that mechanical arm, but she used the same stiff, half-wave we've all seen the queen (or her arm!) employ, and she smiled the whole way. Several people broke through the barricade to walk alongside our car and shake hands. One of them was Roger Percy, son of Chuck Percy, who gave us greetings from his distinguished father, the former senator from Illinois and chairman of the Senate Foreign Relations Committee.

The parade was nearly a mile long and was made up of members of the Armed Forces just back from the Persian Gulf, veterans of other wars, the Boy Scouts of Montgomery, the mayor and members of his council, various school bands, representatives of various local women's clubs, the fire and police departments, six very funny clowns who entertained the crowds that lined Main Street, and, of course, Niki and me. It was a wonderful parade and a great day and as I rode along, an honored guest, I wished that my father, mother, and sister, Niki, could have seen it, and I thought about how much Montgomery has changed since the ugly Ku Klux Klan days.

For this parade, of course, had no resemblance to the ones I remembered from my youth, when the KKK would march down Main Street wearing white cloaks with masks covering their faces and burn crosses in front of the houses of blacks and foreigners. As I thought of this, other memories of my youth came flooding back. I still wonder why my parents settled in a small coal mining town dominated by the KKK.

Probably it was because my father had a job opportunity, and there was no future for him in Greece. But what courage it took, especially for my mother, who spoke little English, to leave her home and her friends and bring her children to a new land. They had their proud name changed at Immigration because *Xenopoulos* was "too foreign sounding." My sister, Niki, chose the name Janus. It sounded like part of our name, Xenos, but it was really a reference to the Roman god with two faces: one looks backward and one forward, to the future.

And as I gazed at the beautiful Appalachian Hills, I remembered the special smells and sights and sounds of earlier days. We always knew the time of day by the C & O train, which would blow its whistles at exactly 8:05 p.m. as it passed through Montgomery. I recall the merry calliopes of the showboat and steamboats which would come down the river from Charleston and the ominous shrill from the coal mines—especially the five or six blasts that meant a cave-in or a mine explosion; the special sights from Eagle Rock, a big and high formation on the top of the mountain overlooking Montgomery, where I used to hike each Saturday with my boyhood pals; the fragrant blue grass and beautiful wildflowers covering the valleys. Yes, they all came back to me on that May day in 1991.

While searching for some dates and names relating to my early childhood, I came across a faded notebook, a kind of diary I kept when I was thirteen or fourteen years old. Currently I've two hobbies that occupy me—collecting copies of Omar Khayyam's *Rubáiyát* and collecting walking sticks. Apparently, as a young man I had another hobby: collecting proverbs and quotations. The notebook is full of them, and now I remember how it started: Miss Jenny, my eighth-grade teacher, started each of her classes by writing a quotation on the blackboard. It didn't necessarily have anything to do with the subject we were learning: it was simply a thought for the day for us to remember.

I was really fascinated by these quotations and began writing them in my journal and adding to them as I came across new ones. The last date in the notebook is July 1926. I was then fifteen years old. Why I stopped collecting quotations I don't know, but I have tried to instill an interest in old sayings and proverbs in my grandchildren. I pay them ten cents for every quotation they find and can recite. I believe I'm making progress because last Christmas my son Lincoln and his family gave me a handsome and interesting painting entitled *Proverbidions*, which illustrates some three hundred well-known proverbs. It hangs in my breakfast room so that I can see it every morning, and when the grandchildren come over they head for the painting to pick up a few more ten-cent pieces.

Following are a few of my favorites collected over that three-year period when I was a boy. I do think they say something about me as a young man—a young man I've nearly forgotten:

"Trifles make perfection and perfection is no trifle." Michelangelo.

"It is indeed a good thing to be well descended, but the glory belongs to the ancestors." Plutarch

"I am not a citizen of Athens or Greece; I am a citizen of the world." Socrates

"Do not train boys to learn by force and harshness, but lead them by what amuses them, so that they may better discover the bent of their mind." Plato

"The helping of man by man is God." Pliny

"We do not say that a man who takes no interest in politics minds his own business, we say he has no business here at all." Pericles

"How a man acts when he wins says a lot about him; how he acts when he loses says everything about him." (I don't know who said this, but I still believe it.)

"Take away a man's illusions and he may not cease to exist, but he ceases to live." Mark Twain

"Life is a theater in which the worst people often have the best seats." Aristophanes

I think that if I can credit any one person with fostering my desire to study philosophy, it would be Miss Jenny. Among those quotations were the words of Plato and Herodotus and other great Greek philosophers. She and my sister, Niki, who had read the Greek philosophers as well, instilled in me the beginnings of a love for philosophy that has stayed with me all my life.

A teacher at Montgomery Grade School would take turns presiding at the weekly assemblies. I remember clearly now the times when Miss Jenny would preside, because she always started the meeting by reading from the Proverbs. I don't know why or how we are indelibly impressed with certain happenings in our lives but hearing Miss Jenny read "Happy is the man who findeth wisdom" was a beautiful awakening for me. I cherish it to this day. I bribed each of my children to memorize the lines. When they were young I would pay them ten dollars each Christmas if they could recite it.

Another grade school teacher I remember at school, but for different reasons, I'll call Miss B. (she may still be alive). Miss B. was the prettiest young teacher who ever hit our school. She was from New York and I believe that this was her first teaching job.

She was very bright, enthusiastic, and beautiful. She taught English. All of her boys loved her, but she was in love with our principal, who was too proper or not bright enough to respond, and he broke her heart. As the Greeks say, "You can't hide love or smoke," and this was certainly true with Miss B. When it came her turn to preside at the assembly she recited the beautiful passage from Corinthians on love:

> Love is patient and kind; love is not jealous or boastful; it is not arrogant or rude. Love does not insist on its own way; it is not irritable or resentful; it does not rejoice at wrong, but rejoices in the right. Love bears all things, believes all things, hopes all things, endures all things. Love never ends,

and everybody knew she was talking about her broken heart, and I wrote the verses in my notebook as part of my collection.

Miss B. was full of surprises, but once she did something that was totally unexpected of her. She had one adoring classmate spanked! Spanking was the usual punishment for misbehavior then, but it seemed uncharacteristic of her. Also, when a student was spanked, the teacher was supposed to do it. In this case the boy, Tony DeVito, was so big (about 6 feet 2 inches and over two hundred pounds) and Miss B. so petite (about 5 feet 4 inches, slim, and I guess under one hundred pounds) that she had the principal of the school come to the classroom and do it. He asked Tony to come to the front of the room and lean over a desk, where he gave him about six whacks with a wooden paddle. Tony didn't cry out and he didn't wince; he seemed almost to be showing off in front of his teacher. The principal asked him if he was sorry. He said, "Yes, sir," and that was it, except that as Tony walked back

to his desk, I saw him wink at Miss B., and she almost smiled.
There was one other thing that we thought remarkable about Miss B. She was a "free thinker" about love and sex, and she let us all know it. On one memorable hayride she organized for Halloween, she had us all singing and holding hands on the warm, moonlit night, and she told us that we must not be afraid to express our feelings. They were natural and what was natural was good. Most of us were too young or scared or shy to be that open, and this certainly included me. But there were several "incidents" on that hayride (one way I know is that when incidents occurred, like kissing, hugging, or so forth, the boy was supposed to call out "Eureka!"—this sounds a bit silly now, but it was supposed to be part of the fun). When this reached the ears of O. K. Robinson, then superintendent of schools in Montgomery, beautiful Miss B. was not invited to return for another year. When she left she gave me a couple of books on Greek architecture and a copy of Will Durant's wonderful *Story of Philosophy*. I still treasure these books, which she inscribed to me. Come to think of it, perhaps Miss B. also put the idea in my mind to become a teacher of philosophy. On a lighter note, as we parted, she said: "Christopher, you have such beautiful black hair. Are all Greek children so handsome?" and she kissed me goodbye!
My mother, brother Alexander, and I left Montgomery in 1926. My father, brother Trefon, and wonderful sister had all died from the devastating flu epidemic (more than twenty-six million people died of the flu that started in Spain and spread worldwide). My father apparently had left my mother a little money, and my brother, aged twenty-two and an enterprising inventor,

now was head of the family. He had some thirty-two patents to his name, including patents on an air conditioning system, a traffic light, and a cellophane machine for preserving documents, but the only patent that brought us any immediate money came about from his pioneering inventions in the vending machine business. I believe he invented and developed one of the first vending machines. It dispensed toothpaste and a toothbrush to be used in rest rooms, railroad stations, and, I believe, on trains.

 I remember the time at the railroad station, when we waited for the C & O train to take us east to New York and New Jersey. A group of friends came to the station to see us off. My classmates at Montgomery Junior High School gave me a class ring. Mrs. Henderson Kelly, postmistress and wife of the mayor, brought us some food to take on the train, and some of my brother's buddies gave him three bottles of moonshine whiskey.

 The saddest thing of all was that I had to leave behind my little dog, Prince. I begged my mother to let me take him but my brother refused—he had enough responsibility, he said, as it was. I cried as we left, and to this day I can still see Prince, wagging his tail but whimpering! and by the look on his face, I knew he knew we were abandoning him. We actually gave him to another family to look after—but we still were abandoning him.

 We ended up in Montclair, New Jersey, where my brother's business partner lived, and this became the headquarters of Evron, the company manufacturing and distributing the toilet articles for the vending machines. I was enrolled first in the Hillside Junior High School and a year later in Montclair High School, from which I graduated. It was quite a transition coming from a West Virginia school (in those days West Virginia was one of the poorest and most underdeveloped states in the union, although I had some fine teachers in Montgomery) to a school in Montclair known for its high educational standards. (I learned later that Harvard looked favorably on applicants for admission who came from Montclair High.)

The first year or two I found it rather tough going in school, but I found something very much in my favor and something that made me quite popular. I had a rather thick Southern accent! It also helped that I joined the staff of the school newspaper and in my first year wrote a column for the paper. It was called "Inside Out," and it consisted of comments on general events and philosophical reflections. As I look back on the column, it seems a rather pompous endeavor for a teenager, but apparently it caught on, for I was later invited to write the same column three times a week for the *Montclair Times*, the local daily newspaper. During my senior year I was elected president of the student body and I don't know what prompted it but the editor of the local paper wrote the lead editorial about me. It was called simply "Chris," and it was about this poor boy from the South, where cotton grew, a son of Greek immigrants, who came to Montclair High School and won the hearts and support of all the students and graduated with honors. I like recalling this experience because I believe the thing that prompted most of my popularity was my Southern accent! (which incidentally I lost in the next few years).

At this time several other important things happened. The angel on my shoulder seemed to be working overtime. Harold Ferguson, the principal of Montclair High recommended me for a handsome scholarship to Clark University, his alma mater, a fine college in Worcester, Massachusetts. Meanwhile, the father of Emily May Phelps, one of my classmates, recommended me for a general scholarship given by the Leopold Schepp Foundation in New York City, which I won and had for all my college years. Then I was introduced to Milton L. Beebe, the president of the local YMCA, and he gave me a part-time job and greatly befriended our family.

My brother's business was making progress, but, despite my scholarship, there was not enough to pay the costs of sending me to college.

This was in June, 1931, and I wanted to go to college in September. Then two things happened that greatly changed the course of my life. The first was that my mother's sister in Athens became seriously ill, and, since it was expected that somehow I was going away to college, my mother went to Greece to look after her—and, I suspect, try to become reconciled with her wealthy but estranged brother, Pan Aristophron, of whom more later. Milton Beebe was aware of this, and he knew my need for help in being able to afford college. He spoke about me to Doctor and Mrs. George Biggs of Montclair, good friends of his, who were among the chief supporters of the YMCA. One day while I was working at the Y the Biggses stopped by to see me, mentioning that Mr. Beebe had told them something of my ambition to go to college and study philosophy. They asked me a few questions and then invited me to come for dinner the following evening. I reported all this to Mr. Beebe and he said that was good news. He told me that the Biggses had provided scholarly and other aid to several young boys and girls and he thought they would do the same for me. Congratulations!

I'll never forget the first dinner I had with the

Biggses. They lived in a small, beautiful house at 16 Rockledge Road in Montclair, and on a clear day you could see some of the New York skyline from their porch. I arrived promptly at 6 o'clock, dressed in a dark suit (I was told they were quite formal people) and I brought some flowers.

Years later Mrs. Biggs told me that she much appreciated those flowers and my good manners, but she thought that they were an extravagance for a young boy seeking a scholarship to go to college, and she had feared that I might turn out to be a spendthrift! We sat and talked in the parlor before dinner, and Mrs. Biggs showed me a copy of Will Durant's *Story of Philosophy*, remarking that since I was interested in philosophy I had probably already seen the book. I told her that I had read part of it, and I loved it, especially the section on the Greek philosophers—in particular, Socrates and Plato. Then Mrs. Biggs asked me something I considered rather weird. "Do you think that Plato was advocating dictatorship as a form of government?"

I answered, "Certainly not, he just wanted the wisest people to run the country and he thought the wisest people were philosophers: it was his 'philosopher-king' concept." Then she asked me if I spoke Greek, and where did I learn it? I told her that I had spoken Greek as a child, that both my parents were Greek, but my father, sister, and brother had all died in the flu epidemic, leaving just my mother, older brother, and me. Then I added that my mother was going to Greece to look after her sister who was very ill and that I was going to college to study philosophy.

"And how are you going to manage that?"

I explained that I had won two scholarships and that I hoped to earn the additional tuition money by waiting on tables in college. Mrs. Biggs said, "I think it's unwise for a student to have to wait on tables when he could be using that time studying and making the most of college life." Then the maid came in to announce that dinner was ready and Doctor Biggs said: "Let's continue this conversation over dinner." We went to the dining room, which was furnished with beautiful but heavy baroque furniture. There were candles on the table and the settings were of gold. I pulled out the chair and seated Mrs. Biggs and stood until Doctor Biggs sat down.

Mrs. Biggs asked me, "Do all Greeks have such good manners?"

I answered something to the effect of, "I don't know, but in such a beautiful room I think everyone would have good manners." Then,

"Now tell us why you want to study philosophy."

Before I started to answer the maid brought in the soup course. It was peanut butter soup. I'd never tasted peanut butter soup before, and it was wonderful, and I said so. Mrs. Biggs explained that it was a specialty of her cook, Duma, who was French and she would be glad to hear that I liked the soup. "When Duma hears that you like it, she will bring you some," Mrs. Biggs said.

I noticed Mrs. Biggs did not say "more" soup, she offered me "some," and that is a nicety I'll always appreciate. And now I ask myself, where did I learn this little nicety—never to say do you want "more" of something. I also wonder, was I deliberately flattering my hosts or just showing good manners? And do you have to learn to seat your hostess or to say something nice about the table and the room? I don't remember being taught manners. In fact, I don't recall being taught anything in our family. I seem to have learned through osmosis, or example. And another thing comes to mind about my upbringing. I don't think I was brought up as a child; I was brought up as a grownup while I was still a child. I remember my boyhood friends always had to ask their parents permission before they could go or play or leave the house. Not I. In fact, at times I felt bad about it and really not cared about, and I would pretend to my pals that I had to get my mother's permission to do such and such when, in fact, I was on my own. But somehow I survived. I've tried to teach my own children first and foremost self-reliance, and they are all so successful that I think this attitude with them worked.

The main course of the dinner was lamb, and I thought to myself, what a coincidence, lamb is the favorite Greek dish. Or was it just more of my hosts' thoughtfulness?

Then I tried to answer Mrs. Biggs's earlier question—why philosophy?

I said I wasn't absolutely sure but that I felt drawn to it, and one day I wanted to write about it and teach it. And then I added that a philosopher's view of life is an eternal view, a whole view of life, and I thought that if you had this big picture yourself, it would make you big and fair and kind, in addition to being wise. These words or something like them came out of my mouth easily and naturally. I really don't think I was trying to sell myself, but apparently I did, and while we were having dessert (vanilla ice cream with hot fudge sauce), Mrs. Biggs said: "You have a good goal in life and my husband and I will help you."

Then they invited me to stay with them after my mother left until college opened. And this was the beginning of my long, friendly relationship with and support from the Biggses, a friendship that has continued, until it now includes their grandchildren. Thus, with their help, I moved on, to Harvard, and Oxford, and worlds far away from Montgomery, West Virginia.

Harvard Years

I recently attended the fifty-fifth commencement exercises at Harvard. I marched with my classmates from 1936, and it was a wonderfully inspiring occasion. After twenty years as president, Derek Bok was retiring and Neil Rudenstine from Princeton (who also has two degrees from Harvard) was succeeding him. Edward Shevardnadze, former Minister of Foreign Affairs of the Soviet Union, received an honorary degree and gave an address that was stirring even in translation, warning of the increasing dangers nuclear weapons pose throughout the world and urging that the United Nations organize an international military force to combat terrorism. Derek Bok in his last address as president of Harvard spoke of the declining quality of education, especially in the United States. He reminded us that the goal and responsibility of a college to provide its students with a good education is not its entire goal: with that education should come a moral responsibility to do good for our society and to each other. His, of course, was not a new or profound proposal but it is one that needs to be emphasized and promoted, especially in these times. I sat with my classmates Lou Perry, Ray Levitas, and Winnie Lee, and I insisted that my daughter, Niki, join me. She was most welcome there, for she has had many associations with Harvard. I must say that some of us in the audience were a bit embarrassed (if pleased) by the over-subscription of many of the class and department financial goals. Harvard is the wealthiest university in the world, with an endowment of over two billion dollars, but it is also, in the minds of its alumni and many educators, the best all-around center of learning that has ever existed. I sensed a great feeling of dedication among the faculty, students, and alumni, and I came away from the exercises feeling very proud to be a Harvard man. I am not just going to hope my grandchildren will go to Harvard, I am not going to listen to that nonsensical advice about letting them make up their own minds where to go. No, I'm going to be arbitrary—I'm going to insist they apply and if they are lucky they will be admitted.

The day after commencement Niki had to return to her home in Woodbridge, New Jersey. Wherever I am, even if I am alone, and especially if I am away from home, there is nothing I enjoy better than taking a walk, meeting and talking with people. On this beautiful June day I walked to the Boston Commons and the public gardens. It is always pleasing and surprising to me how many different experiences you can have if you keep your mind open and walk with enthusiasm. My first encounter in the garden was with a policeman on horseback. Actually I was sitting on one of the benches and he approached me. I don't think I looked like a vagrant, although it was one of the rare occasions when I hadn't shaved and I didn't have on a coat and tie. (I was once teased by some friends that I must have been born with a tie and jacket.) I had been working in

Niki's garden and hadn't bothered to change from my rather shabby working clothes. I did, however, have on a Harvard class of '36 reunion hat. I suppose we all are a little apprehensive when stopped or approached by an officer of the law, and I am no exception, although in this case, formidable and impressive as this policeman was on horseback, he passed me by once and then returned with a rather cheerful greeting. "Excuse me, but didn't I see you on TV at the Harvard commencement exercises?"

"Well," I said, "I was there and sitting not very far from Derek Bok who was the retiring president."

"Welcome to Boston," he continued. "I haven't seen you in the park before." Now once again I began to feel that I was rather suspicious looking, and that he was interrogating me. I explained to him that I was visiting my daughter who keeps an apartment on Acorn Street and that I was from Chicago. Then impulsively I congratulated him on how beautiful the park garden was and how safe it seemed. "Oh, yes," he said, "this is nothing like Central Park in New York. Here you are okay at all hours." Then he surprised me by saying, "You must be a celebrity or very important to be sitting so near the president of Harvard at the commencement events. Are you an actor or something? You look familiar." I explained that no, I wasn't famous but I had written a book or two, and Disney had made a movie based on one of my books. After this remark the officer got off his horse and came over next to me at my bench. "You know, I have a daughter who collects autographs—can I have yours? I sure would appreciate it, and thank you very much."

I pointed out that I didn't have a book with me but I would be glad to give him an autograph for his daughter. "Here," he said, "just put your John Hancock on back of this ticket and address it to Melinda. It will make her day."

A little later I saw the policeman again and he was giving a ticket to a young girl for riding a bike in the park. "It's part of my job," he said and rode off. After this I thought I would treat myself to a ride on the Swan Boat. I handed the girl selling tickets $1.25 and she returned 25 cents saying it was only $1.00 for a senior citizen. I secretly thought I was not too happy at looking so much like a senior citizen. I vowed again to take off some weight and not go out in public again unshaven and in work clothes (although my work clothes could be called English casual—I am not one to wear blue jeans) and to look a little snappier!

After my boat ride (actually these rides are so short and the day was so beautiful, I took two trips), I noticed that there was a group of well-dressed, mostly young people gathered under a tree near the pond. Of course, I had to see what it was all about. I thought someone might have fallen into the pond! Nothing like that. It was a wedding. I listened to the whole ceremony—the bride cried a bit—and then was invited to meet the young couple. The bride gave me a kiss, thinking, I suppose, that I was some relative of the groom. Then they insisted I have my picture taken with them. I also signed a guest book and eventually went on my way. Just as I was about to leave the garden near Beacon Street, I saw a young girl stretched out on one of the benches without backs to them. She had a shopping cart full of clothes with her and two large paper shopping bags. She herself looked rather bedraggled, her hair uncombed, her dress torn, and she wore dirty tennis shoes. I kept wondering whether this young a girl—perhaps twenty or twenty-two years old—could be a homeless person. I stopped by and asked: "Are you okay?"

"Buzz off," she said.

"You look as if you need something to eat," I persisted.

"Oh, yeah, you don't look so great yourself!"

"Haven't you someplace to sleep?"

"None of your fucking business. Now leave me alone or I'll call a cop." (And I wondered what he would say to her—or to me).

Now I felt challenged and very paternal. "Here's ten bucks, go get yourself something to eat, and don't be such a smart ass."

She looked up at me almost tenderly: "Okay, old man, that's your good deed for the day and I hope it makes you feel better." I don't know exactly how it made me feel, but I was definitely sad.

On my way back to Niki's apartment it was difficult to cross Beacon Street and walk along the Charles because there was at least a mile-long parade of gays and lesbians on the march. I was surprised at the number of young and old people in the parade and a bit stunned with some of the shows or acts being performed. There were several large flatbed trucks in the parade, each with either recorded music or a live band. There is a movie called *Truth or Dare* in which Madonna performs some really lewd acts, like masturbating on stage. It seemed to me many of the people in the parade, especially the younger people, were imitating her. Anyway it was quite a spectacle. I am all for protecting the rights of everybody to live their lives the way they want to (though homosexuality is personally abhorrent to me), but why make a show of being gay or a lesbian? What is the matter with keeping your choice private, as all sexual matters should be!

All these little events, which happened during an

hour's stroll in the park, reminded me of how much Boston, and Harvard too, perhaps, have changed since I first went there in 1932 to study philosophy.

One of the turning points of my life and one of my greatest thrills was when I received the letter from Harvard saying that I had been accepted for admission.

And three wonderful things happened to me at Harvard.

First, I studied philosophy with the great Alfred North Whitehead, Ralph Barton Perry, William Earnest Dolking, and Raphael Demos. Whitehead, along with Bertrand Russell of Cambridge, was at the time considered perhaps the greatest living philosopher. (Albert Einstein was not included because he was a scientist more than a philosopher in the traditional sense. And George Santayana, of whom more later, had been at Harvard earlier but was now living in Rome and was out of favor with the Harvard group.)

I took all Whitehead's courses at Harvard—indeed, he was the main reason I wanted to go to Harvard in the first place. I have to confess I could not follow everything he said in his lectures, and this I'm sure applied to many of his other students. There is, however, a clear theme running throughout all his lectures: we are searching for the basic reality of nature and life. What is the one thing that everything has in common? Energy. Everything possesses energy in some form or another. My thesis in his course was to compare energy in nature—the ultimate reality—to that in human beings. Yes, human beings can be reduced to energy, too, but what, I asked, is the best way for a human to identify with energy—with our reality in the universe? I ended up saying that human ecstasy was the answer. In ecstasy you feel and identify with reality: feeling in humans is comparable to energy in a rock. As I look back on my thesis now, it was a very bold assumption. Whitehead gave me an "A" on the thesis adding, however, that it was all a bit confusing! But on the final exams and various theses I wrote for him I never received less than an A-. At the time this pleased me enormously and gave me great encouragement until much later I found that Whitehead gave almost all his students A's!

But one experience with Whitehead saddened me enormously. He invited me to his home one evening for dinner with Mrs. Whitehead and afterward we went to his library for a "chat" and port. Whitehead was very formal in his dress and his manner. He always gave his lectures dressed in a winged collar and cravat and frequently wore a formal, cutaway coat. I felt a little uncomfortable because I had come to dinner wearing a sports jacket and slacks, although I did have the foresight to wear a tie, and I did bring flowers for Mrs. Whitehead. Why I don't know, but I believe that he thought my buying flowers was inappropriate (apple polishing, perhaps!), but Mrs. Whitehead appreciated them and thanked me before she retired as we went into the library. In the library Whitehead asked me to take a comfortable leather chair, poured me a glass of port, and then brought over a volume of Plato's dialogues in the original Greek. "I have some difficulty in reading Plato in the original," he said "but then ancient Greek philosophy is not my field." And then he added: "Professor Demos tells me you are Greek and how is your Greek? Would you read for me?"

Well this is one time in my life when the angel on my shoulder really forsook me. I had to say, "Yes, I'm of Greek descent. I've had several courses in ancient

Greek, but reading it is really my weakest subject. I can't do it. Then I added rather lamely, "But I do fairly well speaking modern Greek."

"Bless my soul," he said, "what a pity. I really thought you might be my assistant."

Then he said something that to this day I find cruel, but perhaps well-meant: "Don't you realize," he said, "especially being Greek, that you won't really make it as a student of ancient Greek philosophy unless you can read classical Greek? I consider professors of Greek philosophy who can't read in the original just plain dilettantes. But you must have another port before you go."

And, of course, Professor Whitehead, as things turned out, was right. I never did become a professor of philosophy, although I did go on to study with George Santayana and C. M. Bowra.

My second most important experience at Harvard was when I became an editor of the *Harvard Crimson*. One of the regular features of the paper was a column that appeared three times a week called "The Student Vagabond." Basically it was a daily review and listing of courses at the college, which students could monitor before choosing. This coincided with a time in my studies when I had discovered the great English diarist, Samuel Pepys. I fell in love with his diaries and especially his style of writing. "Up betimes, and I did put on my new silk robe from China whose red color matched the red of the robin breast now at my window. And this made my heart exceedingly glad and I did . . . ," and so on. I adjusted his style of reporting in writing "The Student Vagabond" and the column was an instant hit. At the end of my two-year stint with the *Crimson*, "The Student Vagabond" was voted the best feature, and the committee of editors, which included

Lewis Perry, Jr., David Rockefeller, Robert Hall, Henry Lerner, and Dick Gilmore (president of the *Crimson* at the time) used some rather extravagant language, calling me "the greatest writer on the *Crimson*." Mind you, this was a comment from my good friends, and they had probably overindulged that evening at dinner before they wrote it. But after my great letdown with Professor Whitehead, the high praise from my buddies did raise my spirits. And that experience, I believe, was directly responsible for my landing—and certainly for my wanting—a job writing for the *New York Times*, and for my continued work in, and love of, journalism.

I have written I was at Harvard, Class of 36, but most of the time I didn't feel I was *of* Harvard, or that I really belonged. My main interest at Harvard was philosophy (my second love was the *Crimson*). I did not seek out much social life—and this was the decade of the debutante parties, there was practically one every week, and Harvard men were high on the invitation list for these parties. I didn't have a girlfriend nor did I look for one, and even when I did go out socially I was really a bore because I didn't care for small talk, treating social gatherings instead to my views on Plato!

I'd like to say something here about the whole concept of belonging. I was born in West Virginia, but being from a foreign family in an area dominated by the KKK, I wasn't made to feel like a West Virginian. In Chicago, where I've lived most of my life, I have many friends and am a member of a few clubs, but aside from having my children nearby, I've never felt any special feeling of being part of Chicago. Many of my friends still introduce me as "my good Greek friend." Would I feel any different if I were Polish or Irish, or if my ancestors had come over on the *Mayflower*? And when I'm in Greece, there again I'm looked upon as an outsider—to Greeks, I'm an American, and, of course, first and foremost I am. But I don't feel as if I have roots anywhere. Socrates said something like, "I am proud to be Greek but the world is my country." Sounds good, but the world is a pretty broad place.

I must say that this feeling of not belonging, especially at Harvard, was greatly changed by a classmate who also lived at Dunster House.

My classmate was Jeffrey Short, who was to become my brother-in-law. In those days, Jeffrey was always full of enthusiasm. He was very bright and charming; he had more girls after him than either he or I could keep track of, and he seemed especially interested in people who spoke a foreign language.

Jeffrey himself was very adept at languages and when he was at Harvard he knew French perfectly, had a mastery of Russian and Spanish, and was well along in learning Greek from me. During the war he joined the State Department shortly after I did and was assigned to Turkey. In a matter of some six weeks he had mastered Turkish and some Arabic. One Sunday afternoon Jeffrey knocked on my door and introduced me to Willie Hunt, another good friend of his, and said, "Come on, put away the books. I'm driving you to Wellesley. We're going to meet some girls and have some fun." We drove to TZE House at Wellesley, one of the college clubs there, and were met by some six Wellesley girls all having tea. Pouring tea was Beatrice Short, Jeffrey's sister. Never in my life had I seen a a more beautiful, elegant girl and I almost dropped the cup when she offered it to me and later asked me to sit next to her.

As I said earlier in these notes, I had not met many girls in my life—what girl wants to listen to a guy talking philosophy all evening—but this was love at first sight. She didn't ask me where I lived, where I came from, none of the usual questions. She said that Jeffrey told her I wrote the "Student Vagabond" column for the *Crimson* and that she had read it several times and liked it very much. Was I planning on a career in journalism? She thought anyone who wrote that well should. For once I thought I'd stay clear of talking about philosophy. This was one girl I did not want to bore. Instead, I asked her if she came into Boston very often. She said she came as often as she could, to go to the symphony and a dance or two. Then I found myself getting serious and again self-centered. Had she by any chance read my Vagabond column on Dante and Beatrice? She said she hadn't seen it. And then I told her I liked the name Beatrice, but preferred the Italian pronunciation "Beatriche." She said she liked that too. Then I said "Okay Beatriche, will you come to the Dunster House dance with me next Saturday night?" She said that Jeffrey had already asked her to go to the dance, then hesitated a bit and said, "But I'm sure he wouldn't mind if we all went together—and we can go in his car." I was in sheer ecstasy. This was my first real date at Harvard and I didn't think of philosophy at all.

The dance at Dunster House was a great success. There was a twelve-piece band and everybody was formally dressed, even the Conant National Scholarship student from the coal mines of West Virginia who had received his first pair of shoes when he came to Harvard! (In contrast to him was an amiable enough young student from Brooklyn who drove a Dusenberg, came to Dunster House with his own valet, and ate in the dining room using his own sterling silver and Irish linen tablecloth). Harvard in those days was still a "gentleman's" college, but President Conant was determined to make it a college with a good cross section of students with great talent but of various backgrounds, and he eventually succeeded. With that success the notion that being a gentleman was all that was required to graduate from Harvard went by the wayside. The couple of gentlemanly C's I got in science and mathematics had nothing to do with being a gentleman; I just couldn't do any better in those two subjects.)

Now to get back to the dance: Beatrice wore a knockout dress of gold lamé, her long blonde hair was beautifully knotted around her head, and she carried the white gardenia corsage I gave her. She stood out from the whole glamorous group not just because she was tall—about 5'10"—but because she was utterly elegant. I was never able to finish an entire dance number with her, so many men cut in. She danced with everyone who asked her unless the student was very short. Then she would often excuse herself and say, "Let's sit this one out." As I recall now the person who cut in on me most frequently was David Rockefeller. He was a bit short, but not short enough to be refused a dance. There were also Edward Melcarth, Willie Hunt, Leonard Eliel, and David Bean, all over six feet, all good friends, and all potential suitors. Here the angel on my shoulder really looked after me, and I shall write more about this later. Suffice it to say now that we were married two years later in Winnetka and in 1987, two years before Beatrice died, we celebrated our fiftieth wedding anniversary with our three children at her sister Marian Harris's house in Glencoe.

An Interlude
with Santayana

Despite the discouragement I had received from Professor Whitehead (any student of Greek philosophy who can't read Plato in the original is a dilettante!), I decided to continue my studies in philosophy at Oxford. I was now not concentrating on ancient Greek philosophy but was studying the works of George Santayana, who, as I mentioned, was not looked on favorably at Harvard. I never found out exactly why, but when I met and studied briefly with him in Rome, he told me he "never liked the taste of academic straw." For me, Santayana's writing is the best philosophic prose since Plato's. He also wrote a best-selling novel, *The Last Puritan*, and he lived with great personal taste and style. I suspect that the Harvard group and others considered Santayana too unorthodox in his way of life (one critic also did not like the idea that he was not married and this included other insinuations!) and style of writing to be listed among the great living philosophers, and yet Santayana's contribution to philosophy, especially his volumes on the "Life of

Reason" are as important, influential, and beautiful philosophical writings as anything written during this century. I decided to go to Oxford, however, principally because of C. M. (Sir Maurice) Bowra of Wadham College, the renowned Greek classicist, and Edward Collingwood of Magdalen College, who was an enthusiastic admirer and proponent of Santayana. There were, of course, other reasons for my going to Oxford. It is one of the most ancient and may be the greatest seat of learning devoted to the humanities in the world. But just the idea of life at Oxford, its beautiful scenery, its ambiance, attracted me. I found unlimited and inspiring academic freedom at Oxford but was frequently irked by the regulations regarding when you had to be within the college walls. At Wadham College (and this applied to most other colleges) you had to be in by midnight and you couldn't go out after nine at night. An exception to this was Christ Church College. There the closing of the gates was at 12:05 a.m. It seems that years ago a student of Christ Church had had an affair with one of the town girls and was caught in a compromising situation by her father, who chased the boy with a meat ax (the father was the local butcher) all the way to the college gates, just as they were closing at midnight. The boy got in safely, but the officials apparently thought that he had had too close a call, so they extended the closing time by 5 minutes thereafter! So the story goes.

    In this respect, my life at Oxford was made a little easier by Bowra, who showed me (after all, I was a graduate student) where there was a break in the barbed wire along the wall of the college and how to climb up to the wall over the coal bin. It was a bit tricky getting back in: you usually had to hire a taxi, have it run up on the sidewalk near the wall, and then get on top of the taxi and pull yourself up and over the wall. More than once I caught my trousers on the barbed wire, but it was fun and it was worth it.

One of my first tutorials at Oxford was with Professor Collingwood, who, I believe, was quite impressed that I had studied with Whitehead at Harvard. I didn't tell him what Whitehead said to me about not being able to read Plato in the original. I found out later, however, that Collingwood himself didn't know Greek very well either. In the beginning I'd meet with my tutor once a week and we would discuss and analyze a paper Collingwood had assigned me to write on some phase of Santayana's philosophy. I remember one of my first papers was to write an opinion of *The Last Puritan*, which had just been published and had become a best seller. "Quite a feat for a philosopher," Collingwood declared.

Toward the end of my first term Collingwood made a wonderful but quite surprising suggestion to me: "Janus, why do you and I spend our time talking about Santayana, when he is just a few hours away in Rome and you might meet and study with him directly? You have a reading period coming up in the spring. (The system at Oxford is for eight weeks of residence study and six weeks of reading period anywhere of your choosing.) Let me see if I can help arrange it for you."

I was delighted with the suggestion and elated when a couple of weeks later I got a letter from Santayana inviting me to come to Rome in March and meet with him at the Bristol Hotel, where he lived. In the letter I was also told to check with Daniel Cory, his assistant and mentor, for help with the arrangements and finding a place to live while I was in Rome. Shortly

An Interlude with Santayana 39

before the beginning of the reading period, however, two memorable events took place: one of great personal importance and the other of international significance. I was in my room at Wadham studying (my quarters consisted of a narrow bedroom about 5 × 10 and a sitting room with a fireplace—my only heat—which some six hundred years ago used to be the small Wadham College library) when my scout, Walter, a third-generation male servant assigned to my section, knocked on my door quite excitedly and said I had a telephone call—"I believe it's international"—and that I should go immediately to the porter's office. I couldn't imagine who could be calling. In 1937 overseas calls were a rarity. The porter told me the call came from somewhere in the United States called Winnetka. It was from Beatrice and, incidentally, it was the first overseas call ever received at Wadham. I asked the porter if he would mind leaving the office for a few minutes, which he obligingly did, and I heard Beatrice's voice saying that her answer was "Yes," she would marry me. I had formally proposed in a letter I had written her about ten days earlier.

Toward the end of our conversation she asked me what was the latest with the king and Mrs. Simpson. I said there was no news that I knew of, and she said that *Time* magazine and the paper in Chicago were full of rumors about them. Actually, I found out later that the British media had been censored in their reporting of the impending abdication of King Edward VIII, and British readers were receiving censored reports from foreign presses. The copies of *Time* delivered to Oxford had several pages torn out of them in the international news section.

I became more aware of and interested in this rather momentous news story when I received a cable from the *Harvard Crimson* asking me to wire them a thousand words on the subject, focusing on the reaction of Oxford students to the king and Wally romance. First I called our embassy in London to find what they knew—and they were quite close-mouthed. I called on the local Oxford newspapers without much luck, and then out of desperation I got in touch with a friend in the U.S. Intelligence office in London. He said that the abdication was a subject he would not discuss on the phone but the next time I came down to London I should give him a call and we could have a drink. I said, "Walter, I have a story to write. I'm coming to London on the next train I can get. Meet me at 5 at the Oxford-Cambridge Club."

His reply: "Fine, I've never been to that club."

We met that same day and he told me in great confidence that it was certain the king would abdicate in December and that Winston Churchill was already helping him write his now-famous address ("I find it impossible to carry the heavy burden . . . without the help and support of the woman I love"). I cabled the story to *Crimson*, together with the reaction of various Oxford students. One rather cynical student's reaction was: "The next thing you'll be telling me is Wally is staying at the King's Arms" (the King's Arms was the name of an inn in Oxford). How my source knew even some of the details of the impending abdication I don't know, but I cabled the story to the *Crimson* the following day and they ran it on the front page, editing the story a bit, and hedging about the part that abdication was certain and would happen in December. I understand some of the Boston papers picked up the story and credited my report in the *Harvard Crimson*. That wasn't the first time the *Crimson* has broken a story of international significance. Just recently they

An Interlude with Santayana 41

were the first to report—in advance of the press release—that Derek Bok intended to resign the presidency of Harvard and that his successor would be someone from Princeton. And the *Crimson* was among the first newspapers to announce that President Roosevelt, a Harvard man, would run for a fourth term.

It is now March 1937 and I am on my way to Rome to meet George Santayana. When I arrived I first called Daniel Cory, as instructed. He had already made reservations for me at a nearby pension near the famous Triton fountain, after which Santayana's collected works were named. (After the war I disposed of my deluxe Triton edition of the philosopher's works for reasons that I'll come to.) After I checked into the pension, which was also near the Bristol Hotel where Santayana lived, I met Cory for a conference before meeting "the Master." Cory told me that ever since *The Last Puritan* became a best-seller in the States, Santayana had become a popular celebrity and that, joined with his solid reputation as a philosopher, had made many demands, most of them unwelcome, on his time. Cory told me several professors (especially from Harvard!) wanted to see him and that he had refused to see any of them. I suppose Cory was telling me how lucky I was to have this opportunity to see Santayana and that I should appreciate it—which, of course, I did. But I also wondered a bit why, if he was refusing to see even Harvard faculty members, he agreed to my visit. I believe that my coming from Oxford (Santayana had been a visiting professor there) and Professor Collingwood's introduction had much to do with it.

My first meeting with Santayana was at the Bristol Hotel. When I first saw him, my impression was, what an elegantly dressed man! He wore a dark, finely tailored pin-striped suit and a Homburg hat and

carried a gold-crowned cane. (I have a particular interest in canes, which I'll go into later.) He was quite a contrast to any professor I had seen at Oxford, with their unpressed gray trousers and well-worn sports coats. But his dress reminded me a bit of Professor Whitehead's formal lecture attire.
 "How do you do?" he said. "And how was your trip from Oxford?"
 "It was a very pleasant train ride, and I'm glad to feel some warm sunshine."
 "Oh, yes, the English weather didn't at all agree with me when I was lecturing at Oxford. And how is Collingwood? He speaks very highly of you, and I understand you studied with Whitehead at Harvard. I have a three-way correspondence with Whitehead and Bertie Russell." And then before I could say much of anything, another question: "By the way, how is your Greek? I am writing some sonnets in Latin and Greek and must show them to you." I thought to myself "My gawd, am I going to have to go through the routine again and confess that Greek is not what I am all about?" I said as much and nothing more was ever said about the subject. Santayana informed me that we were going to have lunch at his favorite restaurant (I don't recall the name now); it had good food and he had a table where it was relatively quiet and conducive to conversation. He said he thought this was a pleasant way to conduct a tutorial. And this became our pattern for discussing various subjects and his philosophy and not once would he let me pick up the check for which, with my limited budget, I was thankful!
 When I say various subjects, I mean we discussed everything, and at this first lunch he started talking about the crystal goblets—did I know they came from Venice? and that the Venetians were famous for their

crystal? He asked me to examine the pattern on the silver: "That's a famous English brandmark, and did I know just what sterling silver was?" Than came comments about the Irish linen on the table. "A gentleman," he said (he did not say "philosopher," but he meant the same thing I suspect), "is interested in everything and awed by nothing." If this is true, Santayana was a model example. I wanted to talk about *The Last Puritan,* which many critics had described as the best novel of the century, but Santayana demurred. He would discuss that at a later luncheon. I did persist in asking him one thing about it, however, Was he Oliver? the main character in the novel.

"My boy, a man is a bit of everything, and we summarize ourselves every second of our lives. Yes, I was Oliver but also Mario and a bit of everybody I wrote about, even Rose (one of the main female characters)." I laughed. "Yes, even Rose. Sometimes I think the best part of our souls is female!"

I was utterly fascinated by our lunch and all the others to come. Our meetings usually lasted until 3 o'clock and I would go to the pension afterward to write my notes.

Following are some of the things I jotted down after one of my meetings with Santayana:

Santayana is a kind of "Mona Lisa of philosophy." His philosophy is beautiful to behold, enigmatic, elegant, and penetrating. But Santayana gives us more enigmas than answers to fundamental philosophic questions. He is a moral philosopher and an idealist but not entirely in the Platonic sense. His ideals are not Plato's, which reside in the blue sky—perfect, eternal, the ultimate reality—but they always are at the point of committing incest with facts.

Santayana's ideal of a perfect man or woman or a perfect situation must take into consideration the facts our senses give us. This is an idealism with a naturalistic basis. And yet he cautions that we can never be sure that facts are indeed facts: our senses are imperfect and may give false or misleading information. And on top of it all, the human mind is also an imperfect and changing organ, probably incapable of comprehending everything in the universe.

In the evenings I usually met Dan Cory, a brilliant man and a devotee and biographer of Santayana. We did not talk philosophy, however, but instead he would take me sightseeing in Rome. We frequently ended up at a nightclub that I believe was called the Coliseum, where there was entertainment, and a telephone at each table connected with numbered tables down in front adorned by one or more lovely girls who were available for dancing, conversation, and, Dan said, "etcetera." "Okay, Chris, what number do you want?" Number 12 caught my eye and I was ready to phone when he said, "Hold it! That's my regular—take anyone else." But then he decided, "Okay, we'll share her." But she didn't know a word of English, and Dan was fluent in Italian. There was not much sharing in any sense!

During that particular evening at the Coliseum I met a classmate from Dunster House who was also an editor of the *Crimson*. He was spending his junior year traveling in Italy and Greece. When I told him I was in Rome to do some work with Santayana, he exclaimed, "Boy you're lucky and why don't you do a piece for the *Crimson*? Santayana is a hot property."

I didn't follow up on the suggestion until a week or so later when I got a cable from the paper asking me to do a thousand words on Santayana, with pictures, if

An Interlude with Santayana   45

possible. I discussed the proposal first with Dan Cory, who said the Master was rather impressed with me and it was worth asking him. Santayana agreed and also to a picture which Dan took of us. The story and picture appeared on the front page of the *Crimson*. When I returned to Oxford some four weeks later I did a longish piece on my meetings with Santayana. Collingwood liked the paper and congratulated me on it but added that he didn't exactly find much new in what Santayana said about his own philosophy (it was new to me). But he was interested in his comments about *The Last Puritan*—and his comments on Irish linen!

I no longer have the paper, but I do have a piece I wrote that was inspired by Santayana and his philosophy. I have always enjoyed writing imaginary letters, either from famous people or from people living in important times. I collected them together in a book called *Only for Your Eyes*, and one of them, a letter purporting to be to Dante from Beatrice's companion, was written soon after my return from Rome. Santayana never approved of Dante's aloofness from world affairs or his attitude toward women. I reprint it here, in the hope that some of Santayana's philosophy will show through.

    CHRISTMAS DAY, MCCCIX
    FIRENZE

        To DANTE ALIGHIERE
        Under secure cover, these:

SIR, I am Lucia Celladora, tutor and lifelong companion to Madonna dé Bardi.[1] My Mistress is distraught, and under the circumstances bids me write you. In all mercy you deserve an answer even though it be an unhappy one and, by comparison, unworthy of your noble poems which out of discretion my Mistress has burned. It is not easy to write words expressing another person's feelings. Something of the writer's own wishes and interpretations may creep in and this, Sir, may still be your best hope. For in this unhappy task I wish that I were bringing quite a different answer.

On this Christmas Day, however, it is easy for me to bring you a little gift, deceptively wrapped, of her favorite perfume. Material things, being limited, are so easy to carry and talk about; they arrive precisely as they were sent. But what messenger of the heart ever carried the precise and full intention of his errand? Perhaps the spiritual should always be enigmatical to protect it against intrusion of uncongenial minds.

FURTHERMORE, I am only a teacher living in the shadows of the experiences of others. Would I prefer her banker to a poet? Am I content to live as an idol of a man's love without the man? Is the promise of a heaven to come enough to satisfy my earthly life? Who knows how I myself would answer the questions my Mistress answers so confidently. No man has loved me even from afar. (No man has even deceived me!) No man has dreamed of me enough to write a sonnet. No man has looked upon me the way you looked at my Mistress at the bridge. Dear Poet, in that eternal moment I secretly hoped you looked at me. What is life without illusions?

However, the things I have missed in life may perhaps make me a better judge of the values you should seek and cherish most. By your leave, My Lady's love is one of them.

MY MISTRESS is aware of your love for her, as is indeed all of Florence; but her message to you, brought with all the limitations of an emissary is this: She does not love you. Do not stare at her in church; do not wait at the bridge. We will not be there. I must also tell you my Mistress is not well.

Women, dear Dante, are happy souls of the earth; it is poets who make them, quite against their will, idols in heaven. Because all poets are vain they are not content to sing of earthly things, but must have idols, as your Beatrice, for their inspiration. But is the earth so unworthy of the beauty of your poems? Is not my Mistress more desirable as a lady than as a veil for your philosophy? Does her husband, a banker, find beauty and virtues and good deeds with her on earth where a poet does not? Of sorry world!

You have vowed eternal love for my Lady. Love, dear Dante, is made eternal not by what happens to it in afterlife, but by what you do to enrichen it in this life. By vowing your love for my Mistress for posterity you lose her while she is just an hour from you today. The trouble with love and mercy and goodness, dear Dante, is that poets and priests claim them as secret words in their own charades.

IT IS infinitely more important that love dwells in the market place than in heaven. In the market place at least, as in the home, it can be increased and it can be tried and exercised, and doubted and strengthened. Love in the market place can save thieves as well as inspire angels thus earning its right to live forever.

If you would win my Mistress' love, do not disdain the earth. Think not so ill of your fellow men. My Mistress, as all of Florence, finds your sonnets beautiful and near God. But the kicks, gossip tells us, you give your servants are also heartfelt. Your violence toward your enemies is violence still and can turn on your friends. Of what use is poetry and faith in the eternal without good deeds on earth? Dear Dante, the helping of man by man is God, and there lies his greatest glory.[2]

MY MISTRESS is looking over my shoulder now. She reminds me to tell you that the little gift of perfume is made from a secret substance found in the sea, wild flowers that grow near Paris and from other earthly things. Alas, I have spilled some! The perfume is called Paradiso.

We wish you the joy of this blessed Christmas Day.

L. CELLADORA

1 The "Beatrice" of Dante's famous works.
2 Deus Est Mortali Mortalem Iuvare, Et Haec Ad Aeternam Gloriam Via, (Pliny H.N.ii 18.7 (5))

I wish my memories of Santayana could be confined to that interlude in Rome and the tutorials we had, but I had another meeting with him later that changed my thinking about him and explains why I disposed of my Triton edition of Santayana's work, as well as of much of the memorabilia I had accumulated about him.

It had to do with the war: the Nazis, Mussolini, and the Jews.

Santayana, first and foremost, was an ethical philosopher. His mission to my way of thinking was observing, thinking about, judging, and writing about right and wrong. I'm well aware that philosophers think of themselves as above the fray, that they must have the eternal view. They must be objective. But philosophers are also human beings, living and reacting with one another in a society, and with a responsibility to other human beings.

When I was traveling from Greece in 1945, I stopped in Rome just to see Santayana, whom I considered a friend and teacher. More than that, I somewhat idolized him. He was living then at the Blue Nun convent. He was rather weak, recovering from an illness, but he was still writing and in full possession of his senses. We greeted each other warmly. He asked me about Greece and what I did in the war and he wanted to know if I had met George Seferis, the Greek poet. (Seferis later won the Nobel Prize for literature.) I said I had met him and in fact gave Santayana an autographed copy of Seferis's poems, which pleased him very much.

Then I asked Santayana the question which had been bothering me for some time.

"As you know, I've been away and have not been able to follow all your writings since the war, so I haven't read about your reaction to the atrocities committed against the Jews or your views about Hitler and Mussolini. As an ethical philosopher, many of us have missed your voice."

Santayana put his arm on my shoulder and said, "No, my boy, I haven't spoken out. Don't you realize I've been a guest in Rome!"

There and then the bubble burst. I lost my respect for Santayana. I disposed of his books and pictures. I put great distance between us.

Should I have asked that question? Was I being impolite? Who am I to judge Santayana anyway? You must remember, however, that hundreds of statesmen, businessmen, professors, poets, and artists had spoken out against Hitler as the greatest evil of our time, and this was before it was fully grasped that he was responsible for killing six million Jews. When years

later I met W. H. Auden in New York, who was also a great admirer of Santayana, and told him the story, Auden replied:
"You were wrong. You were unfair. You're a silly ass. What gives you the right to judge Santayana?"

Maybe Auden was right—but not in my books. Right ethical conduct is, of course, not expected simply of philosophers, ministers, nuns, and the like. We all are equally required to respond and fight the evil embodied in the Nazi atrocities. But when a person's profession is dealing with right and wrong, it seems to me he takes on an additional responsibility to respond to and help maintain ethical justice. I cannot think of Santayana in the same way ever again.

On the Wadham Crew

When I returned to Oxford in the late spring of 1937, the weather was beautiful, and the playing fields were filled every afternoon with students playing rugby and other games. Participation in sports is a custom clearly expected in the Oxford curriculum, and here I should add that most students from the United States in my day were considered good athletes. One reason for this was that the Rhodes scholarship, under which most of them came to Oxford, strongly favored applicants who had special athletic abilities. I was not a Rhodes scholar, but being a Yank I was looked upon as an above average athlete. I'm not sure I was.

Anyway, I was recruited for the Wadham crew. Each college had its own crew and its own boathouse on the Isis River. They didn't compete against each other like the famous Oxford and Cambridge crews. Instead they had a "bumping" race. Boats race away from each other to prevent getting bumped. Once bumped by a rival boat, you are out of the race. The crew that succeeds in never being bumped during the season is winner of all the college bumping tournaments, and each of the colleges, win or lose, has an elaborate dinner afterward.

Our Wadham crew reached the tournament quarter finals without getting bumped and we had high hopes of coming in first for the season. But a strange thing happened. (Strange things always seem to happen in Oxford games!)

I believe I was rowing number two and in front of me was an amiable, fun-loving Argentinean named Carlos Luzzetti, the Prince of Wales scholar. Carlos was a fairly good all-around athlete and an excellent scholar, but he was best known at Wadham for his numerous wild, romantic escapades. He was almost never in college by midnight, and he was known to have hired more taxi cabs to climb on to scale the wall than anyone else in the college.

On the day of our quarterfinal bumpster race, Carlos appeared at the boat house looking very strained indeed. I asked if there was anything the matter. "The matter, the matter," he exclaimed, "you've never seen such a beautiful girl as 'Jane.' Chreese" (he could not pronounce Chris), "I'm in love!"

He changed into his rowing trunks and jerseys, and we all got a briefing and a little pep talk from the coach, and soon we were off and racing. Our speed was strong and steady. The Isis was calm and we were about two lengths ahead of our rival (I believe it was the Magdalene boat). We were on our way to winning. Suddenly, Carlos bent over and collapsed. He had not, however, fainted or had some kind of an attack. I said, "Carlos, what the hell happened to you?"

"Ah, Chreese, the heart is more important than the race!" He was just too tired from his affair of the night before. We then dropped out of the race and headed back to the boathouse.

I was the first to grab Carlos by an arm and leg; three others including the coach joined in and we threw him, one—two—three, into the river. I've said that I thought Carlos was a fairly good athlete, but apparently in Argentina they didn't require swimming in school. Carlos didn't seem to know how to swim. At first we thought he was faking it (he loved practical jokes), but when he went down for the second time, splashing and crying out, the coach, fully clothed, jumped in to save him. As the coach approached him, Carlos suddenly turned around and ducked the coach and swam back to the boathouse. We all had such a good laugh that at dinner that night our elimination from the bumping didn't seem very important and our "heart is more important than the race" crew member was the entertainment of the evening.

Later on in the term, I believe Carlos was the principal perpetrator of an affair that involved my own athletic reputation. I've said that there was a belief at Oxford by faculty and students alike that most of the Americans there were good athletes, and I might have told Carlos that in high school I went out for the track team. This was about the time of the Oxford-Cambridge track meet, and it happened that their star 440 runner had a severe injury and could not compete. Apparently Carlos spread the word that the Oxford team had nothing to worry about. Janus was a star 440 runner back in the States and he could save the day.

Several of my classmates from Harvard had had the same idea I did of studying at Oxford. These included Robert Hall, who got a Henry Scholarship and later went into the investment banking business, Lou Perry, Jr., who planned to get an M.A. at Oxford and go into teaching, like his distinguished father and uncle Bliss Perry. I believe Carlos persuaded my friends to join in his charade (because although I had indeed once run the 440 in high school, I was no star runner), and one night just after dinner a delegation from the Oxford Athletic Department called on me in my rooms and said, in effect, that I owed it to Wadham and Oxford to run. This was an important race. The more I protested that I was not their man, the more modest they thought I was (at last they had met a modest American!). Their final argument was that athletics was not that important at Oxford anyway—this was not an American college—so just run for the sport of it. Be a good sport.

Well, after a few beers and more of this kind of "be a good sport talk," I finally said I would run.

A few days later Carlos came to my room with a copy of the Oxford newspaper, containing a long story by the sports editor evaluating Oxford's chance of winning the meet with Cambridge. The beginning of the story carried the subhead "Dark Horse," and contained two paragraphs about the accident to Oxford's star 440 runner, describing Janus as the dark horse who was taking his place. The story hinted that I was indeed an American track star! This was no longer funny: things were going a long way beyond good sportsmanship. And I had less than a week to do any kind of training. I was determined to do my best, however. And how wonderful, I thought, if I really won. I was beginning to dream of glory.

Anyway, the day came, and it was a beautiful afternoon. The stadium was small but packed. I was very excited. The race was called, and we lined up. I heard the starting shot, and I was off. What I remember most about the race was when I passed the grand stand. I must have been ten yards ahead of everyone, and it seemed to me that practically hundreds of fans stood up yelling: "Bravo, Janus, bravo!" I was going great guns for the first 250 yards. Then I began to feel my knees a bit. Then my feet got heavier and heavier. I didn't feel exhausted, nor even particularly tired. I just couldn't maintain the pace, even though I was still ahead. When a runner passed me, however, and I didn't have the energy to go after him, I knew it was over. My heart and my mind came in first, but my feet came in last. In fact, I barely finished at all. The coach and my colleagues didn't throw me into a nearby river, but I'm sure they felt like it. One thing I do know, however, is that Carlos and his fellow schemers had a good laugh.

I am now looking at the updated diary which I kept at Oxford. I was planning to use the notes for a feature article on Oxford and what life was like there in the 30s, giving some suggestions that might also be useful to any of my future children, who I hoped would go there! I am copying the diary more or less as I wrote it at the time:

Founded more than a thousand years ago by the Saxons, Oxford is situated slap in the middle of some of the most beautiful countryside in England. By rail Oxford is just a 60-minute express-train ride from London's Paddington Station. From London's Victoria Coach Station you can catch a comfortable bus for a 56-mile direct motorway drive. Or, if you have the time, you can book on one of the Salter's fleet pleasure boats for the 112-mile trip on the river Thames. Some Oxford oarsmen and a few athletic tourists have been known to row the journey, but this is not recommended, for among other reasons (like: you probably can't row it in under 20 hours), there is always the danger of running into and injuring the swans on the river, which can result in your being reported to Her Majesty's Swan Keeper and receiving a fine of up to £500!

The poet John Keats thought Oxford was the finest town in the world, but since his day Oxford's population has grown to nearly 150,000, and factories around the area now produce cars, agricultural equipment, printed goods, and the famous Oxford marmalade. But none of these industries has changed the appearance of the town itself or altered its fame. In Oxford, historians tell us, you see it all: century by century or face by face. Oxford is England in miniature.

The visitor to Oxford should plan to devote at least an hour or two to just walking up and down the High, Oxford's main street, where most of the shops are. Here you will find all of the special goods of England and the Commonwealth on display: fine English china, Harris tweed suits for men, the best cashmere sweaters and skirts in the world for women, and excellent leather goods (no one makes better walking shoes and boots). The best way to see and remember Oxford is to get a map and a good walking stick and set out on foot, as I did when I first arrived.

Oxford's greatest attraction, of course, is the famous university which bears its name. According to some Oxford antiquarians the university was founded by King Alfred in the fourteenth century. Today Oxford University comprises thirty-four walled-in colleges, each with its own accommodations for students (some for men, some for women, some for both), its own chapel, garden, library—and at some colleges a museum—and a boathouse on the Isis.

The colleges themselves are private corporations, varying greatly in the value of their endowments but all with their own royal charters. In theory they are perfectly autonomous. They can choose their own students and make their own rules. The university itself, however, awards degrees, arranges the curric-

On the Wadham Crew 57

ulum, accepts State aid, and sets the overall scholastic requirements. Many educators call Oxford University one of the greatest, if not the greatest, seats of learning in the world.

Oxford has well earned its reputation. Among those educated at the university have been Dr. Samuel Johnson, Sir Walter Raleigh, Pope Alexander V, Richard Burton the explorer and Richard Burton the actor, Evelyn Waugh, Dyke Brown, Percy Bysshe Shelley, twenty-two out of forty-six English prime ministers, ten of twenty viceroys of India, Washington's great grandson, Beau Nash, Beau Brummel, and several hundred bishops. President Kennedy's administration contained sixteen Oxford graduates. King James I is quoted as saying if he were not a king he would like to be an Oxford man. The Duke of Windsor was both.

In Oxford Disraeli coined the phrase "on the side of angels," Robert Burton wrote *The Anatomy of Melancholy*, and Lawrence of Arabia propelled himself through an underground stream in a canoe. At Oxford penicillin was given to a patient for the first time. Roger Bannister ran the first four-minute mile on an Oxford track, and it was here in 1987 that Marshall Jones Brooks jumped the first recorded six-foot high jump.

It is worth a visit to Oxford just to see the gardens of the colleges. Christ Church, one of the oldest and most affluent colleges, also has a meadow where sheep graze. Deer roam in a park at Magdalen College. The fine rose gardens, magnificent chapel, and part of the city wall make New College, founded in 1937, unique. Wadham, one of the smaller colleges, founded in 1613, has a three-hundred-year-old garden with one of the most beautiful copper beech trees in all of England.

Many of the colleges have their own boathouses on the Thames, which is known as the Isis whilst it flows through Oxford. Here the various Oxford College crews row and practice, and students and tourists can rent punts for a leisurely and dreamy row along the river. Lewis Carroll first told the tale of *Alice in Wonderland* to four friends in a Thames gig rowing upstream for a picnic tea.

Many of the colleges have excellent kitchens and their own specialties: wild fowl at Christ Church; fondues at Brasenose; venison at Magdalen (from their own deer!); and dressed crab and hare soups at Merton. While at Oxford, the visitor may inquire if there is some special celebration going on in one or more of the colleges and try to get an invitation. Then you can count on a dinner in the grand style, with eight or nine courses, wines for every dish, and high platters of meat, delectably indigestible puddings, and no speeches.

A student at Oxford has his own "scout," or manservant. Some of these scouts are third or fourth generation servants; they are very proud of their work and often play an important part in college life. Pinchings, my scout, comes to wake me with a cup of tea at 7:30 each morning. Then he builds up the fire in my study (there is no central heating), lays out my clothes (making sure I wear my college gown, which is a requirement), and reminds me when I have an examination coming up, an appointment with my tutor, or a lecture to attend. At night Pinchings turns down my bed—on an especially cold night he might have a cup of hot chocolate for me. And if he thinks I am being a bit lax, he will as a gentle reminder lay all my books on the desk for study. All Oxford resident students have to be in their colleges by midnight. Since

I was a graduate student and, as he often reminded me, "an American," Pinchings advised me that if I was determined to stay out after midnight, there was an opening near the coal bin in the barbed wire that circles the wall of the college and that I could use that as my entry—with always the danger, of course, of being caught. Pinchings reminded me that being caught would also reflect on him since I was his "charge." I don't believe I failed Pinchings very often. (His son, incidentally, is now also a scout at Oxford.)

Toward the end of my year at Oxford, I decided to take a shopping trip to London. Even now, one of the things I look forward to when I go to London is the shopping—at least I used to! Where better to find a pair of handmade shoes, cashmere sweaters and socks, a stylish but serviceable raincoat, a good umbrella, a fine leather wallet, or, in the hundreds of book stores, a rare book? London to me has always meant "quality." I used to look forward to the time I would shop for a Rolls Royce, but I've had to put that off for a while.

On this, my first shopping expedition, I was looking, of course, for a Harris tweed suit. Sir Maurice Bowra recommended a tailor, who, he said, was good and not too expensive. With an introduction from Sir Maurice, I was welcomed with a certain amount of respect and consideration. (I found that you needed a proper introduction to a tailor—the same as a proper introduction to a club—in order to be fully appreciated.)

At Woodwards, the tailor took me into a private room and brought out a score of swatches of Harris tweed to choose from. The first material I picked out the tailor objected "with all due respect" was not a good color for me. The second I chose he also rejected (a good tailor is a fashion dictator) because it was too thin a material for Oxford weather. We finally agreed on a beautiful gray tweed, and he started taking my measurements. He was meticulous about every detail, including wanting to know on which side of my thighs my testicles hung. These English tailors! We agreed on everything but he was shocked at my last request. I wanted a zipper on my trousers. At that time this tailor's establishment, at least, had either never heard of such a thing or simply did not approve. "A gentleman always had buttons on his fly," etc. But on this I was not to be coerced, and I insisted, even offering to have some zippers sent from the States. My tailor very haughtily told me that would not be necessary and he would see what he could do.

We made an appointment for my first fitting to take place in two weeks. The day arrived, and I went to try on my first Harris tweed suit with some excitement. First, I tried on the coat. He had done a wonderful job, and we picked out the silk for the lining and the buttons. Then came the trousers. I put them on; they felt comfortable, but what is this? The silly ass had put the zipper on the outside of the fly! I explained to him to his annoyance that the zipper should be on the inside covered by the fly. He said he would discuss it with the cutter and to come back in three days. When I came back, the coat was finished and beautifully made. Then I put on the trousers and found that he had, indeed, put the zipper on the inside, but he had covered it with a fly that buttoned! I suppose he thought he was giving me the best of all possible worlds—a fly with buttons in the traditional English sense and a zipper underneath— the American way.

I gave up and took the trousers the way he made them. Later, I had my own tailor at Marshall Fields install the zipper the proper way. The tailor at Fields could only exclaim when he saw the zipper: "What on earth could he be thinking of—was he just trying to make sure you Oxford boys would keep your flies closed!"

My second shopping expedition in London was to have a pair of fine shoes made at Maxwell, the world renowned Bond Street shoemaker. Here, again, it was important to have a good introduction, and I got one through my classmate Keith Joseph, whose father at the time was Lord Mayor of London. My plan was to go down to London on Friday, see a couple of shows after the shopping, do some sightseeing, and return on Sunday.

Even though I was a graduate student at Oxford, I still needed permission from the Warden (Sir Maurice) to be out of residence for the weekend. When I made my request, his reply was, "Okay, but you Americans seem to waste too much time on sightseeing." I took the rebuff calmly, boarded the train from Oxford to Paddington Station, and went directly to Maxwell, where I presented the letter of introduction from Keith Joseph's father. I was received with great courtesy and asked to be seated while the right person was assigned to look after my needs. A salesman appeared, a man in his early forties, wearing a wing-tip collar and striped pants. "I see you want to open an account with us and we are very happy to accommodate Sir Keith, Lord Mayor of the City. But I must tell you there is quite a long wait for delivery, but we'll do the best we can." He showed me various samples of shoes: loafers, dress shoes, ordinary Oxfords, and walking shoes. "Step into the next room and we will take your foot measurements for your last." He asked me if I'd ever had a last made before. When I admitted that this was my first, he responded, "You Americans don't really go in for lasts and handmade shoes." I agreed with him and added that that was why I was there. I ordered a pair of loafers and a pair of walking shoes. The price was the equivalent of about $60 a pair and he said it would take anywhere from three to five months for delivery. (I have amused myself by looking up prices of other items in 1937: designer women's dresses, $5.84 to $16.50; a permanent, wash, and set, $2.75; a Stetson hat, $5; kid gloves, $2; custom-made tux, $45; sterling silver flatware—8 place settings for $39.95; shrimp, 18 cents a pound; Kenmore washing machine, $36.48; Sears tires, $3.45 (terms as low as 33 cents a month); Buster Brown shoes $3.50. So those walking shoes were not cheap.

I told him that I was a student, planning on taking a walking tour of Greece in March, just six weeks away, and that I'd appreciate having at least the pair of walking shoes ready by then. He hemmed and hawed a bit but said he would do the best he could for a friend of Sir Keith's. He had both pairs ready in about just thirty days, and I could not have been more pleased. After I wore that pair of walking shoes for more than twenty years, I had them done over and gave them to my son Chris, who wears exactly the same size shoe I do. He still has them.

When I was in London in 1989, I could not wait to call again on Maxwell to order a few pairs of shoes. The morning after my arrival I took a taxi from the Carleton Hotel directly to Bond Street, but Maxwell was not at the same address. I left the taxi and walked up and down the street, asking where Maxwell was located. No one seemed to know, and I felt quite depressed. Could they be out of business? After all it was only a matter of some fifty years since my first visit! Just as I was about to give up I ran across an English bobby, and they certainly have not changed in fifty years (though in some instances I understand they now can carry firearms). He knew immediately where Maxwell had relocated: a block away on the corner in a basement.

I didn't like the sound of "basement," but when I found them they didn't seem to have changed a bit. There was the same smell of fine leather, the same comfortable private rooms, the same courteous but pompous service. I introduced myself, explained that I had bought two pairs of shoes from them some fifty years ago and wanted to order more shoes. They asked me to be seated and in a few moments brought out a dusty book and, sure enough, there was my name: Ch. Janus, 1937, pr. loafers, 2 walking shoes. I was very pleased and surprised and congratulated the salesman on his records. He wasn't surprised at all. "It's our business, sir!"

He brought out samples of the shoes and again I ordered a pair of loafers, some tan walking shoes, and a pair of Oxfords. He took the order, and noted that they had my last but there would be at least a four to five week wait for delivery. It was just like old times. I thanked him and expressed the wish that he might be able to make a quicker delivery. He said he would try, although they were very short of help. "A good shoemaker these days is hard to come by." Just as I was about to leave, I remembered that I had not asked the price.

"And what's this going to set one back?" I asked.

He did a little figuring and noted: "It averages out at about $885." I knew prices were high in England, but I was still thinking somewhat in terms of what I paid during my Oxford days: about $60 a pair. But my initial shock was very little compared to the final shock. I wanted to make sure that the $885 was for the three pairs of shoes I had ordered. "Oh, no sir, it averages out at $885 for each pair."

I said, "Thank you very much, but put the order on hold for a while," and I walked out. I could not bring myself to pay $885 for a pair of shoes even at Maxwell—but I must say I still have the original pair of loafers they made for me in 1937. English quality is still available—for a price.

Decisions, Decisions, Decisions

In June 1937 I returned to the States from Oxford. At that time, I had three important decisions to make: whether to continue my studies at Oxford or Harvard, get my doctorate, and teach philosophy (I had been offered an instructorship from the Harvard philosophy department to support me while I was getting my doctorate); whether to take a job I'd been offered through an introduction from Margie Altschul to the Sulzbergers, whom I had met briefly at Oxford (Arthur Hays Sulzberger was the publisher of the *New York Times*), to work in the Sunday Magazine department of the *New York Times*; and whether to marry Beatrice right away or wait until I could better afford it.

Beatrice and I were very much in love and wanted to marry as soon as possible, but although I had several potential prospects, I was without a job. I felt it was irresponsible to take such a serious step without being able to support a wife fully, and in those days girls of a certain class didn't work. Indeed, Beatrice's father, Jeffrey Short, would not hear of his daughter working. When she got a summer job on her own anyway as a secretary at the Cook County Hospital, he had her dismissed!

I was close friends with Beatrice's brother, Jeffrey (we were classmates at Harvard), and he had recently married Barbara Allen, a beautiful, wonderful girl from Smith College. Jeffrey wrote me a long letter which greatly influenced me. The gist of it was: "Forget academia, join the world of action and make some money; take the *New York Times* job now and marry the girl you love. Life is not doing one thing and then another and then another. Life is doing a lot of things at the same time. Get going!" I say Jeffrey greatly influenced me, but when you are in love, you don't need much influencing to get married. It's what I wanted, too, and as soon as possible. So that is what we did, but to this day I'm not sure that leaving the world of academia for the *New York Times*, or any other job, was the right decision. Of course, it changed the course of my life, but I wonder whether the angel on my shoulder was watching.

How I joined the *New York Times* is interesting. My first interview was with Edwin James, the managing editor. When he saw my academic credentials and some samples of my writing for the *Harvard Crimson* and the *Montclair Times*, James said he thought I would be most suited for the Sunday Magazine section rather than on the news desk. And anyway, he said, he didn't have any openings in the news department. He sent me upstairs to see Lester Markel, editor of the magazine and one of the best people in journalism at the time. Markel was known as an editor's editor. As I walked into his reception room, Alice Sheely, his secretary, greeted me cordially and said, "Go right in. Mr. Markel can see you now."

He was on the phone, talking apparently to the *Times* correspondent in London, discussing a piece he wanted on Winston Churchill, who was then a member of Parliament. He motioned me to sit down. "I'll be finished in just a minute." After he hung up he said, "Did you ever meet Churchill when you were in England? There's a man who is going to make history." I said I'd never met Churchill but I did hear him speak at Oxford.

Then quite abruptly, Markel said: "First and foremost a newspaperman must have news sense. Being able to write clearly helps but it's the news sense that makes the difference. Why do you want to be a newspaper man?" I'm not sure I'm reporting all this accurately and in chronological sequence (this was over fifty years ago) but suddenly I did recall, yes, right in the middle of this meeting, what Professor Whitehead had told me at a dinner in his home, when he was in fact interviewing me as a possible assistant: "Bless my soul, if you can't read Plato in the original (and I couldn't), you can only be a dilettante philosopher."

I can't say I answered Markel with complete honesty—I wanted the job!—but I did say, "I like to write, it's in my blood. I can only say I have to write. It's like a calling. Furthermore, the *New York Times* is the best in the business."

Completely honest or not, apparently I said the right things: Markel said, "I hope you know what you are doing but first let's see what news sense you have. By tomorrow morning bring me a list of ten suggestions you think would make good stories for the magazine. Where are you staying? Give Mrs. Sheely your address and phone number."

I thanked him, and on my way out I gave the secretary my phone number (I was staying at the

Harvard Club), and asked her if there was somewhere I could go to make a few notes and write a memo. She suggested the *Times* library and I spent the next hour or so dreaming up ten ideas for magazine stories. I don't recall all the ideas now but I do remember two suggestions. At this time Robert Moses was rebuilding New York's highways and bridges (among them, the Triborough Bridge and the East River Drive), and he was known as the most independent man in the local government as well as a bit of a tyrant. He also happened to be an Oxford man. I suggested a piece on Robert Moses.

Another suggestion was a bit more far-out, but I took a chance on it. There was to be a meeting of the American Philosophical Association at Princeton, New Jersey, at the end of the week, and I suggested that I take that meeting as the occasion for a journalistic essay on philosophy. I really didn't think that suggestion had much of a chance on being accepted as a *New York Times* magazine piece, but to my great surprise, when I met Markel the following morning (I'd turned in my suggestions that same afternoon), he picked out the philosophy suggestion and said: "Okay, give me two thousand words—make the theme something like the meaning of philosophy in everyday life—and let me have the piece as soon after the meeting as you can."

What a break for me! At least that was one subject I knew something about, and I actually started writing the story before I even attended the meeting in Princeton. I turned the story in promptly, and apparently Markel liked it. He featured it in the Sunday Magazine, illustrated with Rembrandt's painting "Aristotle Contemplating the Bust of Homer," gave me a byline, and I seemed to be on my way to becoming a journalist. I remember observing sometime afterward that of all the writing I did for the *Times*, this, my very first article, was the only story I did in which not one of my words was changed!

Sometime later Markel apparently took another look at my list of suggestions and called me in the office. "I like your suggestion for a story on Robert Moses, but we have a problem. He doesn't give interviews, and he doesn't care very much for the press. We've already asked the mayor's office to help us, but no luck. You want to try? Good luck. Here's his phone number."

I loved this challenge, and I got on the assignment immediately. But I didn't phone his office. I thought I'd take my chances and just try to see him. Sometimes the less experience you have in these matters, the more courage you have.

I went to his office and introduced myself to his secretary. "I'm from the *New York Times*. I'd greatly appreciate setting up an appointment to see Mr. Moses for a possible story on the great job he is doing for New York." His secretary politely told me Mr. Moses did not give interviews, but I might talk to the press secretary. There was something about the secretary's accent (she was also quite good looking) that caught my attention. It sounded Greek to me, and I took a chance and spoke to her in Greek.

Sure enough she was Greek, but born in New York. Now she felt she had to be more than polite to me (not all, but most Greeks stick together), but she still told me that it would be difficult for her to help me because Mr. Moses just didn't give interviews to newspaper people. She was almost apologetic. Then I think the angel on my shoulder went to work again. A picture on the wall caught my eye. It was a picture of Oxford, with its towers and spires and meadows. "What a lovely picture," I said. "Does it have any special significance, or is it just a decoration?"

"Well, yes," said the secretary, "Mr. Moses has a degree from Oxford." And then she added: "In fact, he is going to attend the Oxford-Cambridge boat race dinner tonight."

Well, you can imagine my next actions. I couldn't wait to get back to the Harvard Club, get into my dinner jacket, and attend the dinner, to which I had also been invited. I managed to meet Moses during the cocktail hour, told him I was just starting out at the *New York Times*, and I'd greatly appreciate coming to see him: it would be a great break for me, and I needed a break. How could one Oxford man refuse another such a small favor? Moses was very cordial and said he would be glad to see me but that he could not promise to give me a story. I thanked him and two days afterward I was in his office asking the same secretary to announce to Mr. Moses that I was here.

"Mr. Moses is expecting you! Go right in," she answered, and rather proudly added, "Congratulations."

Moses greeted me warmly and asked me what I had read at Oxford and how long I had been in New York. I felt that we hit it off, and he didn't seem much like a tyrant to me, but he didn't agree to a story right away.

"I'll tell you what you do," he said. "I want you to walk all around the periphery of Manhattan. Take your time, make a two- or three-day project of it. Talk to some of the workers on some of the projects. Be careful going through Hell's Kitchen, and I'd do that during the daylight hours. Tell me what you think of the Battery, the Triborough Bridge project. Take a look at Harlem. After you've done all this, if you still want to do a story on me and my good works, then come back and we will talk again."

It was the best advice anyone could have given me. I spent nearly four days on this walk; I learned a lot about New York and I've loved Manhattan ever since. I met Moses again. He gave me the interview, and aside from a problem he raised by insisting on reading and approving the story before we printed it, I finally got the piece done. Markel would not agree to having Moses approve the story before it was printed, but I worked that out privately with Moses—I slipped him a copy of the draft and made a few changes that he requested. I received warm congratulations from Markel and was beginning to be recognized in the department as a promising young man. I've regretted all my life that I didn't make a career as a newspaperman on the *Times*.

In the meantime, Beatrice and I were making plans to marry. I told Beatrice and her family that my income from the *Times* was modest and that our way of life in New York would probably be quite different from what she was accustomed to for a while. These things don't appear much of a consideration when you are young and in love and the whole world is ahead of you, however. So we decided to marry come what may, and the wedding was set for December 28, 1938, in Winnetka, Illinois, at the Congregational church. Dr. Sam Harkness was the minister. It never occurred to me at the time that this might cause me, who had been baptized in the Greek Orthodox Church, some problems later with the Greek community. I had never been active in the Greek church and had little contact with the Greek community in Chicago and elsewhere until I became active in Greek war relief later. Only then did I really identify with Greeks and Greece. To this day the

Greek church has never forgotten that I married a Protestant and in a Congregational church. (I'm sure they have forgiven—don't all religious people forgive?) Indeed, just recently, when a Greek doctor, a friend of mine, died, and the services were held in a Greek church, I went to the church office to make a hundred-dollar donation in my friend's memory, and the secretary refused it. "Too much of religious policy," as some wise man said, "is based on fine print, and too little is based on love."

But our wedding, Congregational church and all, was what the *Chicago Daily News* and other newspapers covering the event called one of the most beautiful marriages of the year. I think this was because Beatrice was one of the most stately, beautiful women of her time. She was tall, elegant, and patrician. Even more important, she was always kind, fair, and just. One of the papers romanticized me as a Greek of royal blood, which was sheer nonsense, but I certainly felt royal, if that is indeed the word. More to the point, we were both very happy and continued to be so for over fifty years.

After the ceremony, Beatrice's parents gave the reception in their beautiful home on Pine Street, in Winnetka. There was champagne and music and a good time was had by all of the two hundred or so formally dressed guests. As Beatrice and I were getting ready to leave the six bridesmaids gathered round and she tossed the bouquet, which was caught by her best friend, Betty Dale Evans, and we were off to the Blackstone Hotel where we spent the night. Beatrice had changed into a beautiful gray Chanel suit and I into a deep brown Harris tweed outfit, which I had bought in Scotland while I was attending Oxford. I say "deep" brown, because I think it was more yellow-looking than brown, and I don't think it came off very well in that crowd of formal white ties and glamorous gowns! Why I remember this I don't know, but Beatrice remarked jovially on my suit for many years afterward. I finally gave it to the janitor in our building in New York.

The following morning all the Shorts, all the bridesmaids, my usher, and a big crowd of guests were at the LaSalle Street Station to see us off to White Sulphur Springs in West Virginia, where we spent our honeymoon. And why a summer resort in December? It was hardly the season, but something in me wanted to include West Virginia in our marriage.

I don't know how the news of our marriage reached Montgomery, West Virginia, but from the hour we arrived at the Greenbrier the phone seemed never to stop ringing, with calls from all my gang of friends in Montgomery. These included Meredith Arbaugh, Jimmy Dupey, Henderson Kelly, Tommy Robinson, and others, and the next day flowers arrived and a jar of West Virginia honey. We spent just a week there and had a quiet but wonderful time. Beatrice beat me at tennis. I beat her at croquet. She couldn't stand drinking the sulfur water (it does smell something awful), but I, being a bit of a water freak like my father, drank eight glasses a day and took the sulfur baths every morning. We both loved the flowers that were sent us, and after the Chicago weather (it was snowing when we left), West Virginia felt brisk but beautiful. I also remember Beatrice remarking on the furniture in our small suite. The chairs were the same Chippendale chairs as in her home in Winnetka, but obviously, I remember her laughing, these are copies. Then she said, "But I love this place and these days and I love you."

I mention and remember this expression of affection because Beatrice never talked much about her feelings, nor was she very articulate about her views on politics, morals, or society. "She didn't talk about her feelings," as her friend Patty Nielsen said at the memorial service, "she was her feelings and everybody knew it." But she felt very deeply about things. She was against the Vietnam war when all her Indian Hill friends were for it, for example, and she marched in an anti-war parade in Washington. She came from a WASP-ish family but she was the most tolerant, kind, and loving person I've ever met. She had an unwavering sense of justice, and she was unconditionally loyal to me throughout the best and worst of circumstances.

At the end of our week at the Greenbrier, I went to the cashier to pay our bill, where I was told that it had all been taken care of. Franz Wangemann, who had made the reservations for me (he was in the hotel business in Germany) had escaped from Germany at the beginning of the Jewish persecution. I had played a small role in helping him to get connected with hotel people in the States, and Beatrice and I, while at college, had been his friends. Wangemann had somehow or other arranged for our stay to be free—or maybe he had paid for it himself.

One does not look for kindness to be repaid and sometimes one doesn't understand how important a kind act is. Franz came to the States at a time when anyone from Germany, Jew or not, was looked upon with some suspicion, or at the least made to feel unwelcome. Beatrice and I befriended him just because he was a nice person and we liked him. Many years later, when he had become one of the senior vice presidents of the Hilton Hotel chain and was managing the Waldorf Astoria in New York, he told me that he had never forgotten our hospitality. We were among the few people who were kind to him. How sad it is that human beings can be or are unkind to each other. "Kindness," George Santayana said, "is the last wall of human thought." For me, kindness and loyalty transcend almost all other virtues. In the minds of some people, this emphasis has made me at times into a bit of a "patsy." I really don't mind. I'm strong and self reliant enough to afford kindness and hope that people can be influenced by example.

Beatrice and I returned by train to New York and took a lovely apartment (but not in the fashionable area Mrs. Short had suggested) on East 86th Street. The Shorts had given me a beautiful Sheraton desk as a wedding present and that was the second piece of furniture in the apartment, and most of the other furniture we bought in New York. Our apartment was convenient for the subway to Times Square and my job. Now everything fell in place for a happy life and a promising career.

We loved New York. First of all, Manhattan is an island, and for some reason I love islands. This has something to do with my sense of direction—which I totally lack. But on an island, I always seem to know where I am. I knew the East River was on one side and the Hudson River on the other. And I knew that the Battery was the end of Manhattan! But more important, life in New York in the 30s, despite the Depression and the unsettled conditions in Europe, was exciting and in those days *safe*.

Beatrice and I used to go everywhere, including Harlem to the Cotton Club—even to some of the dance spots in Hell's Kitchen, which we were warned against. We would picnic on Sundays in Central Park and walk there at night. We were never threatened or accosted.

New York had some rather interesting what today we would call low rent neighborhoods, but we found them friendly. They were noisy, with frequent domestic fights using four-letter language that I'm sure Beatrice had never heard before, but she found them entertaining and not in a patronizing way. She really wanted to get to know the people around us, especially the young wives and their many children.

I liked every aspect of New York. Its very rich, its immigrants (I did not feel any hostility in New York, only great ambition and vitality). I felt in a way that New York provided a cross section of America, because so many people, especially young people, came from farms and small towns, all wanting to "make it big." It was a favorite saying then and still is that if you can make it in New York you can make it anywhere. And I wanted to write about this kind of New York as I saw it.

I asked Lester Markel for this kind of an assignment for the Sunday Magazine. He said, "Okay, you can start with a piece on Hell's Kitchen."

I told Beatrice about my assignment and asked if she wanted to go with me. She said, "Of course," and off we went one late morning, stopping first at Sardi's for a snack. Bringing Beatrice with me was a mistake. First of all, she was so well-dressed, tall, and patrician looking that it was difficult for me to get honest interviews with some of the more disreputable characters (and it was a rough neighborhood) with whom I wanted to talk. She was definitely distracting. One man I tried to talk to first asked, "Hey are you a reporter or a social worker? We don't need no charity here!"

One block of Hell's Kitchen was known for its prostitutes and from this section came, I found out later, most of the prostitutes working Times Square

Decisions, Decisions, Decisions 77

and upper Manhattan. I was able to interview one of the girls (I had to pay her $10 an hour, the same rate as for her customers), and she talked freely about her life and profession.

She was a black girl from Rockford, Illinois, aged twenty-two, and had come to New York to work at the Copacabana Club. She thought she was going to be a dancer but ended up as a cigarette girl and eventually went into prostitution, first for the club, with which she had to share her payments, and then later on her own, so that she kept all her earnings. I felt rather uneasy talking to a prostitute in front of my wife, but Beatrice struck up a good conversation with her.

Their conversation went something like this: "Well we both are from Illinois and I've just come here. Do you want to stay here and try to get into show business? Eventually, I suppose you want to get married and start a family. My husband knows a lot of people. Maybe he can help you." Beatrice talked to the prostitute just as if they were classmates at Wellesley. And her attitude didn't come from not knowing the difference in their situations in life. It came from her sheer compassion for the girl.

At the end of the interview—which went over the agreed upon hour, the girl refused additional money for the overtime!—Stella said: "Man, you've got a great gal there—I hope you know it. And when you first came over I thought you wanted some three-way action!"

I went on to write other articles for the *Times*. There was one on William Russell, Dean of Columbia College; an article on Pan Am and the first round-the-world airline route; something on the Legal Aid Society in New York, which gave free legal advice to those who could not afford it; a piece on the great theater in New York—in the 30s an orchestra seat went for $3.00; a piece on an astrologer and the many clients she had among the stockbrokers on Wall Street; and a score of other articles that gave me great pleasure to do and allowed me to know New York better. That was the time of my life. That is, until a year or so after I'd begun, when money raised its ugly head.

Though I had some savings and Beatrice received a small dividend from stocks, my income from the *Times* was not enough to support us with anything left over. If we had given it three or four years, I'm sure I could have made it, but one night I received a call from my father-in-law, who said that there was an opening at the advertising firm of J. Walter Thompson in Chicago (Henry Stanton, head of the firm, was my father-in-law's best friend), at a salary of about three times what I was making from writing for the *Times* and was I interested?

He told me that I would be working on the Elgin National Watch, the Northern Trust Bank, and the Kelloggs cornflakes accounts, all important, big-billing accounts. I didn't want to stop writing for the *Times* or leave New York, which I love to this day, but the salary was very tempting. Then Henry Stanton himself called me—at the urging of my father-in-law, no doubt—and told me he had read some of my articles. He reminded me that J. Walter Thompson was the number one advertising company in the world, and that, if I did well, the sky was the limit, and that he saw no reason why inside of a year or two I shouldn't expect a vice presidency in the Chicago office, and so on. All this attention was pretty heady stuff for a poor, young journalist. I talked it over with Beatrice, who assured me she was happy the way we were in New York but that I should do what I thought best. I much appreciated her response. She also reminded me that back of all this was her father's desire that she be in Chicago. She was her father's favorite (I couldn't blame him there), and he would pull any strings to get us back home.

So I took the job at J. Walter Thompson, and it turned out to be one of the biggest mistakes of my life. In the first place, going from reporting and writing feature articles for the *New York Times Magazine* to writing copy for cornflakes and watches is, to put it mildly, rather uninspiring. I, with a view to the future, could have handled that, but unfortunately I was working under a character who obviously was a good advertising man but was also a religious freak. On every bit of copy that he wrote, and everything that I wrote as well, including memos, he insisted on putting at the top the initials "JMJ" (for "Jesus, Mary, and Joseph"), after which he would bless the copy and cross himself!

The copy certainly turned out to be a great success—both his and mine—but I didn't think that that was due to divine intervention, and I couldn't take the praying, the blessings, and the kneeling. He would ask me to kneel and pray with him in the office. (This now reminds me of President Nixon asking Henry Kissinger to kneel and pray with him during the Watergate crisis.)

Of course, everybody else in the office knew about his idiosyncrasy, and none of his assistants lasted very long despite the handsome salary. Co-workers told me just to laugh it off. But then I was the one who had to put up with it. One day the senior vice president of the company, I believe his name was Kenneth Heller, asked me to write a speech he was about to give before a group of investment bankers and economists, sponsored by Bache & Co. I wrote the speech, and it was wonderful to get back to some real writing, even for a few days. Then my director asked to see the speech before I gave it to the vice president. I said this was not part of my advertising copy, and I thought that it was a personal matter between me and the vice president. He insisted, however, saying all copy had to go over his desk. So I finally gave him a copy of the speech. "This is very good," he said, "Congratulations." And then he started to bless the speech and write the initials on it.

This was too much for me. I became so angry, I grabbed the pen from his hand, broke it in half and threw the pieces on his desk and said, "Fellow, there will be no fucking initials on this," and I took the speech and left. The next day I felt I'd had enough and resigned. (Incidentally, and with all respect to the religious freak, although the vice president liked the speech and said something like "Old boy, you deserve a raise for this," it did not go over very well with the economists, and he did not get the Bache account he was angling for.)

My father-in-law was unhappy with my resignation and asked me why I hadn't complained to Henry Stanton earlier. I think I answered something rather pompous like, "That's not my style," and let it drop. For the record I was offered another job in the company, but I felt I'd had enough of the advertising business.

Actually there was another reason why I did not hesitate to resign or accept a new offer that came my way soon thereafter. The war in Europe was heating up, and I was itching to get into it. At this time the various countries involved, especially Great Britain, France, and Greece, were conducting war-relief drives. I don't remember where or how I met Mitchell McKeown, but he was the best fund-raiser for charitable purposes in Chicago, and when he found out I had left J. Walter Thompson he asked if I would join him for a special fund-raising drive for Navy relief, which was designed to help the families of Navy personnel. This was a temporary but well-paying job. Having nothing else to do, I accepted and joined Raleigh Warner, who was then president of the Pure Oil Company and chairman of the Navy Relief Drive, hoping to raise, I believe, three hundred thousand dollars for the cause. This goal was like shooting fish in a barrel; the war was on, and patriotism was at a high pitch. Our boys were risking their lives, so who in good conscience could refuse to help Navy relief? In less than six weeks we raised nearly twice our goal and with more money coming in Warner, to his credit, ended the drive. McKeown congratulated me for my effort, and Warner gave me a special citation signed by the Secretary of the Navy for "a job well done." This was my first crack at raising money for charity, and I learned a lot that helped enormously the next time I took a fund-raising assignment, this time one that I chose for myself, Greek war relief.

Greek War Relief

Greece and Greeks in the early 1940s were suffering enormously under German occupation. We could not get relief supplies into the country because Great Britain, fearing the supplies would fall into German hands, had established a blockade. Meanwhile, more than a million Greeks were dying of starvation.

The purpose of Greek War Relief, which was headed nationally by Spyros Skouras, president of 20th Century Fox, was to raise funds for food, clothing, and medicine, as well as for the ship to transport them to Greece. Greek War Relief was also determined to persuade the British to lift the blockade, even if this meant that part of the relief supplies fell into German hands.

As I've mentioned earlier in these memoirs, although I was of Greek parentage and of course was proud of it, I had never really felt Greek—I'd never mixed much with Greeks, and I didn't go to the Greek church. In fact, on the only trip I'd taken to Greece up to that time, that walking tour in 1937, I'd had to insist on my American nationality to stay out of the army. I'd been showing off my knowledge of Greek at the customs line, and the official's response had been, "If you're Greek, you're Greek—where are your military papers?" But during the war my heart and spirit went out to Greece, and I wanted to help.

I volunteered my services to the Chicago Greek Relief office, which at the time was headed by a group that included John Manta, George Phillips, Andrew Kanelis, and Milton Baldji. To my amazement I found that they were not soliciting funds from Americans or American corporations, but only from Greeks and Greek businesses, and they had only raised about thirty thousand dollars! Was this more of the famous Greek *philitoma*, or pride? In this case, when Greece was fighting and suffering not just for them but for our allies, it seemed to me sheer stupidity not to seek help from all Americans, and I told the committee so. The group did not know me (perhaps they knew that I had married an American girl outside of the Greek church), but they seemed willing to listen. I made them a proposition: you go ahead and raise funds from Greeks. Triple your goal. Let me organize a Chicago Citizens' Committee that doesn't have any Greeks on it to raise funds from the Chicago community, mainly non-Greeks. I suppose they felt they had nothing to lose, so, with the condition that they be allowed to approve what I did, they agreed. I didn't feel that they entertained any high hopes for my success, however.

    I, on the other hand, was fired up. I immediately got in touch with my father-in-law and asked his help. He introduced me to Clarence Randall, then president of Inland Steel, and Howell Murray, a vice president of A. G. Becker Company, an investment banking firm. I met with each of them individually, gave them the statistics of Greece's great suffering, and asked them right out to head up a drive to raise one million dollars for Greek relief among Chicagoans and Chicago corporations. Now these were two very successful, tough businessmen, widely known and respected in Chicago. Neither of them had ever been to Greece, however, and I suspect that they knew little about the country. But I seemed to have touched their humanitarian spirit (perhaps my angel helped in this), and each of them accepted leadership of the Chicago Citizens' Committee for Greek War Relief with enthusiasm.

In less than sixty days we had formed a committee of more than sixty people, representing the top families and businesses in Chicago, and we raised more than a million dollars for Greek War Relief. Needless to say, although Randall and Murray deserve most of the credit, I became a bit of a hero in the Greek community and was asked by Spyros Skouras to join the National Board of Directors of Greek War Relief to raise funds nationally. That campaign also made me even prouder of my Greek heritage, and I feel that I have been more Greek ever since.

Greek War Relief now had the money for food and medical supplies—nationally we raised more than five million dollars—and also we had two ships to transport the supplies, given to us by the Swedish government. The problem was that the British were still refusing to lift their blockade. How they really came to do it is rather extraordinary.

Spyros Skouras, always direct and usually blunt, believed in getting to the bottom of matters and dealing directly with the top people involved. But even he couldn't see Winston Churchill, as he wanted to do, so we had to settle for the British ambassador to Washington. A meeting was arranged for our Secretary of State, Cordell Hull, the British ambassador and one of his staff, one of the people working on Greek affairs (who was as I recall a lawyer), and me. The agenda was simple and clear: what can be done immediately to lift the blockade, so that these two ships can deliver foodstuffs to the starving Greek people? The lawyer presented the agenda. Mr. Hull expressed his support for lifting the blockade, and then the British ambassador spoke.

Now before this meeting took place, I had been asked by the lawyer to remind Spyros Skouras that this was simply a meeting to present information, so could he please take care to observe protocol. When I asked him what the protocol business meant, he explained that Mr. Skouras must not make any demands that could not be met and would therefore embarrass the British ambassador.

The ambassador was a portly man, with a watch chain across his rather large stomach. He spoke eloquently, expressing his great admiration for the Greek people, who by their resistance of the Italian invasion and their prolonged engagement of the Germans were delaying the Nazi invasion of Russia. He was aware of their great suffering and starvation, but his government could not agree at this time to lifting the blockade, because such a course would also help the Nazis. There was a bit of silence after he spoke.

Up to this point, Skouras had said nothing. The secretary of state then asked Mr. Skouras if he wanted to make a statement. Skouras picked up his briefcase as if to leave and walked over to the British ambassador, who then also stood up, and said:

"Mr. Ambassador, the only reason you don't lift the blockade is that your fat stomach is full (and he patted the Ambassador's stomach) and the Greeks are starving, and you don't know or give a damn about the difference."

And to the shock of everybody present (however, I thought I detected a bit of a smile on Cordell Hull's face) he walked out. But I was told later that by the time Skouras returned to his office at 20th Century Fox in New York, the blockade of Greece had been lifted.

At this time I was a member of the State Department, which I had joined in 1942, to Skouras's disappointment. (He promised me anything I wanted after the war—a job in Hollywood even!—if I'd stay and head up the Greek War Relief effort, but I was eager to go overseas and be a real part of the war.) Soon after I was sent to Greece, to administer aid directly, under the aegis of the newly formed UNRRA (United Nations Relief and Rehabilitation Association). While I was in Athens, I came into contact with Skouras again, this time in connection with the relief of his home village, Skouharou. His behavior in that situation was as high-handed, and as effective, as ever.

Skouras, in his capacity as president of Greek War Relief, had decided to pay a visit to Athens to help coordinate the activities of UNRRA with Greek War Relief. This was the end of November before the outbreak of the civil war, but it was nonetheless a time of great distress in Greece, particularly, Skouras found out, in his village in the Peloponnisos, Skouharou, which is named after the Skouras family. The Germans had blown up parts of the railroad leading to the village, and the main road was impassable. There was no airport either in or near the village, and it seemed that all communications were down. Yet word got out—Greeks are very enterprising—that there was starvation in the village, that there were no medical supplies in the small local hospital, and that help was desperately needed.

I reported this situation to General Scobie, head of

the British armed forces in Greece, and involved with UNRRA. He sympathized but responded in effect that Skouharou was only one of a hundred villages in the same or worse situation and nothing could be done immediately. Of course, this was not a satisfactory reply for Skouras. Skouras was determined to help his village and now! He got in touch with the State Department in Washington and later with our Defense Department, and within twenty-four hours, in true Skouras fashion, he got action. The Defense Department flew in a special plane from our base in Egypt for Skouras, and then we did two things.

First, with Oscar Broneer, the renowned archaeologist and excavator of Corinth who was helping with our relief efforts, Skouras and a helper and I flew low over Skouharou, circled the village several times, and dropped a red bag containing a message that we would be dropping food and medical supplies at noon the following day, and would they please stretch out a white sheet in the village square indicating where best to drop the supplies.

At noon the next day, our plane, loaded to capacity with bags of flour, powdered milk, powdered eggs (the Greeks hated powdered eggs), beans, olive oil, other foods, and medical supplies (including the newly developed penicillin), circled the village and what did we see? Not one sheet stretched out in the village square but hundreds of them all over the village, including sheets on practically every house top. That's Greece for you.

We parachuted the supplies down, aiming for the village square, and with the parachutes went my prayers that the supplies would be equally and freely distributed, and not fall into the hands of the black marketeers. I had found in my experiences dealing with relief matters, that no matter how much starvation and misery there was, there was always a black marketeer who could being relief if you could afford it. During the worst days in Greece, even while it was under German occupation, you could still get a loaf of bread for a fifty-dollar sliver of gold (gold was the only currency accepted). The rich carried ribbons of gold with them and cut off whatever amount was needed for a purchase. A bag of flour could cost as much as $150; even the hated powdered eggs and soup would cost $30; a package of American or British cigarettes cost $25; a jar of honey came at a premium in Athens of $250.

The word we got back from Skouharou after we dropped the supplies was "Long live the U.S.A.—and Long live Spyros Skouras."

And I must happily admit that it was only because of Skouras that we were able to do what we did. For this and his many other good works Boston University some years later gave Skouras an honorary degree. Tom Pappas, a Boston financier, and I had a little something to do with this, and Skouras remarked to us after he received the honorary degree: "My dear friend Chreese, this is pretty damn good for a shepherd boy from Greece who never got beyond the sixth grade in school." And so it was!

I Enter the War

To backtrack a bit, Beatrice and I had invited Ann and Phil Weld (Phil and I were classmates at Harvard) over for lunch at 1200 Lake Shore Drive, Chicago, where we had a small but beautiful apartment, convenient to the Wrigley Building on Michigan Avenue, where I had been working for J. Walter Thompson. Among other things, I wanted to show Phil our new Lafayette radio, which he had recommended I buy. We turned on the radio and after some sputterings heard for the first time the momentous news: the Japanese had attacked Pearl Harbor.

For those who were too young or not around at the time, it may be difficult to appreciate the patriotic impact that the Japanese invasion had on most of us. Before Pearl Harbor many citizens, and especially Colonel Robert McCormick, publisher of the *Chicago Tribune*, were either lukewarm or absolutely against our getting into the war. But after Pearl Harbor anyone who didn't want to fight for his country became suspect.

I was caught up in the fever to enlist immediately and volunteered for the Navy. I had just completed my work for the Navy relief effort. Through some friends on the *Chicago Daily News*, I also had some contact with Colonel Knox, the Secretary of the Navy. I enlisted their support, but not for favored treatment. Rather, I knew I had a weak left eye, and I was hoping the Navy would make an exception and accept me.

I went down to the Board of Trade, where the Navy had their recruiting office, and I passed the physical—until we got to the eye test. Try as hard as I could to fake it—"Now put your right hand over your right eye." I put my right hand over my weak left eye!—it didn't work, and without further ado I was flatly rejected.

"Don't you need someone who knows Greek?"

"Sorry, buddy, no exceptions!"

After the end of the war, when they did need someone who knew Greek and Greece, the Navy did look the other way and enlisted me as a first lieutenant, but this was in 1946 and I never saw any action. But meanwhile I joined the State Department in Washington and worked there from 1942 until I was sent overseas.

At that time, as I mentioned, Cordell Hull was Secretary of State, and former Governor Herbert Lehman of New York was invited by President Roosevelt to be his special assistant in charge of foreign relief matters. I had met Governor Lehman through his niece, Margaret Altschul, and I believe that she told her uncle of my interest in joining the State Department, and working on war relief, especially for Greece.

I had another contact to the State Department in Doctor Raymond Geist, our former Consul General in Berlin, whom I met though my old friends the Biggses. I mention these contacts not to indicate that I was trying to get special treatment at the State Department.

I Enter the War 91

In fact, they were necessary simply to receive any consideration for a job at all. I found out several years later that I had almost not gotten the job of assistant in the Greek war relief efforts: the reason—I was Greek! (Well, I was of Greek descent.) In those days it was against State Department policy to offer an ambassadorship, for example, to a person whose family came from the country in question. It was feared that the person would feel mixed loyalties and not work fully for the interests of the United States. When John Kennedy became president all that was changed, I believe.

In my case, the position I was being considered for was way below ambassadorship status, but the fear of conflict of interest was a serious consideration. Anyway, I joined the department, and my job was to help prepare the relief program for Greece—as soon as we could get rid of the Germans, who were nearly starving her to death. (More than two million Greeks died of starvation and related causes during the German occupation.) At about the same time I got the offer to join State, Raleigh Warner called me to say that he had talked to "Wild Bill" Donovan, head of the Office of Strategic Services (OSS), the forerunner of the CIA, about me. Donovan thought that they could use me as an agent in the Middle East. Spy work has never interested me (and I don't like motorcycle cops who hide behind billboards and bushes to catch speeding motorists either), and I turned down the offer.

Meanwhile, we moved. My wife, Beatrice, and new-born daughter, Niki, came to Washington with me. I tried to prepare for the time I would be sent to Greece to implement the relief program. Part of my work at the time was also to help form UNRRA (United Nations Relief and Rehabilitation Association), which Governor Lehman headed up. I was a delegate to the conference in Atlantic City, New Jersey, that saw UNRRA officially come into being.

Finally in April 1943 the word came that we would be on our way to Greece via Egypt soon and to be ready to leave at a day's notice. We left from Norfolk, Virginia, to join a ninety-eight-ship convoy to Egypt, which took us twenty-nine days at the rate of four or five knots. That long trip was quite a revelation to me. Traveling seems to bring out the best and worst in human character, and if in addition you can throw in a poker game or two—now that is a real test of what kind of people you are traveling with.

In our running poker game, for example, were two high-ranking State Department officials, the head of an OWI (Office of War Information) department, three OSS officials (whose official status was "Weathermen") and myself. The makeup of the group varied but these were our regulars. I like the observation among poker players: "How a person acts when he wins says a lot about him; how he acts when he loses says everything about him!"

I think it was on our seventh or eighth day at sea that we had our first, shall I call it incident, at poker, at the same time that we had an incident at sea. Earlier in the day we underwent our first enemy submarine alert. Our ship, the *S.S. Morrison*, lay about in the middle of that ninety-eight-ship convoy (were we such important cargo?), and I don't think there was much danger of a submarine torpedo getting through to us, surrounded as we were by other liberty ships. Nevertheless, we were told to wear our helmets while we played poker that night. There was a bit of nervousness at the table. I can't say I was nervous because once I start playing poker, I am totally and happily engrossed in it, and I think of nothing else, not even a submarine alert.

Maybe that helped cause the "incident." We usually played seven card stud. The maximum bet was five dollars on the last card, with a one-dollar bet on each card dealt. Rarely did any one player win or lose more than a hundred dollars during an evening.
The bet on the table was four dollars for a pair shown. The player who caused the incident was one of our key State Department people, and he was having one of those nights when you just don't get the right cards, or worse still you always have the second-best hand. Anyway, after he had lost another big pot—he was now down about sixty dollars for the evening—he cried out, "I just can't bear it any longer, I just can't bear it!" and he actually burst into tears! We were all quite embarrassed for him but in addition to sympathy for him, I couldn't help thinking, "This is a policy-maker for the Middle East. What will he do if the going gets tough in dealing with a German or an Arab, or even a polite Turk, known as they are for their cunning diplomacy and cruelty to friend and foe alike?" Anyway, we didn't invite him to play with our group again. Poker demands gentlemanly competition and, above all, fun and excitement, not problems.
A more serious incident concerned the OWI man. He seemed scared from the moment he boarded the ship in Norfolk, and he wore his helmet at all times—at meals, in the john, even, we suspected, when he slept. Another thing I noticed about him was that he always wore thick-rimmed glasses when he played poker, but never for reading, or at any other time. And I've never seen a man draw to more inside straights. Finally one of our players, one of the OSS "weathermen," said, more kiddingly than in accusation, "I've never seen such luck. Are these cards marked? Take the pot!"
With that the OWI player stood up, drew out a

large knife, plunged the knife through his accuser's cards lying on the table and shouted: "Oh, yeah, does anyone want to make something of it?"

At that moment I could not control myself. I jumped up, grabbed a whisky bottle from the table (I'm not sure what I was going to do with it, break it like they do in the movies and attack him?) and shouted: "No, nobody is going to do anything about it—just take the money and leave, you're out of the game and I'm taking two dollars for the deck you've ruined." To my relief he backed down (most cheaters do when caught), but he left his knife still stuck in the cards, and he did not take the money. The next day he apologized and said he had been drinking. Nevertheless he was never invited to play with us again.

Shortly after we had crossed the Atlantic and entered the Mediterranean, we had another submarine alert. This time one of the outer liberty ships was disabled and we had to abandon it. That was understood before we set out. One of our destroyer escorts was able to rescue some of the crew. This attack made us all a little more apprehensive. As civilians, which most of us were, we were never as appreciative of the danger we faced as were the seasoned military personnel on board.

As a result of this last scare another incident occurred in our little civilian group which to this day still enormously amuses me. This happened not at our poker table but in my cabin and involved my roommate. I'm purposely not mentioning some of the names, for as far as I know most of our group are still alive, even some fifty years later. My roommate, like myself, was of Greek descent, but unlike me he was a trained military man, a proud member of the U.S. Marines. As we were about to retire in our cabin, he seemed

unusually nervous. I asked him what was the matter. He said an astonishing thing: "Chris, do you realize that the lower bunk in this cabin (I had the top bunk, he the lower) is practically on the same sea level that a torpedo travels?"
 I think all I could say was, "Oh?"
 "Chris, I'll give you fifty dollars if you will change bunks with me."
 "Fellow, are you crazy? What difference would it make whether you are in the lower or upper bunk if a torpedo hits us? Go to sleep!"
 "Chris, I'd sleep better."
 As a matter of fact, I preferred the lower bunk. It was a little roomier and easier to get into. So I said: "You're a fool," and took the fifty dollars.
 A few days later off the coast of Sicily, we had a rather heavy air attack that left our ship untouched. That night I said to my roommate, "Boy, am I glad to be on the lower berth with all that protection from bombs. For another fifty do you want to change again?" I don't think my roommate appreciated the humor or ridiculousness of it all. But we all survived, and after twenty-nine days of this sort of boredom alleviated by tension, we arrived in Port Said, going on to Cairo by motor convoy.
 In Cairo I was booked into a rather small Egyptian hotel not too near the center of the city. As I'd already heard of the world-famous Shepheards Hotel, I thought I'd pay it a visit, before even checking into my own hotel. After seeing Shepheards and meeting the concierge, who happened to be Greek, there was no way I was going to stay in my place if I could possibly get a room at Shepheards. It was unlike any place in this world. Among other things, it had a small zoo in its palatial gardens out back, featuring gazelles. The

rooms were large with high ceilings and silent ceiling fans. The bar, famous for its drinks know as S & Bs (suffering bastards), was a meeting place for foreign dignitaries and the press in particular, and the large outdoor terrace in front of the hotel facing one of the busiest streets in the city was perfect for sitting and, as they say, "watching the world go by."

Shepheards was also known for having the most famous checkroom in the world. It was run by a third-generation Egyptian family. In addition to managing the checkroom, they also had a little silver business, mostly making cigarette cases, key rings, and copies of ancient silver slave bracelets. In ancient times these bracelets were used to measure the size of the female slave's wrists, the smaller the wrist, the more costly the slave.

There is the story that Winston Churchill, a young army lieutenant in World War I, checked a bag in Shepheards's checkroom. When he returned to Cairo in 1942 he went to the hotel and asked if by any chance they still had his bag (some 27 years later). Without blinking an eye—so the story goes—the young checkroom attendant said, "Of course," dusted off the bag, asked Churchill to sign for it, and gave it to him. Perhaps because he was so amazed, Churchill didn't leave a tip! (A colonel in the U.S. army, who apparently was an autograph collector, was staying at the hotel at the time and heard the story. He bought the autographed coatroom check for $10.)

When I arrived, however, I was told that the hotel was completely booked, with a sixty-day waiting list, and even my offer of "baksheesh" (money) had no effect. (Baksheesh isn't regarded as a bribe exactly; giving it is a common practice in Egypt, no matter what you want to do or get. Hungry children ask for baksheesh on the streets.) I was discouraged a bit, and to console myself I had a drink on the terrace. My angel apparently had plans for me, however, for no sooner had I sat down when a man in a swanky U.S. officer's uniform slapped me on the back. "You old bastard, what are you doing here?" It was Johnny Irving, a friend from Chicago, masquerading as another "weatherman," but a member of the OSS! Soon we were joined by a couple of his buddies and two WACs, also from the U.S. Army. (Actually, privates in uniform, like the WACs, were not supposed to mingle with officers and guests on the terrace, but these girls from Mobile, Alabama, were too attractive for anyone to deny them our company.)

Johnny insisted I join them for dinner, but I explained I had to return to my hotel to check in and get organized. "Hey, you can't stay at that dump. I'm leaving tomorrow for a little mission (I found out later that his "little mission" was being parachuted back of the German lines in Greece) and you can stay in my room—and I'm getting a special rate. Just, under no circumstances, give up the room. They are as scarce as hen's teeth. I must be gone a month or more." At that point, I didn't care what the rate was (actually it was about $15 a night), and I accepted his invitation immediately.

Before we went out to dinner (we had roasted pigeons for the main course), he introduced me to the room clerk as a very important State Department official. He also showed me the room, which was small but overlooked the back garden and the gazelles, and I moved in the next morning. My living quarters wherever I travel have always meant very much to me. I don't mind roughing it when I have to, but living in Egypt constituted a health hazard under the best of circumstances, nor is it particularly comfortable, so I was pleased to be staying in one of the most luxurious, as well as one of the strangest, places in Cairo.

Later that same day I reported to the State Department officials not far from Shepheards that I was ready for work. But as it turned out, they were not quite ready for me, nor did they know what to do with me. I had been sent overseas to head up the UNRRA Greek Desk for relief matters. It seemed that the post was already filled by an Englishman. In a very pompous fashion he offered me a desk and offered, "No problem, old chap, you can work for me!"

As diplomatically as I could, I said that this was a matter I'd have to take up with Governor Lehman's office. I returned to Shepheards and drafted a private cable to George Xanthaky, who was head of relief operations for Greece. In a few days Xanthaky cabled back regretting the mix up but advising me not to make an issue of the matter with the English; we had enough disagreements with them as it was. He assured me that they were working out another slot for me that would ensure my getting into Greece and working on relief matters. In another week I got my assignment and to my great surprise, and a certain amount of chagrin, it was as chief of Balkan intelligence, but with an addendum that this would be an interim assignment. I go into such detail regarding this matter because it led to rather interesting developments and mysterious repercussions.

As may be rather obvious, in the diplomatic world there are really no secrets, and apparently the word got out quickly that I had landed a prestigious, secret, and important job. I must add here that I never did any intelligence work; the whole idea of spying is not very agreeable to me, regardless of the cause, as I've said before. But apparently the title Chief of Balkan Intelligence was enough to bring me invitations to all the important social and government functions in Cairo. And I got the impression that the experts thought I was perfect for the job because who would suspect that anyone (and these are not my words) "so open, kind, and soft"—they didn't quite use the word *naive*—could be head of the tough and often necessarily vicious intelligence department.

In passing I should say that my view of life is quite different. I believe that only the strong, self-sufficient, courageous, and unconditionally loyal person can afford to be "open, kind, and soft." It's often the weak and cowardly who must be cruel, biased, or revengeful, and join others of like nature to survive. Well, that's my sermon for this morning.

But being Chief of Balkan Intelligence got me some interesting assignments and perks in Greece. A wise man does not question these things.

When in September 1943 the Germans were driven from Greece, all of us in the UNRRA-State Department contingent were cleared for entrance. There was some hitch when our ship arrived in Pireaus. Demonstrators from the growing menace, the Greek Communists, who didn't want us in Greece at all, caused a fuss. But apparently General Scobie, head of the British Armed Forces in Greece, intervened and was able to get clearance for us to land. Along with other members of our UNRRA contingent, I was given comfortable accommodations in a hotel near Omonia Square. No sooner was I settled in my room than I got a call from Colonel Michael Lubbock, who was the head of the Armed Forces in Athens and whom I had met briefly in Cairo at some social function.

"Chris, this is Michael Lubbock. You remember

we met in Cairo, but we have never really had a chance to talk, even about Oxford. I'd like to see you, now that we are going to be working together in Athens. Can you come for tea tomorrow at 4 o'clock, 21 Americus Street, top floor."

I said, "Fine," and was glad to accept, though I wondered why he had really sought me out. Probably, the old "Chief of Balkan Intelligence" thing again.

When the next day I went to 21 Americus Street, I noticed that the apartment I was going to was in the name of Eliopoulos. I learned later that the British had simply asked Mr. Eliopoulos to move and requisitioned the penthouse apartment for their office use.

Michael greeted me at the door like an old friend and introduced me to the other British officers living with him. One was Colonel Robert Lauder, head of the Quartermaster Corps; another was Colonel Victor, head of the British Military Police, another officer, whose name I can't recall, was head of all transportation in Athens, and there was Colonel Galofka of the U.S. Army, who was Lubbock's opposite. The only person not present was General Scobie. After the various introductions, Michael showed me around the duplex penthouse, which had a fine view, and then said to me, "Chris, why don't you come and live with us? There is plenty of room and you can have the den overlooking the terrace."

I thanked Michael very much for the invitation but told him I'd have to check with the State Department. Michael said: "That is really not necessary, but do talk to them if you want." I was very busy over the next few days and didn't have time to respond to Michael's invitation. But at the end of the week, I returned to my hotel, only to be told by the manager that my things had been moved to 21 Americus Street, where I had been "ordered to stay."

So, I followed my belongings to 21 Americus Street—after all, it was an order (Greece was under the British sphere of influence). I didn't ask any more questions and lived out the Greek civil war in the company of all the top military people in charge of Athens' political, military, legal, and economic affairs.

The Greek Civil War

The Greek civil war, in which more Greek lives were lost than during the entire German occupation, had broken out in December 1943, immediately following the expulsion of the Germans. This was essentially a war between the Greek underground forces, which we had helped to organize and support during the war in order to harass the Germans, and the regular Greek army, which wanted to restore the legal, exiled Greek government. The regular Greek army was revived after the Germans left Greece. The underground forces, later dubbed Communist, refused to give up their arms (which had been supplied principally by Great Britain and the United States).

Churchill could have been speaking of Greece when he said that there is no more vicious, emotional, or dedicated conflict than a civil war. In a normal war you know where and who your enemy is. In a civil war, brother fights brother, and the woman who sells you flowers in the morning can be delivering a machine gun to your opponent at night. The Greek civil war was one of the saddest conflicts in all of Greek history, one that I, as a civilian, was quite unprepared for.

About two months after we arrived in Greece, the civil war broke out in great fury. At one point the Communist forces were within some 1,500 yards of the Grande Bretagne Hotel, which was General Scobie's headquarters. By capturing Athens, they would have controlled most of Greece. At this point, the State Department ordered all American civilians not essential to the present crisis out of Greece, and this included me. But I was damned if I was going to leave Greece after all I had gone through to get there.

I asked Michael Lubbock to intervene on my behalf, as well as Laird Archer, who had become head of UNRRA in Greece. I was finally permitted to stay, along with eight other Americans, one of whom was head of the Red Cross in Athens. Each of us did the best we could, which included a little bit of everything. One afternoon Laird Archer asked me if I would drive a truck to help pick up the dead killed on the streets of Athens the day before. With two Greek helpers, I picked up thirty-nine bodies of men, women, and children, all within a few blocks of the Grand Bretagne Hotel. We buried them with just a minimum of identification in a ditch in the Palace Gardens. This experience left me very shaken; to calm my nerves as well as to lessen the stench of decaying bodies, I first started smoking. Some years after the war when I revisited Athens, I went to the Palace Gardens where I'd buried the bodies, but they had long before been dug up and given a proper religious burial.

A few days later Rodney Young, who was working with the Red Cross, asked me if I would help deliver food and medical supplies to five hospitals in Athens, three of which were behind Communist lines, "but it will be all right because you will be riding in a Red Cross truck, white flag flying." We loaded the truck with olive oil, beans, flour, powdered milk, and some medical supplies and drove off toward Omonia Square, which was still in Communist hands. I was driving, with three helpers in the back of the truck. At the moment that we crossed into the square, I heard machine-gun fire and our right rear tire was hit. Fortunately, there was an alley just ahead, which I quickly drove into, and we changed the tire. Meanwhile, I walked into the street, where I met some men in rather ragged uniforms and asked in the best Greek I could manage, "What the hell is going on? Can't you see we're a Red Cross truck carrying supplies for the hospitals?" The soldiers asked to inspect the truck and told me afterward that just the day before that same truck had been used to transport ammunition. At this point, I was ready to wring Rodney Young's neck, though I realize that he may not have been responsible. But this adventure is mild compared to what happened later.

We delivered supplies to four hospitals and were on the way to the fifth when again I took over the driving. I had been riding in the back of the truck most of the way. One of my three Greek helpers rode in the cab with me, the other two were in the back of the truck sitting on the last of the sacks of flour, beans, and other supplies. As I approached the hospital I saw a group of people waving. I thought they were just a welcoming committee. It turned out that they weren't waving greetings, but waving me to stop or go back. My helper, sitting next to me, shouted "Staso, staso" (Stop!). But it was too late. We ran over a German land mine.

The cabin was blown off the truck with my helper and me in it; the rest of the truck was destroyed, killing both of the young Greeks in back. My helper miraculously escaped without a scratch. My eardrum was hurt, but with the exception of a few relatively minor cuts on my forehead that were bleeding profusely, I was shaken but unhurt. All of us were taken to the emergency room of the hospital. They just cleaned me up a bit and eventually gave me a ride back to our headquarters at the Grande Bretagne Hotel.

Laird Archer was shocked to hear what had happened, and the reporters, whose headquarters were also in the Grande Bretagne, covered the incidents widely, with headlines claiming that the Communists were now attacking the Red Cross. The story also appeared in the *Chicago Daily News*: "Janus Hurt in Mine Explosion," but Archer had already wired my wife, who was back staying with her family in Winnetka, that I was okay.

During the civil war I met and became good friends with General Alex Melas, who was among other things (I believe he was working with the OSS) a special assistant to General Plastiras, then the prime minister of Greece. I never did check into Alex's Greek military credentials, especially the "General" part (at times Alex was fond of "civilized lies," as he called them), nor did I care to. He was an extraordinary character, a good man with a great sense of humor, and a good friend. He used to show me his wounds, received in various Greek battles, and I would tell him that they looked more like wounds from duels with irate husbands! Alex was irresistible to women of all ages and all nationalities. I asked him why he had never married and he said simply, "Because I can never bear to hurt a woman and it would be impossible for me to be a faithful husband."

Alex was a nephew of Heinrich Schliemann, the great adventurer of the last century who had uncovered the ancient city of Troy. Schliemann's excavations have always fascinated me. One day Alex showed me a trunk full of letters (about seven hundred of them) written by Schliemann, which had been unknown to Robert Payne at the time he wrote *Gold of Troy*, an excellent book about Schliemann and his discoveries. It occurred to me that these letters would add tremendously to Schliemann's story, and with the full cooperation of Alex, I arranged for Lynn and Gray Poole to do a new book on Schliemann, which was published under the title *One Passion: Two Loves*. I am now trying to interest a movie company in doing a full-length film on Schliemann and his excavation of Troy.

However, back to the civil war. With the encouragement of our State Department, I began to work closely with the Greek prime minister and Alex Melas to help bring about a cease-fire and an end of the vicious war. I attended several of the Greek cabinet meetings and met secretly with the Communist leaders in Athens. My job was more to listen to the discussions than offer an opinion but at least I felt I was participating in something important, at long last doing something useful.

Even with the help of the British 8th Army, Athens and all of Greece were at various times in great danger of falling to the Communists. More than fifty thousand Greeks lost their lives in the civil war, and hundreds of British troops were diverted from the rest of the war in Europe simply trying to keep the peace and help normalize Greece's political situation. Only when General Scobie was able to bring in the Reminie Brigade, then stationed in Italy, were the Communists overcome. But even then there was no peace, for the defeated Communists would not give up their arms. And this became the main point of contention. Not until Winston Churchill came to Athens in December 1944 and personally intervened was the issue of the arms settled, and Greece returned to some sort of political stability. At that point, we were finally able to bring in and distribute much-needed food and medical supplies, railroad equipment, road-building machinery (the Germans blew up many of the railroad tracks and roads as they left Greece), and other construction materials and machines.

Life for the average Greek was very grim. Even with the food and medical supplies UNRRA brought in, there was still a great food shortage, because a great deal of the food fell into the hands of the black marketeers. The wealthy Greeks survived very well. I remember visiting various food stores to see which of the supplies that we had brought in were there. Many were not visible but hidden under the counter or in a back room reserved for buyers who could pay for them in gold. I saw many wealthy Greeks using gold sovereigns or ribbons of gold, which the proprietor would cut off and weigh to pay for their shopping.

The countryside of Athens, especially Mount Hymettus, was devastated. It was estimated that 80 percent of the trees were cut down and used for firewood. After the war Kaity Argyropoulou, wife of Alexander Argyropoulou, the Greek ambassador to China, started a worldwide drive to replace the trees, especially those on Hymettus, and was responsible for the planting of more than one million trees.

At the end of the war, when the time came to make the final accounting, we discovered that there had been a great deal of waste in the UNRRA program throughout the world—about 70 percent, in fact. In war and postwar times, such problems are understandable, almost expected. But the UNRRA program in Greece as it was evaluated years later was one of the most successful of any of the countries where the organization operated. I can't and don't take any direct credit for any part of the success of the overall program, but I am glad that at least I was part of a successful mission that helped save a proud but devastated country, the country of my origin.

The help we gave to Greece was general—we helped thousands of people—but it was also personal. I'm still friends with many of the individuals we helped. I can't tell all their stories, but here is one that had an intriguing ending, and led me to a new friendship.

One of the tasks I had at UNRRA was filling the 150 or so jobs with local workers. At that time jobs were terribly scarce in Greece, and, of course, people were starving. We announced that we would begin filling the job vacancies the next day. We must have had 2,000 applicants, so of course by the end of the day, all the jobs had been filled. The next morning, when I arrived for work, I found a thin, scruffy sixteen-year-old girl waiting for me on the steps.

"I've come for a job," she told me.

"I'm sorry, but they've all been filled. I don't have any more."

"You don't understand—I have to have a job."

Well, I admired her persistence and intensity, so I decided to try and find her some work around the office, easy tasks, but enough so that we could pay her a small salary. By the end of a month, Helle Tzalopoulou (Elli) was running the office. Bright and determined, she took charge.

I was so impressed with her that at the end of the war I wanted to help her out if I could. Greece was still devastated, and there were few opportunities for a gifted girl. It occurred to me that if she could go to college in America, she'd have a much better chance when she returned to what I hoped would be a healthier Greece. So I got in touch with Beatrice and told her my plan. Beatrice eagerly endorsed it and, as she was a graduate of Wellesley, she told the administration there about Elli. They agreed to enroll her if she could get the money to come.

Now, of course, I had to find a scholarship for her. I approached a wealthy friend of mine, Bodossakis Atheniades, whom I had helped during the war when he was imprisoned in Egypt. He provided valuable intelligence for the Allies during the German occupation. I told him Elli's story. A scholarship, I pointed out, would allow her to get the education and training to make her of real value to Greece when she returned. He thought for a few minutes.

"How many scholarships do you want?"

I hastily assured him that I needed only one, but Bodossakis was sold on the idea, and he established a dozen! They were for boys and girls both, to study at American universities and had as a proviso that the students must return to Greece after they graduated. Those scholarships continue to this day.

Elli, meanwhile, did take up her scholarship and went to Wellesley. Naturally, she had some trouble adjusting, but she did graduate and, in fact, went on to take a graduate degree in painting from Yale. When the time came for her to return to Greece, however, she came to me in great distress. She had fallen in love with an American, Willis Barnstone. They wanted to get married, but the time had come when she needed to return to Greece.

I told her not to worry—I'd arrange something so that she could stay in America, but she didn't want to do that—she was committed to returning. In the end, she and Willis married and they both went to Greece. So Greece got two gifted scholars for the price of one scholarship in that deal.

Well, I've described a little of the devastation in Greece, but nothing can really make it vivid. I once tried, in one of my imaginary letters, to get at the feeling ordinary individuals had as the war ended. I called it "Christmas Day in Wartime Athens":

Christmas Day
Athens, 1945

My dear Chris:

Forgive me if today I sound sentimental. These have been unusual times. Our youngest daughter, just four, was blinded with the butt of a Nazi rifle. We have been starved. We have seen our home bombed, our cattle shot, our books and furniture burned. The Acropolis, though undamaged, was defiled. Worst of all, we have lived in fear. At times there was nothing left to do but pray, and our prayers were not answered.

Some would say we had a right to doubt that God was mindful of us or our little country. How can you justify the suffering of a child? Yet something within us would not let us deny Him, or the justice of our cause.

It is strange, dear Chris, that as our hardships increased somehow our faith increased also. The worse it became and the weaker we grew—the more we resisted. Now that I look back upon it, it was uncanny. If in these cynical times evidence was ever needed of a greater power beyond ourselves—here it is. Believe me.

The Greek Civil War

And so, my "Merry Christmas" to you today is not quite like my greetings of the past. But with faith renewed and the wish that now and always you fight tyranny and cherish freedom.

Dmitri Xenopoulos

One of my final assignments in Greece came in 1945, when I was asked to help the program that was bringing back and rehabilitating Greeks from the Aegean Islands who had escaped the Germans during the occupation and fled to Turkey and Egypt. I was assigned a British mine-sweeper with which to visit the islands and the refugee camps established in Egypt. This was a comparatively pleasant assignment, and I was able to visit Mytalini, Chios, Samos, and other islands, and also the Moses Welles refugee camp in Egypt, which took care of some five thousand Greeks. What astonished me however, was that many of the Greeks who had fled did not want to return.

One of my final stops was on the beautiful island of Samos. I left my ship to have lunch and a bottle of the famous red wine of Samos at a nearby taverna and there I heard the sad news that President Roosevelt had died. As we prepared to return to Athens, the captain of the mine-sweeper suggested that we make a quick trip to Smyrna, just across the way from Samos, and I remember his saying: "Sir, it's a decision you can make; my orders come from you." I should have known better, but perhaps I was too elated that my job was over, and it was a beautiful day, with the shore of Turkey in full view, so I said, "Let's go." It was a mistake. Turkey was a neutral country—they always seem to be neutral in a crisis—and we were a military ship, with no clearance to enter Turkish waters. Nevertheless, they let us enter. I did have the sense to call on the U.S. Consul General in Smyrna, who received me coldly but politely. I asked to use his phone to call Jeffrey Short, my brother-in-law, who was an aide to our ambassador in Ankara.

I asked him what news he had had from home and also told him that during the trip my captain claimed that he saw a German submarine that apparently had not managed to leave Greece. (I understand that the submarine was later captured by a British destroyer in the Aegean.) In the middle of our conversation, the Turkish authorities, who had been monitoring my phone call, simply cut us off. When I told this to the Consul General he said sternly, "And what did you expect?"

To put it mildly, our reception in Turkey by the U. S. authorities was not very friendly, and perhaps they were correct in their hostility. The consul did, however, invite me, but not the captain of my ship, to tea. I probably made another mistake in not showing up (I was annoyed that they hadn't invited the captain). The report sent by the consulate on our illegal trip to Turkey was very critical of me for entering the Turkish port without permission, although I was told when I got back to Washington to forget it. "Just another striped pants report." As against this blemish on my record, however, I was also shown a letter of commendation from Prime Minister Plastiras praising me for my contributions toward ending the civil war in Greece and my dedicated efforts in bringing peace to the country.

The letter of commendation also mentioned the incident when we drove over the German mine, claiming that I had shown great courage and nearly lost my life. This exaggeration could only have been dictated by my dear friend Alex Melas—and I loved him for it! Years later when I went to Athens for a visit, Alex took me for dinner at his favorite taverna just below the Acropolis. We finished a bottle of retsina and he asked me again about the mine incident. I said I was just lucky, but that I had gotten a busted eardrum out of it. "Let me see," he said. "Ah, it looks to me like something an irate husband did to you." And we both laughed and we did a Greek dance together, and people applauded us, shouting "Oopahs" and throwing plates!

On Tour with Hitler's Car

One of the reasons, I think, that my publisher has urged me to do these memoirs (but I like to think and hope there are many better reasons!) is the fact that I once owned Hitler's armored parade car.

After World War II I went into the export-import business in Chicago. As an exporter I always tried to accommodate a customer, however curious the request. Once a prominent Chicagoan in 1950 wanted a pair of genuine Abyssinian cats—the kind that the Egyptians memorialized in statues. Abyssinians are supposed to be the ancestors of all cats. Well, I found out that Emperor Haile Selassie owned a cattery, where he raised the rare felines. Through an agent in Addis Ababa, I had the cats flown to Chicago. They were a great success—they were even televised. Marlin Perkins, the director of the Chicago Lincoln Park Zoo and later the host of TV's "Wild Kingdom," called them priceless. Later on, however, someone discovered that while the cats were being shipped through Cairo the priceless pair had been cat-napped, replaced with a pair of common Egyptian alley cats. The Abyssinian cats would have been worth over $1,000 apiece, but luckily I did not pay anything like that price for my specimens.

When I bought Hitler's car, however, I got the real thing: especially built by Mercedes Benz, it was a twenty-foot-long parade car that weighed 5 tons, was armor-plated, and had bullet-proof glass and two gasoline tanks. It had five forward speeds and could cruise at 125 miles per hour. It was used in parades and other ceremonial functions for Hitler but Hitler also used it to go with Eva Braun, his mistress, from Berlin to Berchtesgarten. It had a special section in the right front door for an automatic weapon.

In 1948 I had exported some machinery to Sweden worth about $27,000. When the time came for payment, the buyer in Sweden asked me if I would accept Swedish kronor instead of dollars, for there was a great dollar shortage in Europe and elsewhere. This was unacceptable to me, and I demanded payment in dollars as we had originally agreed. My buyer came back with another proposition. He had in his possession Hitler's car, built originally at a cost of nearly $47,000, and it was in excellent shape. There was a shortage of cars in the United States in 1948, so I was tempted to accept the car for that reason alone, but I had other ideas as well. I thought that Hitler's car would be a great attraction to raise money for charity, and, incidentally, to get my investment back and even make a profit.

But first I wanted to discuss the project with people who knew show business, and the first person who came to mind was my old compatriot and fellow fund-raiser for Greek war relief, Spyros Skouras, then president of 20th Century Fox Film Corporation, and universally known for his unerring instinct in picking themes and pictures that made a great deal of money.

(Although even he guessed wrong about *Cleopatra*).

When I told Spyros my plan to import Hitler's car, his first reaction was "You must be out of your mind! Chreese, are you crazy? You want to get involved with that monster Hitler? What will people say? You have been an important person in our State Department and you are a hero of Greek war relief. Do you want to ruin your reputation?" And then, more practically, he added, "Furthermore, who is going to pay to see Hitler's automobile? He is the worst person who ever lived." I explained to Spyros that I agreed with his view of Hitler, but that I wasn't getting involved with Hitler—I was just buying the car as a business proposition to try to recoup the money from the machinery I had exported. "Take the Swedish kronor," he said, "and play roulette at Monte Carlo. Your chances of success are infinitely better!" And he hung up.

When we ask for advice from a friend, we often really want them to agree with us. This had been my motive for calling Spyros Skouras. So I went ahead and imported the car. It was shipped from Copenhagen on the *S.S. Stockholm*, and I went to New York personally from Chicago to receive it. Word had gotten out (I believe that the shipping line tipped off the reporters) that there was an American who had bought Hitler's car, and when I arrived at the 57th Street pier to pick it up, I was greeted by no fewer than twenty reporters and cameramen. The picture of me receiving the car appeared on the front page of the *New York Times* and was wired to newspapers all over the world. One of the first reporters to call me after the original story appeared was Philip Hamburger of the *New Yorker* magazine. He wanted to interview me and drive the car himself through Central Park. Everybody seemed to wave at us, although some people booed as well. It made a great story, which was featured in the "Talk of the Town" column of the *New Yorker*, and that was the beginning of what seemed like a thousand more stories that came out during the two years I kept the car before giving it to a museum in Boston.

Among the people who wanted to make use of it was the New York recruiting officer of the U. S. Marines. He thought the car would make an effective come-on in their recruitment program if he put the car on display to attract attention. I gave the Marines a free loan in exchange for the great publicity they generated for the car. (Shortly afterward, I had a call from a marine in California who claimed to have Hitler's personal automatic luger. He offered to sell it to me for $500, but I declined.) After leaving the car with him, I returned to Chicago, not knowing exactly how I was going to exhibit it there. The matter was solved for me that same day by a call from Governor Dwight Green's office: "Would I agree to lending the car for the opening in September of the Illinois State Fair?" We could split any profits. I also got a call from Mayor O'Dwyer's office in New York. They wanted to use the car for some charity for two days. I agreed to that also. A third call came from the Athens College office in New York (I was a member of the Board of Trustees) asking if we could show the car to raise money for the Athens College Scholarship fund. I'm not sure how much the college raised but it was more than $2,500 for a three-day exhibit.

Meanwhile, I had to arrange to bring the car to Illinois for the state fair in Springfield. The head of public relations for the fair had a brilliant idea: Why don't we have the car driven from New York to Springfield and have Mayor O'Dwyer give some kind of a Freedom Torch as a symbolic gift from the mayor of New York to the governor of Illinois? The mayor went along, and it was then proposed that the car be given a motorcycle escort all the way from New York to Springfield. Governor Green had special license plates made which spelled HITLER. Everything fell into place, and when we were ready, each state we passed through provided a motorcycle escort for the length of the state. In effect, we had two policemen on motorcycles all the way from New York, New Jersey, Pennsylvania, and Ohio on to Indiana, and finally the Illinois police brought us to the Springfield fair.

The trip from New York took three days, what with stopping along the way in the various towns and cities, which did local interviews and stories as we came through. We achieved fantastic publicity (Irv Kupcinet, Kup, of the *Chicago Sun-Times* had been the first to report that I bought the car), and the Hitler car was on the way to becoming known all over the country. I had hired a driver from New York and Jack Mabley, then of the *Chicago Daily News*, came to Springfield from New York with me to do a story for them. UPI did a series of feature stories on it, and the car became very much in demand for charity and other promotions.

All in all, more than fifty charities benefited from showing the car. We exhibited it from coast to coast three times in two years, and grossed more than a million dollars. To top it all, 20th Century Fox, of all studios, wished to use the car for their film *The Desert Fox*. I charged $2,500 a week for three weeks, after which I got a call from Spyros Skouras: "You lucky bastard, only you could have pulled it off—but I congratulate you and next time I come to Chicago I want to ride in that awful machine!" (For those interested, the last scene of the movie shows Rommel, played by James Mason, driving away to what was to be his death in Hitler's own armored car.)

I'm not sure what has happened to the car since I gave it to the museum, but I have heard that some car buff in South Carolina later bought it for something less than $300,000. My own profit from the car was not bad for a $27,000 investment, and it was fun. Having bought Hitler's car, however, I apparently seemed the ideal person to invest in another of Hitler's prized possessions, his yacht. I was first approached with the proposition in the late 50s, in Chicago's prestigious Pump Room.

In the 40s and early 50s, Chicago's Pump Room in the Ambassador East Hotel was the stopping off place for many of the actors and actresses and other celebrities traveling from Hollywood to New York. Non-stop plane travel between the coasts had not begun and as the ads said "though hogs on their way to slaughter did not have to change trains, people on their way to the coast did," and in Chicago, this usually meant having to spend the night, and the most popular hotel seemed to be the Ambassador East Hotel, home of the famous Pump Room.

I first became acquainted with the Pump Room through Ernie Byfield, its originator and first owner. But I came to use it frequently because of a charming gentleman from Turkey who was a good friend of Jeffrey Short, my brother-in-law. Jeffrey and Victor Lutfalla first met when Jeffrey was attached to the U. S. Embassy in Ankara. Victor and I became good friends, and we spent a great deal of time together (as I look back now, much to my growing family's loss). Victor became very popular for the beautiful parties he gave, and with his European charm and manner he was much in demand at many of Chicago's social functions.

There are many stories about happenings in the Pump Room, but few more remarkable than the following, which happened to me. I had invited Victor and Mario De Fretas, the Consul General from Brazil, to lunch. This was election day in Brazil, and, because Victor was such a good (and well-known) patron of the hotel and De Fretas was the distinguished Consul General, we were seated at the prestigious "Booth One," which had a special telephone. From the moment we were seated, De Fretas started using the telephone, first to call his wife and then his office, trying to learn the latest election results in Rio. After De Fretas' third or fourth telephone call a man came over to our table, pointed to De Fretas, and said: "The boss would like to see you at his table." His table was just across the way, occupied by three rather tough looking men, all dressed in black suits and light colored ties.

De Fretas looked very puzzled, as I was, and he looked toward me for guidance, thinking perhaps that these were friends of mine. Without waiting for a reply, the man pulled out a gun from underneath his jacket and said, rather ominously, "Come! Move."

Mario said, "I'm the Brazilian Consul General. What do you want?" but he was already moving to the table.

The man seated at the middle of the table said, "Please sit down," and then he asked, "Were you calling the police?"

Mario said, "No, no, I'm the Brazilian Counsel General. I'm trying to find out if I still have a job in Brazil. I don't if President Vargas is defeated."

But one of the other men said, "You got any identification?" Mario pulled out his wallet and showed them his diplomatic card.

"Oh, that's fine. I'm Mickey Cohen."

Apparently Mickey Cohen, the notorious mobster, was at that time in trouble with the law. He was not supposed to leave the state of California, and his picture had been in all the papers. He had suspected that Mario had recognized him and was calling the police. With great presence of mind, Mario told him, "Ah, Mr. Cohen, but you're famous. My son collects autographs. Will you sign the menu for me?"

"Of course," said Cohen.

Mario then waved to me to join them. He introduced me as his "distinguished friend, a banker," and Mickey Cohen ordered another round of drinks for all of us. Afterward we returned to our table where Victor, late as usual, joined us, and Mario delighted in telling him the whole story. Victor did not think this incident particularly funny and felt uneasy. Victor had just become a citizen of the United States and probably felt, rightly so, that he didn't want to be seen with gangsters.

A little later Ernest Byfield joined us and Mario repeated the story again. Byfield went over and shook Mickey Cohen's hand and bought the group a drink on the house. Afterward he came back to us and said, "We get all types here. That's what makes the Pump Room the Pump Room!"

It was as we were having dessert that Victor brought up the subject that he thought might be of special interest to me since I had acquired Hitler's car: one of Victor's best friends in the Middle East was George Arida, a prominent businessman from Beirut who was presently serving as Lebanon's Consul General in Madrid. George Arida had recently acquired Hitler's beautiful 425-foot yacht, the *Grille*. Apparently Arida had been traveling to Beirut via England, where, an avid yachtsman, he had gone to

Southampton. While in Southampton, a friend of Arida's had pointed out to him that Hitler's yacht was in a dock nearby, and it was worth seeing. They were given a tour of the yacht, in which they saw Eva Braun's private stateroom, Hitler's study and bedroom, and some of the art work Hitler had collected or as their guide said, "probably stole." The yacht had been given to Hitler as a birthday present by German housewives, friends, and businessmen, and it had reportedly cost over five million dollars. The guide told them that the yacht was up for sale at auction and probably could be purchased for a fraction of its original cost. Arida's response was, "Who wants to own a yacht owned by Hitler?"

According to Victor, more as a kind of joke than as a serious bid, Arida made a bid of $250,000 for the yacht. When Arida returned to his office in Beirut a week later, he found a telegram on his desk signed by his friend. "Congratulations. You are the owner of Hitler's yacht."

When Victor finished telling us this, Byfield remarked, "Hey, that's an interesting story. What's he planning to do with it?"

Victor answered, "Actually he wants to sail it around the Mediterranean this summer, and then he wants to sell it. And he asked me to discuss it with Chris, who had a very successful experience with Hitler's car." Byfield was still interested, so Victor gave us the specifications of the yacht: it had some fifty cabins, a cruising speed of over seventeen knots, and was reported to be in prime condition. Byfield then surprised us by saying that he and some of his associates were looking for a luxury yacht to run between their hotels in Los Angeles and Mexico—and he thought that the *Grille* might be ideal for this purpose.

Victor, who is a very keen Lebanese businessman, took all this in quickly, and by the time dinner was over he had promised Byfield to cable the information to Arida, get more specifications, and, if some agreement was reached, have Arida bring the yacht over by the end of the summer.

Within some thirty days, Byfield and his associates, with me acting as broker, made Arida an offer of $1.2 million for the *Grille*, subject to inspections, clearances of title, and the usual contractual arrangements.

So Arida, along with his wife, son George, and a crew of fifty, set out for New York from Beirut. They were scheduled to dock at Wall Street just before Labor Day. And they brought along on deck a new Lincoln Continental for use in New York. They made a stop in Alexandria, Egypt, on the way and invited King Farouk to come aboard to see this beautiful ship. The story, as Arida later related to us, was that Farouk was delighted to accept the invitation. They had tea, and then Farouk was given a tour of the yacht. When they were in Hitler's stateroom Farouk picked up a pair of binoculars with a swastika on them, and Arida pointed out that they had belonged to the Führer. "They are beautiful," Farouk exclaimed.

And Arida answered, "Your Majesty, they are yours."

Later in the captain's cabin, Farouk saw a small painting, supposedly done by Hitler. Farouk admired that too and, again, Arida insisted he take it. Then Farouk gretly admired the ship's compass, but Arida demurred: "Your Majesty, we need that to cross the ocean!"

The *Grille* arrived in New York on schedule and, of course, it was a great media event. Every paper, including the *New York Times*, did a feature story on it, with pictures of the Aridas. There was unusual interest in Eva Braun's cabin. "Where did Hitler sleep when they were on board—in Eva's room or his own?" one of the tabloids asked.

Now, in my mind this whole thing was simply a business deal, but to try to lessen any stigma that might accrue from dealing with a Hitler property (for me, *another* Hitler property), I suggested that we give a party on board to benefit various charities in New York. I forget now what the admission fee was, but it was modest, and eighteen different charities were listed as the sponsors, and thousands of people were given a tour of the yacht.

I invited Dorsey Connors, who at the time had a television show on NBC, and some of my newspaper friends from Chicago to come to New York and do a story. The stories of the benefit were even more numerous than the coverage of the yacht's arrival, featuring pictures of probably every celebrity in New York, including the mayor and governor.

I go into some detail regarding the publicity surrounding the event, because all this attention apparently went to Mrs. Arida's head. She was a portly Lebanese woman, who, unlike most Middle Eastern wives, had considerable influence over her husband. I believe the message she got to her husband was, "Watch out, I believe this Greek (meaning me) is taking advantage of you. This is a very important ship and you must ask at least $2.5 million for it. And, remember, I've just had the ship's living room furniture upholstered!"

In a conference with Arida, with Mrs. Arida present, I tried to explain that selling any yacht in the million dollar price range was not an easy thing to do (at least not in the late 50s), and that the $1.2 million Byfield and his associates had offered was fair—in fact, we were lucky to have it.

Mrs. Arida was adamant, however, adding that they already had other offers (which was not true). For a while I felt I was in a Middle East bazaar, not a conference room. But I had no authority to offer more for the yacht and would not have approved it anyway. I knew from Victor that Arida had paid only $250,000 for it. I tried to plead with Arida to accept the offer, and I believe (although I'm not sure) that Victor, who was speaking to him in Lebanese, backed me up. The long and the short of it is that the whole deal fell through, and with expenses piling up—supporting a crew of fifty and dockage and other charges—the beautiful *Grille* was finally sold in Hoboken for scrap, about $35,000. Such is the result of too much publicity mixing with vanity and bad business sense.

It's sad for me to realize, however, that there seems to be a resurgence of sick individuals who idolize Hitler and are collectors of his memorabilia. About fifteen years ago, I sold an amber bound copy of *Mein Kampf* for $2,500, the license plates to Hitler's car for another $2,500, and its black wool headlight covers, which had a little yellow slit for driving during blackouts and bombing raids, for $1,000. I donated the proceeds to charity and was glad to be rid of these last few mementos. To this day, however, I am labeled "the guy that bought Hitler's car," and I'm a bit tired of it. I like to think that that project, however widely publicized, is the least of what the angel on my shoulder has guided me to—or perhaps, as some of my friends and family insist, inflicted on me! I sometimes feel that my angel (no, I'm not trying to put all praise or blame on her—-we and we alone are responsible for our actions) has enjoyed having fun with me, or, put another way, has enjoyed testing me.

Dancing Girls in Winnetka?

After the war, as I mentioned, I went back to Chicago, where I began in the import-export business. Beatrice and I moved to one of the prestigious suburbs there, Winnetka (population 2,200). Beatrice had grown up there, but for me, the small, affluent, WASP community was an enormous change over Athens, New York, or Montgomery, West Virginia. I've never been entirely at ease with the people, however friendly they've been, and I'm not sure they've been entirely at ease with me, especially since the affair of the dancing girls.

Winnetka is many things: its teachers and schools are among the best in the country; its per-capita wealth is second only to Kenilworth. Many of the top CEOs in the Midwest make their homes in Winnetka, and the houses in which they live are beautiful and well kept. Winnetka has been compared to Palm Beach, Florida, and Santa Barbara, California, as one of the best-run communities in the country, and its reputation in these respects is well deserved.

As for its residents, and the Jeffrey R. Shorts, my family-in-law, were among them: they tend to be honest, decent, well-meaning, successful people, who usually exceed their goals each year for local and united charities. Their private social and golf clubs, like Indian Hill, are legally open to all residents, but actually closed to blacks, certain ethnic groups, and residents with too liberal views. Winnetka is a comfortable nesting place for some of our best-known and most able WASPS. And, of course, up to a point, that is their privilege.

I must say I really liked and respected my family-in-law, although I never felt part of the family. I think the barrier started building up when I came from New York one Christmas to court my wife. No family could have been nicer to me, but Jeffrey Short charged me eight cents a mile to use one of his cars. This was not stinginess. It was simply his kind of tradition, quite alien to my background and way of thinking.

The question I've often asked myself for some forty years is, What was I doing there? The obvious answer, of course, was that I happened to be married to Beatrice, one of the beautiful daughters of the Shorts. I don't know how it happened but Beatrice was not politically a Winnetka kind of WASP: she was not a Republican, and, despite her family and environment, she was a dedicated liberal. When all her Indian Hill crowd and Women's Athletic Club bridge-playing friends were extolling the Vietnam war (I remember Tom Brooker, Arnold Maremont, Gerald Gidwitz, and the like calling Vietnam part of the Marshall Plan; we had to be there because of the Domino theory, for if we weren't then the Russians would be), Beatrice was in Washington marching against the war. She also marched in Washington and other cities defending the right to abortion and other liberal causes. She was not articulate about what she believed in, she was just there; she was what she believed. I once asked her, a year or so before she died, how it happened that she was not part of the mold, and she answered with a jovial compliment I'll never forget: "Well, I had to live with you, didn't I?"

We had many friends in Winnetka, despite having different values and different political views. I sometimes felt I was accepted because I was a bit of an oddity—a Harvard/Oxford Greek in Winnetka—and, as my good friend, Art Nielsen, would say, I was entertaining. It is not difficult to be entertaining in Winnetka because most of the residents are so utterly dull, at least to everyone but their own limited kind. As for conversation in Winnetka and, indeed, most of the North Shore, it's a lost art, if the art ever existed there. Time and time again I found myself in a dinner group of four or six or eight, where it was impossible to have only one conversation going on at a time. Even with four people, there were usually two different conversations; in a group of eight, four conversations. I was brought up to believe that this kind of thing is rude. But perhaps my dinner companions had a limited attention span. I once spent a good part of a dinner conversation listening to a lady boasting that the grass in her lawn was the oldest in Winnetka! I asked her if she saved the grass cuttings for posterity, but I don't believe she thought that was funny.

I must also mention the churches of Winnetka. They serve the spiritual and cultural needs of the community exceedingly well, especially the Congregational Church, where Beatrice and I were married and our children baptized. I am not a religious person in the ritual sense, and there is a minimum of ritual at the Congregational Church. I've been asked to read the

Scripture two or three times a year, which I have enjoyed doing, and I've found much support and comfort in talking with Paul Allen, the present minister, and Sam Harkness, the minister who married Beatrice and me. I've never agreed with the practice of inserting editorials from the *Tribune* or the *New York Times* into the sermons. The last thing I want to hear in a church is a rehash of current events. But ministers tell us they are trying to make their sermons relevant to what's going on in our lives. I prefer sermons with moral or spiritual uplift over and above secular happenings.

A very bold thing once happened in Winnetka (bold for Winnetka, at least); we had a little robbery in our White Oak Lane neighborhood home. A meeting was immediately called of the neighborhood residents. There were comments like: "Have you seen any blacks in the neighborhood?" "A lot of our servants are Polish or Jamaican. Could it have been one of them?" "Has anyone seen any suspicious characters around—the south side type?" They asked the chief of the police department to come to the meeting and give his opinion. When he suggested that the thieves could have been some young people from our own village on a spree, the group was shocked and denied anything like that could have happened. Finally it was suggested that we should form a vigilante group, with flashlights, to patrol the neighborhood at night. Hands went up to be the first to volunteer and it was asked: "Shall we carry guns?" The chief of police wisely discouraged such a move. I flatly refused to be part of such stupidity and left the meeting. "Shall we watch your home?" asked one of the group. And our hostess, ever so polite, said I must take some cookies before I left, which was thoughtful of her.

Dancing Girls in Winnetka?   131

The culprit was found. He actually turned himself in: the sixteen-year-old son of one of our wealthiest residents. He did it, he was quoted as saying, because he was bored.

Yet I must add, that all of our three children grew up in Winnetka. They are a product of their home life and environment and, apart from often not understanding their father, they have turned out just fine—good looking, public spirited, with a strong sense of family, and, all in all, above average.

I now come to the matter of the dancing girls. If I've said that the Hitler car received worldwide publicity, you must realize that its publicity and notoriety were small compared to those of the dancing girls episode. It starts with an uncle: Pan Aristophron. He was my mother's brother. You have probably heard or read that most Greeks suffer from megalomania. If that's true, my uncle Aristophron could have invented the disease. He was the most pompous, vain man I ever met, and I met him only once.

He had his butler shave him every morning and insisted that the shavings be saved for posterity. Like royalty, he never carried money, although he had a lot of it. Some of his fortune came from his Egyptian cotton business. At one time he owned more than 3,000 acres of the most valuable cotton land in Egypt. Then he married a very wealthy Greek widow who dyed her hair blue and kept several gigolos on the side, but otherwise was a faithful if vain wife. She did not like to be spoken to unless she spoke first. The exception, of course, was her friend King Farouk and his royal relatives.

After he married the widow, my uncle decided to change his name from Xenopoulos (our Greek family name) to Aristophron. (I believe he equated the name with aristocracy). Although my mother had reared him until the age of seventeen, had helped send him to the Gymnasium (college), and was one of his early backers in the cotton business, they had had a falling out, and he never spoke to her after his marriage. He felt that our family was no longer his social equal. The Greeks in Athens and Alexandrians applied a rather vulgar expression to the Aristophrons. "They think their *skata* doesn't smell." You can translate the Greek word yourself!

Pan Aristophron did, however, do at least one memorable thing. He discovered the site of Plato's Academy in Athens. Like his hero and model Heinrich Schliemann, who against all odds had discovered the ancient city of Troy and its gold, Aristophron had an obsession: he knew where Plato's Academy was. None of the archaeologists of Greece agreed with him, and they made fun of this rich Greek dilettante who pretended to be a scholar and archaeologist. But Aristophron claimed that by reading Plato carefully you could be led to where the ancient academy had stood. Against all expert advice, he excavated, and he did discover the site (but no gold). He and his wife vowed to build a world university on the ancient foundation. Unfortunately, they both died before they were able to build it, but he did leave money for the purpose. (The trouble is that the site is in the middle of the business district in Athens; but the foundation is still trying to build the university.) Aristophron also wrote a book on his discovery of Plato's Academy. It was published by the Oxford University Press and in true, vain, Aristophronian fashion, he insisted on (and paid for) one edition that was printed on vellum to endure for posterity, just like his shavings.

It so happened that I was a graduate student at

Oxford in 1937 when the book appeared, and the one time I met him was when he was invited to Oxford to give a lecture on his book and findings. (I had tried to meet him when I was on my walking tour in Greece, but he refused to see me.) Because I was the son of his estranged sister, however, both he and his wife once more refused to see me at his hotel afterward. She answered the phone when I called—and I suppose she felt she did me an honor by speaking to me at all—but the gist of what she said was: "We really have nothing in common (and here I was at Oxford studying Plato!); please do not try to see us." I was so furious, both for myself and the insult I felt to my mother, that I wrote them a very strong letter, threatening to tell their society friends in Athens what had happened. I never carried out my threat, but my letter (on Wadham College, Oxford, stationery) apparently led to the further vendetta against our family, that eventually resulted in the dancing girl episode I referred to at the beginning of this story.

Pan Aristophron died in Alexandria in 1952. Though he was a resident of Egypt he was still a Greek citizen, and the will was therefore probated according to Greek law. That law specified that a sister (my mother) was entitled to one third of his estate, but Aristophron's widow contested the court ruling. Because Aristophron was such a vain, controversial character anyway, a great deal of publicity ensued, including a detailed listing of his assets. My mother was seriously ill at the time, so I decided, quite against the advice of the lawyer we had engaged in Alexandria, to compromise on a settlement. It may have been a mistake, but my mother was at least able to enjoy some benefits of the cash we received, along with the ownership of some of the cotton lands. News of our settlement was reported in the papers in Alexandria, and eventually the wire services picked it up, and it was even reported in the Chicago papers. I'm not sure today whether it was my friend Irv Kupcinet, one of the best reporters and columnists in the profession, or another friend, Jack Mabley, who always had a keen sense for a good story, who first called me, but the reason they both called was that among the assets listed, we had inherited, according to the reporters' interpretation, "Three dancing girls"!

Under Egyptian law, I was told, when you inherit farm property you also inherit, or at least are responsible for, the people who live on the property and farm it for you. The bottom line was that since my mother had recently died I, a married man (married, no less, into an established, WASP family in staid Winnetka), had inherited three buxom dancing girls.

It was not long before the press got pictures of the girls in Alexandria and those, along with pictures of me in Illinois, were shown all over the world. The whole matter might have died down or been passed off as just a rather humorous incident if the Egyptian government had not issued a statement insisting that there was no slavery in Egypt, and therefore I could not have inherited dancing girls nor any other human beings from Egypt.

Even then the whole thing might have rested, but it snowballed until eventually the matter was brought before a human rights committee of the United Nations, who issued a press release: No, there is no slavery in Egypt. I had no right to the ownership of the dancing girls, but I did have a certain obligation regarding the people who lived on the land. The publicity and notoriety lasted for several weeks. It was a strain on my family, but I tried to handle the matter lightly, as if it were a laughing matter, and I had to admit to some of my reporter friends that it made a good story. At least two movie companies sent me treatments for a movie about it, and I still hear about it occasionally.

But it was no laughing matter in the Winnetka community—at least not at the Indian Hill Country Club. The tennis membership we had at the time was not renewed. I also received a call from the Social Register in New York, in which we were listed. In the early 50s, the Social Register was quite important to the sort of people we lived among, and it considered itself the arbiter of acceptable and correct social behavior. (My wife, to her credit, always thought it a bit of a joke). Suspecting what the call from the Social Register was all about, I did not call back. Apparently they took the whole matter in a jovial spirit. In any event, we were not dropped from their august listings.

Eventually, I was able to sell the cotton land in Egypt, and that ended the story. I've naturally been curious about what happened to those three dancing girls, and some years ago I got a letter from the lawyer in Alexandria telling me that all three girls had married, and now had children. He claims that they are fatter than ever and have never had a clue they once "belonged" to me, or of all the publicity that ensued (apparently they were illiterate and no stories reached them).

Goldmining at Maravilla

Europeans have always been more interested in possessing and trading in gold, coins as well as bullion, than most of us in America. This is because most European countries, including Greece, have been through devastating periods of inflation. In my own lifetime I've seen German marks, for example, become almost worthless for a time, and right after the war I paid a hundred thousand drachmae for a newspaper in Greece.

As a young boy I remember discussions between my father and mother about the importance of owning gold. My mother always had a few gold coins stashed away, and on birthdays and anniversaries and at Christmas a gold coin was the most appropriate gift.

I mention this to try to explain (or even understand) my own little obsession with possessing gold, which led me in 1952 to become involved with Maravilla, a small gold mine in Brazil. I've always liked the feel of a gold coin; it's solid, not like paper currency. The coin itself is often quite artistically designed: the Mexican 30-pesos piece, for example, is one of the most beautiful coins in the world, and so is the U.S. 20-dollar gold piece, the one-ounce gold Maple Leaf, and the Krugerrand. And some of the ancient gold coins, like the Alexandrian coin, are still works of art. I still have the first Greek gold coin that was given to me by my mother on my twelfth birthday and have given each of my grandchildren gold coins on their birthdays.

Now to come to Maravilla: while on a vacation trip to Brazil (to visit my old classmate from Oxford, Carlos Luzzetti), I was sitting at the swimming pool at the Copacabana Hotel in Rio, where I struck up a conversation with an older gentleman who turned out to be the chief geologist for U.S. Steel. He was in Brazil looking for monocyte (the sandy element from which the trigger for atomic weapons is made), and in his exploration, he told me, he had come upon a small gold mine that he thought had great potential. From drinks we went on to dinner, and the more he talked about the mine, the more interested I became. It needed a large mill, some expert help who knew modern mining methods, and, of course, an influx of cash. The idea of owning a gold mine and actually turning out my own gold pieces has always fascinated me. I persuaded Charles Mitke, the geologist, to take me with him on his upcoming visit to the mine, and to cut a long story short, I, along with Edwin Maynard of Winnetka and another investor from Philadelphia, who also had a mania for owning a gold mine, eventually bought Maravilla.

Before we invested, however, I recommended that we get a second geologist's opinion on the mine reserves. So I convinced Harry Burgess, a geologist friend from Winnetka, to come down. Harry had never flown in a plane and was deadly afraid of flying. Brazil is many, many miles from Chicago, and to get there by train and ship would have taken more time than I was willing to wait. By upping his fee considerably and trying to persuade him that flying was actually safer than driving a car, I got Harry to fly Pan Am with me from New York to Rio. (We took the train to New York!) Harry was actually perspiring with fear as the plane took off, but we had beautiful weather, the clouds were fascinating, and, after a couple of drinks, Harry appeared to be relaxed and reassured. Then it happened. I had the aisle seat, having given Harry the window seat so that he could enjoy the view. Well, about four hours into the flight his window blew out! Fortunately, he still had on his seat belt, but it scared the daylights out of him (and me!). The co-pilot came back to the cabin and assured us that the plane was not in danger. He sealed up the window and after some twelve hours we arrived safely in Rio. Harry was too polite to discuss the matter with me, but I did say rather lamely, "You see, Harry, even in an emergency like this the plane was safe."

But now we had another plane trip to take, and this one was not in a big Pan Am airliner but in a Beechcraft. To my great surprise, however, Harry did not balk. "What the hell, Chris, let's go." I think he was resigned to the idea that whatever was going to happen would happen. That was a wise emotional decision, because what did happen could have been very serious indeed.

I should mention that we were traveling during Carnival time in Rio, and everybody was in a holiday mood. There was dancing in the streets and parades, and hardly anyone spent much time sleeping. There was also a lot of drinking. Nevertheless, we had reserved a Beechcraft to fly to Maravilla; there was the pilot (who arrived at the small airport a half hour late), an interpreter (the pilot did not speak any English),

Harry, and myself. When I reserved the plane I had given the officer in charge our destination, time of departure, number of people flying, and other information. When we got in the plane and were waiting to take off, I said: "Maravilla," to the pilot, and he smiled and said, "Okay." Then I asked the interpreter if he knew where we were going and he said, "Oh, yes, oh yes." We took off exactly at noon. It was ordinarily an hour's flight (I had been there twice before), and I understood that we had fuel for four hours of flying. (I believe this was the legal reserve.) We had a pleasant, uneventful flight for the first hour. Harry seemed relaxed; the interpreter was taking a little nap, and in fact I dozed off a bit myself after take-off.

But when I woke up and looked down all I could see was jungle, not a sign of the little clearing we had made for planes to land. It was now about 1:15, an hour and fifteen minutes into what should have been a one-hour flight. I woke up the interpreter and said we should be over the mine location now—ask the pilot where we are. The pilot reported that we had run into some headwind but that we would soon be there. I let it go with that explanation, but after another half hour (now we were running on reserve), I nudged the pilot and said, "Where are we?" The interpreter became a bit anxious. Harry was perspiring, and I was not feeling too happy myself. Then the pilot pulled out a little address book and looked at the map in it. That's when I realized that if that was the best guide he had we were lost—and we were lost.

I then had the presence of mind to say to the interpreter: "Tell this jackass to forget about the mine, just get us out of this jungle. Head for the ocean. That's an order." Then I added, "Does he know where the ocean is?"

Fortunately the pilot did know in what direction the ocean was, and he insisted that he had been given the wrong directions to Maravilla. After another half hour of flying we came out of the jungle and saw the ocean, but there was only a very rocky beach. It looked as if we were going to have to go for a water landing when, miraculously, we saw what looked like a farm with a field, where we landed. It wasn't exactly a normal landing. We hit the ground, and the plane actually turned over. We were all shaken up but no one was hurt. And the first thing I thought of as we were coming down was, "Now what was I going to tell Harry?" But he was a good sport about it and also about what happened next.

Many of the Indian tribes in Brazil, even today, are not particularly friendly to intruders; some tribes are known to be cannibals. We had landed not in a farm but in a small Indian village, and we wondered how helpful or friendly the inhabitants were going to be. Nothing happened for about fifteen minutes after we crash landed. Then several Indians began to appear out of the bushes. Our interpreter came forward, raised his arms in a friendly gesture, and said something that I'm not sure they understood, but at least they did not appear to be violent or hungry. Our interpreter apparently was able to communicate with them, for before long the Indians brought us several horses and directed us to a place on the coast where we could get help and try to return to Rio. Two of the Indians, carrying a small lamb, accompanied us (our interpreter gave them cigarettes and a knife for guiding us), and on the way we had to cross a river. Before we crossed, the Indians slit the lamb's throat and threw it in the river. Harry had a look of sheer astonishment on his face, but I realized that they wanted to attract and corral the piranhas in the water while we crossed, riding with our legs on top of our horses. For a man with a fear of flying, who didn't want to go to Rio in the first place, Harry was having a rather unusual trip.

But we eventually made it to Rio and Harry returned home with a great story to tell (as did I) for many years to come. Actually, flying up from Rio was frequently an adventure. Once superstitious natives shot arrows at the small Beechcraft plane, forcing us to land on a beach. But other natives befriended us, and we finally got to the mine.

As the new owner I was virtually apotheosized by the natives. I vindicated my exalted standing by shooting a jaguar, but almost ruined it one night when a mouse startled me in my hut. My serving girl saw me jump at the mouse and told the other villagers about it. At once the native's hero-worship changed to dislike and on the following morning I found a chicken bone outside my hut and within the next three days three more chicken bones. The natives were using them to put a voodo curse on me. The curse never took effect and I enjoyed my stay in the Amazonian jungles.

Since Harry never made it to Maravilla, we never did get a second opinion on the mine reserves, but we still increased production and were well satisfied with the quality of the gold we recovered. For nearly three months after we began operations, all went well, but we didn't allow for two things—which a geological report would not have uncovered anyway.

First was the theft. We would dynamite at midnight, and after the smoke had cleared the following morning the workers would go down into the mine and recover the quartz for grinding in the new twenty-ton mill. But we discovered that some of the miners, with or without gas masks, would work in the smoke right after our dynamiting and recover the largest and choicest bits of gold. They would carefully leave us with enough to work the mill. We finally suspected one specific worker and searched his hut, where we discovered he had accumulated (stolen) nearly three pounds of gold. There were some twenty miners working this phase of the operation, and we estimated that almost half of our production was being stolen. At one time we had close to two hundred people working the mine, and it was simply not feasible to provide enough supervisors to prevent the stealing. And, quite frankly, there was always the question of who would supervise the supervisors. This was a mining camp one hundred road miles from the nearest point of civilization, and this was Brazil!

Brazil, in fact, was the second problem, which was just as serious, although the average person might not suspect it. Maravilla indeed lay in a paradisial setting. The mine was bordered by a beautiful waterfall, with banana and orange trees always ready for picking. I've never seen more magnificent and lush tropical greenery growing wild anywhere in the world, and the climate, despite its proximity to the equator, was ideal. And the living was easy and the girls were always pleasant and easier! After a few weeks in this paradise, a man could lose his perspective as well as his sense of values, however rigid.

I discussed the problem with Ed Maynard and two other investors who wanted to come in with us (which included our lawyer: he wanted a "piece of the action" and sensed that the price of gold was going to skyrocket from $35 an ounce). We agreed that what we needed was a manager to administer the mine, preferably a rigid German (I'm not sure why now) who was older, experienced, disciplined, and, above all, dull enough not to succumb to the easy pleasure of paradise living. We interviewed some twenty applicants, mostly from the United States and Canada. We didn't find a German, but one of our Canadian applicants seemed ideal. He had traveled in Brazil but not worked long in a tropical setting. He was, however, known as a tyrant of a gold-mining operator. He was honest and feared. Married, with three grown children, he was a no-nonsense guy. It was agreed he would go to Maravilla, establish himself, and then after a few weeks arrange for his wife, a buxom, equally no-nonsense woman, to join him. It looked like we had the right man. To help insure it, we promised him a bonus as he increased production.

In the first six weeks, we got regular reports and he raised production by more than 30 percent. His reports were crisp, clear, and very promising. His estimate of the reserves at Maravilla were almost twice what our original geologist had given us. After three months or so, he reduced his reports from daily to weekly. That seemed all right. We would have settled now for a monthly report. But after three more months, it became difficult even to get in touch with our ideal manager. I thought he probably had become ill—very easy for a Northerner in Brazil—but after a while, we finally heard from him. He said things had been going very well; it was beautiful at Maravilla, but he didn't think it wise to arrange for his wife to join him. "It was not her bent of life." That to me was a sure tip off, and, with our lawyer, I decided to pay a visit to Maravilla.

I flew to Rio, made sure I had a pilot who spoke English and knew where he was going, and we arrived in Maravilla at 1 o'clock in the afternoon. I did not go there to spy on him or catch him by surprise in any misconduct. I had wired him three days before of my proposed arrival time. When we set down at the little clearing about five miles from Maravilla, there was no one to meet us. The pilot asked if he should wait or return in three days as arranged. We waited about an hour before our manager showed. He was sorry, he said, he had misread the time of my cable. That was alright with me, but not the way he looked. This cleanly shaven, pants-and-coat man we had sent to Maravilla six months ago now had a long beard. He wore torn shorts, his breath smelled of alcohol, and his speech was slurred. With him in the truck was a young girl, daughter of one of the miners, whom he introduced as his girlfriend. He took our bags, put them in the back of the truck, then asked the girl to get in the back as well, and drove us to our mine.

There is not much point going into further detail here. Suffice it to say he had gone completely native, which, as any sociologists would say, was to be expected. Our environment shapes us more than our genes, especially, as they say, in paradise.

We did try another manager and later a team of managers, but we could not really control the stealing much less the environment. Despite our problems with theft and management, I was still hoping that we could continue operating Maravilla. We all felt the price of gold was going to skyrocket, and, eventually, it did. But a visit from a representative of the Government Mining Office in Rio left me with no choice but to abandon operations, at least temporarily. In effect, the government demanded a tax of 5 percent of our gross revenues. In situations like this, especially in South American countries, you couldn't be sure whether such a demand constituted a tax or a bribe or both.

I tried to explain to the government agent that 5 percent of our gross could represent our whole profit for the year. I offered him instead 10 percent of our net. We could not agree; at first I thought he was just bargaining, but he was adamant, and in addition, unlike most Brazilian businessmen, he was also obnoxious. I told him goodbye, please leave our property, and we eventually closed down.

We still have title to Maravilla, and I'm sure that gas-masked miners still make a bit of a living from stealing, but according to Brazilian law if a mine remains idle for three years or more it passes on to the government. One day I'm going back to Maravilla, just to see, and even sample, a bit of paradise—paradise lost, once more.

I felt very sad to leave Maravilla; it had seemed like an opportunity of a lifetime (and with gold going from $35 to over $800 an ounce, it was). To console myself, I decided to return to the States by way of the Amazon River, going all the way up the river to its source in Iquitos and then from Iquitos over the Andes to Lima, Peru, and eventually on to Chicago. It was truly a wonderful trip: everyone should see the Amazon rain forest, the greatest and most vital to our global ecology—and diminishing daily. The Indian tribes along the three-thousand-mile river (and hidden sometimes a hundred miles inland) are still among the most primitive peoples on earth. Some are cannibalistic; some have never seen a white man.

As well as being the greatest rain forest on earth, the Amazon is also the home of some of the most interesting, unusual, and dangerous Indian tribes in South America. They might also be called an endangered species! When I was on the Amazon in the early 50s there were numerous newspaper stories about unscrupulous land developers hunting and shooting Indian tribes from the air, machine-gunning them or killing them at night when they were asleep—even leaving poisoned food and liquor to kill them, so as to get them off the land. The Manaus Indian Society was formed by concerned Brazilians to help protect the Indians and diminish this human plundering. But it still goes on today, especially in areas where gold has been discovered recently.

I was an ardent supporter of the Indian Society and became friendly with several of its officers in Manaus. One evening I was visited by Ruy Alencar, who asked me whether I would be interested in going on an exploratory trip in the interior to find an Indian tribe that purportedly had never been in contact with "the white man." It was also the purpose of the Indian Society to study various tribes and, when advisable, to bring them into contact with what to the Indians was the outside world.

I accepted the invitation with alacrity. Ruy said it would probably be a two-or-three-day trip by boat, horseback, and foot. There were to be seven of us in the group, plus a reporter from one of the Rio papers. To our great surprise the reporter who showed up turned out to be a blonde girl in her twenties. She was a niece of one of the owners of the newspaper, and reporting on the Indians and their plight was her specialty. This was all acceptable enough except that the leader of our group explained that when we finally met the Indians it was very important that we not be conspicuous or look too much out of the ordinary.

What he meant was that just before we finally met the tribe we would have take off all our clothes and be just as naked as the Indians! "You really wouldn't be comfortable doing that, would you?" our leader asked the reporter, and then he added, "Our advance scout has not really told us too much about this tribe. They

Goldmining at Maravilla

could be dangerous. They might also be cannibalistic." (Earlier in the year two missionaries seeking out a tribe near Iquitos had disappeared, and the conclusion was that they had met up with a cannibalistic tribe known to be in the area.)

Our reporter said she was aware of all this: she had in fact written a story about the missing missionaries and was prepared to do whatever was required of her during the trip. She was, indeed, a very good sport during the trip, telling us of her writings about Indian tribes. She spent a lot of time with our advance scout learning as much as she could about the tribe we hoped to meet. She also asked me about my gold mine: she thought that a gold miner from Chicago in the Brazilian jungle would make a good story. All in all, she was an asset to our group except for her decision at the last part of our trip.

After many days of travel, we ended up in the center of a clearing about half the size of a football field. Our guide had read various signs from the Indians (all a mystery to me)—a broken arrow, twisted tree branches, the skull of a wild pig—that told him that the tribe knew we were here and that we ought to go no further. Meanwhile, the leader of our group placed various gifts around the border of the clearing: strings of colored beads, various pots and pans, wire, several machetes, and some honey in colored glass containers. To this day I don't know if the Indians ever ate the honey or what it was supposed to mean. Of course, he was trying to lure the Indians out of the bush to take the gifts, which would gradually, because he had placed them progressively nearer to our circle, bring them into direct contact with us.

I said that our young reporter was a good sport, but now, when it came to undressing, she demurred, saying that she didn't think it was necessary. The rest of us took our clothes off. Our leader said he wouldn't force her, but at least she should stand in the middle of our group to be partly hidden. He refused to be responsible for the consequences of her refusing to strip, however.

After most of the gifts were picked up by the Indians (darting out from the bush, picking up the beads, etc., and then darting back), the chief of the tribe emerged. A tall—about 5'8" (which is tall for an Indian)—well-developed warrior, wearing a colorful leather headband and bracelets on his upper arms, he had painted cheeks and wore only a kind of G-string. He also carried a spear, his special symbol of authority.

Fortunately, our interpreter was able to communicate adequately with him and explained that we were coming in peace, bringing gifts, and would be going on to other places. Everything was going rather well until he spotted our fully dressed reporter. I don't know whether he thought we were bringing her also as a present, but he approached her and began fingering her clothes. Our interpreter, thinking quickly, shouted to the reporter: "For God's sake, give him your blouse." It was rather a tense moment, for none of us knew what to expect next. The reporter quickly took off her blouse and also her bra and handed them to the chief.

We all breathed a sign of relief when he accepted the blouse and bra (obviously he had never seen clothes before), walked to the interpreter, and in effect said "thank you" and invited us to meet his tribe. We spent the afternoon with them, taking pictures and making recordings of some of the conversation and drum music. They offered us fish that they had just caught and cooked, which was delicious, and some corn-like mush, which I couldn't eat. Meanwhile, our reporter, still bare-breasted, made friends with other women of the tribe. They gave her neck, nose, and ear ornaments, and she gave them Polaroid pictures and a small compact mirror which made a great hit.

There were no further incidents with the chief of the tribe and a good time was had by all. After we left, I loaned my safari jacket (I seem never to go anywhere without a coat) to our reporter, which she put on, but as things turned out didn't seem to think was absolutely necessary! I am determined one day to see if civilization has taken the tribe over, assuming it still exists. In any event, it is a wonderful experience to remember.

The experience I want to write about connected with my final trip home from Maravilla, however, has nothing to do with rain forests, but only with nature, human nature in this case, and some of its sad failings.

While I was in Iquitos awaiting the Fawcett Airline plane to fly me over the Andes to Lima, I met a charming young man, an Ivy League graduate who was on a photographic mission for the *National Geographic*. I'll call him Sam. Sam and I had lunch together, and then we joined a couple of the people who worked in the little airport, and also two gentlemen who were in the Chicklet chewing gum business on behalf of Wrigley's, for a friendly game of poker. There is no better way to find out about a man than to play poker with him, as I had discovered on the *S.S. Morrison*. (There is no better way to find out about a woman, according to my friend Ann Landers, than to travel with her.)

Sam, as far as I was concerned, passed all the tests while playing poker. He never complained when he lost and he was modest when he won. Once he got a straight flush; he knew he had to be the winner (it comes only once in 65,000 hands), but when I, with a full house, raised the bet, he did not raise me but only saw my bet (and that, according to Somerset Maugham at least, is the correct etiquette for a gentleman). I liked him a lot. But then, according to some other sage, you really don't know a man until you see how he handles women, and this is where Sam disappointed me.

To get from Iquitos to Lima, you have to fly over the Andes, which means flying at over 24,000 feet. Our Fawcett twin-engine plane was unpressurized, so when we started climbing, the stewardess instructed us to put the oxygen tubes provided at each seat in our mouth, breathe normally, and keep them there until she told us we could remove them.

When we had boarded the plane, the stewardess had welcomed us and told us to sit anywhere. (Of course, there were only three other passengers and the plane had twenty-eight seats). When Sam saw the stewardess, however, a really beautiful Indian girl, with a square jaw, olive skin, and long black hair, dressed in a very smart uniform, he seemed transfixed. "Chris, I've never seen a more beautiful girl in my life."

I agreed that she was beautiful—certainly compared with anyone else we had met in Iquitos. Some of the South American women, especially Brazilians, are a mixture of Indian, Black (brought over from Africa as slaves), and Portuguese. I do not believe this combination produces the most attractive look, although I realize that this is a very superficial observation on my part. But this girl—her name was Maramia (her father had named her after a character in the *Arabian Nights*)—was an exception. And she was attentive and friendly, especially to Sam, who literally could not keep his eyes off of her.

As we climbed to 15,000 feet she instructed us to insert the oxygen tubes in our mouths, and then she went up to the cockpit to see the pilot. I dozed off with the tube in my mouth, so I'm not sure what happened to Sam. Either his oxygen tube was defective or he was love stuck by Maramia, but he didn't use the tube. When I woke up, Sam had passed out. Just then Maramia returned and saw what had happened (apparently she had had the same problem with other passengers). She gave him oxygen from a portable tank, which revived him. When he woke up, she was holding him in her arms administering the oxygen—like giving milk to a baby. When Sam looked into her eyes, I felt he was ready to pass out again, but he came to, thanked Maramia, and was ready for the snack she served us.

"Are you alright, Sam?" Maramia asked as she felt his head.

"Oh, yes, thank you. You make me feel wonderful," and Maramia blushed a bit.

Afterward Sam told me again that he had never felt so elated looking at a girl, and he asked whether we could possibly meet her in Lima. This was no infatuation, but, at least on the surface, love at first sight. Since I myself fell in love with Beatrice at first sight and we had fifty good years together, I may be more willing to see it in others.

I answered: "All you have to do is ask. I think she likes you!" And then I added that according to the ad in the newspaper we had on board, the opera in Lima was having its opening night that evening, so why not invite her? I'd already found out that Maramia loved music and the theater. (In fact, I had been about to invite her myself!)

Sam finally got up the courage to invite her to the opera, and she accepted immediately. It was arranged that she would meet Sam at 6 o'clock at the Carllion

Hotel, where we had booked reservations. Sam did suggest, rather lamely, that I could come with them if I liked, but I thought I'd better leave these two lovebirds to their own devices. Anyway opera is not really my cup of tea, especially unaccompanied. I did say, however, that I'd have a drink with them.

Now here I should add that Lima is a sophisticated city, probably one of the most civilized cities in South America, and the society ladies of Lima, who pride themselves on being of pure Spanish descent, are among the best-dressed women of the world. They import most of their clothes from France—at least they did in the 50s. I haven't been back recently, and I'm sure the poverty and fighting have changed things considerably.

Sam and I, as I mentioned, were in the bar of the Carllion Hotel. It was filled with many of the people going to the opera—*Madame Butterfly*—and the ladies were dressed to the teeth. And then it happened, and my opinion of Sam was a bit shattered.

There was a silence, which caused me to look up, and there was Sam's date. But she was not the Maramia we had met on the plane in her trim, French-designed, stewardess uniform, but Maramia, an Indian girl dressed in full Indian dress. She did not look like our popular conception of an American Indian, but she did wear a long woven dress of leather and fabric, with many beads of turquoise and silver, and a beaded headband. She was still beautiful, but there is no other way of saying it, she looked like a young Indian squaw.

Sam exclaimed, "My Gawd." Everybody in the room looked at her. Before she sat down, Sam said quickly and simply: "Chris, I can't go through with this." And it seemed to me at that point that Sam's Ivy League education had taught him nothing. It had only made him a snob. Sam apologized to Maramia, explaining that he had an attack of "stomach trouble" (he was too sensitive to say "diarrhea"), handed me the tickets, and, without another word, left us. I apologized to Maramia, saying that I hoped she didn't mind going with me and that *Madame Butterfly* was a favorite opera of mine. (Actually, it's the only one I can really take!)

And she answered, "But I thought you were coming anyway."

We had two excellent seats, just a row back of the dress circle. Maramia was familiar with the music and, of course, knew the opera's sad story, in which the American lieutenant deserts his loving Japanese wife. I could see tears in her eyes during parts of the performance. At intermission, we had refreshments in the lobby, and she told me how much she appreciated being taken to the opera. Then she said: "Mr. Janus, I'm off tomorrow. Will you let me show you Lima?" I answered it would be a great pleasure for me—and I thought to myself I didn't care what she wore.

She stopped by the hotel the next morning at nine; we had coffee and a sweet roll and I rented a car which she volunteered to drive. "I'm a good driver," she said, "and one day I might even be a pilot."

She was an excellent driver and guide. We saw the famous underground gold museum and the National Museum of Art. We had our picture taken together in a carriage that had been used by the Royal Family of Peru. Then she took me to lunch in a charming restaurant where we had Pisco Sours, a delicious but potent native drink. Maramia ordered for me, and when I asked for the check, the maitre d' said it was already taken care of. I protested to Maramia but she said, "You're a guest in my country. You must let me be a good hostess."

That evening I took her dancing at the Carllion. We had a wonderful time together. Is there anything more wonderful than a warm, genuinely attentive girl whose main mission seems to be to please you? And afterward I asked her if she would like to have a nightcap in my suite. She answered that it would be a great pleasure for her, but her parents worried if she stayed out so late at night and anyway, she said, rather sadly I thought, "There is no way the management of this hotel would allow you to take an Indian girl to your room, even for just a drink."

We talked a bit more over a brandy in the bar and then she told me: "By the way, you must understand that I wore my Indian dress to the opera not because I don't have anything better but to make a statement for our people. I hope you understand."

I said, "I do understand, and you looked beautiful and more power to you." I kissed her good night and put her in a taxi.

A year or so after this, I got a letter from her, from Madrid. She had married an elderly Spaniard, apparently of some royal rank, and was very happy and expecting a child. She said she would never forget me or the opera and the dance.

I saw Sam the next morning before he left for the States, and he asked me, "How did you make out?" I told him that I had had a wonderful time, and, by the way, that headdress Maramia wore was that of an Indian princess, and fellow, you don't know what you missed.

And it's true, the Sams of the world don't know what they are missing.

Bache and Company

When Robert Hall (Bobby), my classmate at Harvard and Oxford and a senior vice president of Bache & Co., at that time the biggest investment banking firm in the United States, called me from New York, he started the conversation not with a "hello" but, "Chris, it's time now. It's time you started focusing your life."

I answered, "Bobby, it's great hearing from you." We hadn't been in contact since our Oxford days in 1937, and it was now 1955. "How is the world of finance?"

"Chris, that is what I want you to find out. I've been reading about you and the Hitler car and the great job you did with Spyros Skouras and Greek war relief—by the way, Skouras is a customer of ours and a good friend of yours. Chris, we want you to join Bache & Co. Now it's time!"

I answered Bobby that indeed I did want to start "focusing my life" but I was thinking more of going back to my first love, writing. I also said I didn't think I was really cut out for business (I'm not).

"Chris, your problem (or blessing) is you're cut out for many things. We're not running the 440!" he laughed, "but you could really make it big with a firm like Bache. Anyway, I want you to come to New York as our guest and talk to Harold (Bache). He personally wants to see you. Come on down and we'll also take in a couple of shows. I'll make a reservation for you at the Harvard Club, unless you'd rather stay with Imogene (his wife) and me."

I think it was the prospect of seeing a couple of Broadway shows that persuaded me to go to New York, rather than the prospect of a job with Bache, but I accepted the invitation and appointment with Harold Bache.

Actually I had met Harold several years ago through Frank Altschul and his daughter, Margie. Bache & Co. at this time was at 2 Wall Street, and Harold's office was on the sixth floor near the elevator. As you entered Bache you had to pass by Harold's office, and he always kept his door open—perhaps so that the staff could just pop in and see him at any time, but more likely so that he could see everyone who came in and at what time the employees arrived. Harold was an early riser and was usually the first person in the office in the morning. This kind of supervision may be good for business, but it didn't suit a more or less free spirit like me!

Harold was very charming. One of the first things, however, that caught my eye in his office, in addition to an excellent piece of Greek Cycladic sculpture, was a framed picture of some kind, consisting of the word *listen* repeated about fifty times. After seeing this, I thought I'd better take the hint. And this is what I heard:

"Chris, Bobby has been telling me about some of

the good things you've done, such as the money you've raised for charity, and your friend Spyros spoke to me about you, too. We want you to come aboard, and this is a good time because we're going to open an office in Greece, which I'm sure you could help with. Chris, with your contacts and background, I think you could become one of our top producers. We'll start you off with a nice salary and commissions for the first six months; then you'll go on your own on a straight commission basis. What do you say?" Before I could answer he added: "Bobby tells me you want to write. I've read your articles in the *New York Times*. They're excellent. And you should continue to write. Chris you can do both—but if you write about our company, you have to clear with me first. But write, do a novel, whatever. So long as you produce, you're your own boss."

I must say I began to like what I was hearing, but a big problem remained in my mind. I was not ready to move back to New York, and I told Harold this.

"Chris, you don't have to move to New York. We want you in our Chicago office. There's Bud Fairman there, whom you know, and Jack Harris, who heads the office. You'll be with friends."

"More important," I thought to myself, "I won't have to pass by your office every morning and check in!"

I did join Bache, where I was very happy, although there was a time, just a few years after I got there, when it looked like I wasn't going to stay or at least would take a leave of absence. That was when I became involved in what might be called my ambassadorship awash.

Some of the best things in my life have happened (or tried to happen) when they were not expected or planned for, and my being recommended for an ambassadorship to Greece was one of them. In 1957 I received a telegram signed by Charles Percy and his friend Art Nielsen saying that Percy had been visiting with President Eisenhower and had recommended me to the president for an ambassadorship—preferably to Greece, which country I know and whose language I speak. At this time Percy was the golden-haired hope of the Republican party. Eisenhower admired him, for he was young and exceedingly able. He was one of the youngest presidents of a leading company (Bell & Howell) in the country, and he became the head of the Republican party of Illinois.

In addition, he was self-made. He had become rich and was married to a wonderful and attractive wife, Loraine, with four exceptional children. Sharon, one of his daughters, is married to Jay Rockefeller, and if the long-range program of the Rockefeller dynasty is successful and the Democratic party ever comes back into power, Jay may well be president of the United States, which would make Sharon the first lady of the land. I predict that she'd be even more successful at it than Jackie Kennedy was—she has the potential to be a worldwide stateswoman and a star. (In many ways Sharon has more political acumen than Jay, and that is saying a lot, because Jay Rockefeller is a dedicated, honest, and concerned statesman, and everyone who knows him thinks he will make a good candidate for president in 1996).

Arthur Nielsen, Jr., Percy's New Trier schoolmate and his lifelong friend, is equally able and dedicated, one of the world's finest businessmen. He followed in his father's footsteps as head of A. C. Nielsen Co., the world's largest marketing organization, and contributed greatly to its growth before Dun & Bradstreet bought it, which made the Nielsen family one of the wealthiest in the country. (Incidentally, they are also the Nielsens of the famous television ratings.)

With the endorsement of Percy and Nielsen and, apparently, Eisenhower's blessing, it seemed to me that I might indeed be offered the ambassadorship, even though I was not a great contributor to the Republican party (actually I'm a Democrat). I've also mentioned the resistance our State Department had to sending an ambassador to a country of his own ethnic origin. Under President Kennedy's administration, however, I believe this policy was changed.

During the preliminary negotiations, I sought my friend Christian Herter's advice. He urged me to go for it even though he said, somewhat jokingly I think, that he didn't know why anyone would want to be an ambassador in today's world, since world diplomacy is now run "electronically" from Washington, and an ambassador is just a glorified errand boy, without even the striped pants anymore!

My next step was to check in with Senator Everett Dirksen's office. Dirksen was the distinguished and powerful senator from Illinois and, of course, I was warned I'd have to deal with Harold Rainville, Dirksen's able senior assistant. I did, but I was never sure what his final action or recommendation would be.

This was a time in my career when I felt that a change of course—at least for a while—would be desirable. I had been working for Bache for two years, and I had not quite settled in, as I was later to do. I also knew that my wife, Beatrice, would bring great distinction to whatever country we were assigned. She, of course, agreed she would go wherever I was assigned, but aside from helping my career, she admitted honestly that the entertaining and politicking expected of an ambassador's wife was not at all to her liking. She was a very private person, and all the publicity that goes with embassy life was much against her nature. The publicity had, in fact, already started, with my picture and a story appearing on the front page of the *Chicago Daily News* that said I was a strong contender for the ambassadorship to Greece.

As it turned out, Beatrice really didn't have to worry. I got a call in my office at Bache at around 11 o'clock in the morning from the Secretary of State's office in Washington, asking that I be in my office around 2 o'clock Chicago time. The Secretary of State would be calling to tell me what country I had been assigned to. I immediately called my wife, who received the news with some surprise and not much enthusiasm, but nevertheless she said she was proud of me; Congratulations! I also called Harold Bache and told him I would be taking a leave of absence for a couple of years. Harold was very enthusiastic with the news—thought it was good public relations for Bache & Co. He added, "Your being ambassador to Greece won't exactly hurt our office in Athens!"

I told him I wasn't sure what country I was going to, but I don't think he really heard me. He didn't have to. I was in my office at 2 o'clock waiting for the call, and I waited for it until 4 o'clock. The call never came. Some two weeks afterward, I found out from a friend in the State Department that a "fat cat" from Palm Beach who had given over $250,000 to the party got the job. And that is how it's done and that's politics!

So I remained at Bache, and for nearly twenty-five years we had a fine relationship. I never did become their number one producer, which I'm sure disappointed Harold, but I did bring in some profitable deals, especially when Dan Walker was governor. He sent some city and state business our way. Overall, however, I'd have to say looking back that my production at Bache was at best uneven.

On the more positive side, I met some of the world's top business people while I was at Bache, some of whom ended up doing business with the firm. One of these was Aristotle Onassis. My first contact with him was over a business matter that ended unfortunately, but many years later we became friends, principally through Valerie Valentine, who knew Onassis socially and worked with him on *Greek Heritage* and Olympic Airlines.

That first business matter came about because the U. S. government had decided to sell its liberty ships, which had served us so wonderfully during the war, at an extraordinarily low price. I met with Onassis and two of his business associates at the Harvard Club in New York. Onassis, who was building up his fleet of cargo ships, wanted to buy all the liberty ships he could get. There was, however, a problem. Liberty ships could be bought only by U. S. citizens, and Onassis was, of course, Greek. Would I buy the ships in my name for him, or commission someone else to do it? This is one time I almost wish that the angel on my shoulder hadn't been there! But she whispered loud and clear in my ear: "No! It's illegal." And there went a commission that could have run into over a million dollars for me.

I did say, rather lamely, "I'll try to come up with an alternate." But Onassis said to forget it. He had simply been trying to do a fellow Greek a favor (!), and we had another drink and went for lunch.

Onassis did eventually acquire several ships from our government which almost led to an indictment, but the matter was settled with a fine which mattered very little compared to the enormous profit he made on the ships.

It was about this time that I also became friends with Huntington Hartford. He was no financial genius but he had impeccable taste in art and good intentions, and he was, on the whole, a charitable and charming person to be with. Life has been generous but not fair to Hunt, endowing him with a good name, good family, and keen judgment in many matters, but leaving him rather blank when it comes to women. That is a separate story, however, already told in gossip columns and at least one book.

I first met Hunt in connection with the development of Paradise Island in the Bahamas, when he was trying to obtain a casino license from the Pindling government. He and his sister had each inherited about fifty million dollars in A & P stock, and they already owned a large part of Hog Island when I met him. He had just leased the Werner estate on what was later named Paradise Island and built the wonderful Ocean Club on part of the terraced garden land. My role was that of friend and financial consultant; I was eventually to try to raise the additional funds necessary to build a casino on the island.

The only advice I gave him then—and he needed it—which was echoed by Jim Vanderpoel, his staff financial consultant, was not to spend any more money on the island and the casino project until he actually got the casino license from the government. License first, investment later. One did not need to be a financial genius to offer such commonsense tactics. But Hunt's response was: "Pindling is my friend. We trust each other. I've been promised the license." Well, the long and the short of it is that he never got the license. He lost most of his $30 million investment in

Paradise Island, and eventually Resorts International got the license instead, giving him some kind of token payment. They made a great fortune not only on Paradise Island but later on Atlantic City casino projects. At Bache I saw the stock of Resorts International soar from $2 a share to $210 a share, of which (thanks angel!) I had quite a few shares, as did my clients.

During the course of his unsuccessful venture, Hunt called me one evening when I was in New York, saying he had seen Ari Onassis at El Morocco, and could I arrange an introduction. Onassis had been a big investor in Monte Carlo, but was at that time having differences with the Grimaldi family and wanted out. Hunt, meanwhile, hoped to interest him in Paradise Island. Or, in any event, Onassis was a man he would like to know. I told Hunt that Valerie was a close friend of Ari's, and it probably would be more effective for her to arrange the introduction.

Valerie agreed immediately, pointing out that with the big party Onassis was giving to celebrate the opening of the Fifth Avenue offices of Olympic Airlines, which he owned, she had a perfect opportunity. She could invite Hunt to accompany her, and then perhaps the three of them could go on to El Morocco, Onassis's favorite club in New York, afterward.

I forget now why I couldn't attend the Olympic Airways party, but I did meet them at El Morocco. I arrived first and told Angelo, the prestigious maitre d', that I would be with the Onassis party, soon to arrive. I didn't have to suggest that they would expect table number one—Angelo said he would hold it for them. He did not ask me to sit there in the meantime, however, but suggested that I wait at the bar. For those readers who don't understand or care about such matters, I should explain that in cafe society in the 50s (or even now), celebrities were very sensitive about where they were seated at prestigious restaurants and clubs. One night at El Morocco after the theater group had arrived, I saw the Duke and Duchess of Windsor walk out because they were asked to wait a few minutes before they could be seated at table number one. On the other hand, Prince Rainer and Princess Grace turned it down and asked to be seated way in the back of the room (the part called Siberia), because they wanted privacy.

That night, I must have been in the men's room when Onassis, Hartford, and Valerie arrived, because I didn't see them come in. I first saw them, Onassis on Valerie's right arm and Hunt on her left, coming down the stairs from the second floor. What they were doing upstairs is a bit of a story. It seems that after Valerie introduced Hunt to Onassis they had a drink at the Olympic Airways party and then rode to El Morocco in Hunt's limo. On the way, Hunt said to Onassis—and I'm quoting Valerie who was terribly embarrassed— "Mr. Onassis, you have much more money than I do, and my wife Diana who respects money above all else is in Reno getting a divorce. May I ask a great personal favor? Would you call her and talk to her. With your money she might listen to you. Perhaps you can tell her we two are friends—she'll love that—and that I'm not such a bad guy."

Valerie told me that Ari looked rather astonished at such a request, but in good humor he agreed to call Diana. That is what they were doing on the second floor. I asked Valerie if she knew Diana's response to Ari's call. In essence it was: "Mr. Onassis, if my husband were as nice a person as you make him sound,

I probably would be in bed with him instead of being in Reno getting a divorce."

Later on in the evening when Hunt had excused himself for a few minutes, Ari turned to Valerie and said "Wasn't that a strange thing for him to ask me to do?"

Valerie told him, "Ari, Hunt is a bit eccentric at times, but he is a sweet person and really loves his wife, and it was wonderful of you to be such a good sport."

"Let's dance," said Ari. And that's the way the evening went.

Some years later, after Onassis had married Jackie Kennedy, they were cruising in the Bahamas on the *Christina*, and they docked at one of the landings on Paradise Island. For some reason Ari did not call Hunt. Hunt told me that this was a slight (I don't believe it was intentional) he would not forget. Such is life in café society.

All of which reminds me of an amusing incident involving Jackie Onassis. She and I have met several times briefly, usually at some charity function, but the last time I saw her was in an elevator we shared at Henri Bendel in New York. I asked her what she was shopping for, and she said a nightgown, and I was with her when she picked one out. I remarked that it was a lovely color on her, but she replied: "Oh, it's not for me, it's for Caroline." I forget now what I bought but it was something that my wife asked me to look for, and we went to the counter together to pay for our purchases.

Jackie handed the nightgown to the cashier and said, "Please charge it."

The clerk to my surprise (and I'm sure Jackie's), replied, "What's the name, please?"

"It's Mrs. Onassis," responded Jackie rather curtly.

Without blinking an eye the clerk picked up the telephone, called the credit officer, and said, "$168 item, Mrs. Onassis. Doesn't have her credit card with her."

The reply, of course, was, "Onassis, A, credit okay."

After taking care of the purchase, the clerk turned to me and said, "Yes sir, what have we here?" And I did have a credit card.

On the way out Jackie didn't say a word about the transaction, but she did say to my great surprise, "Sorry you couldn't come to dinner with the Weisses." I had to think hard to figure out what dinner she was referring to, but then I remembered that she had invited Edward Weiss, his wife, Ruth, and me to dinner—but this was six months ago.

I said, "Oh, yes, but I was out of the country at the time." I'm not sure where I was. "I hope you'll give me a raincheck."

Jackie did not answer. One does not refuse a dinner invitation from Jackie. I feel it was my loss, however, because even shorn of her celebrity status and her many good works, I've always considered Jackie Onassis to be one of the most lovely and utterly appealing ladies in the world.

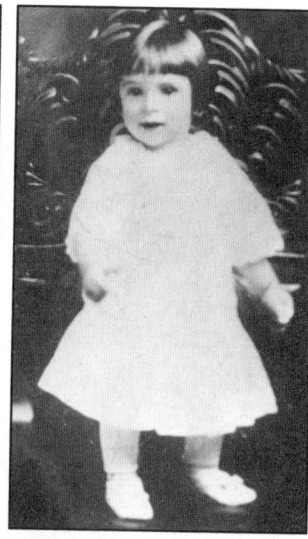

Clockwise from top left: *Author's parents, George and Olympia Xenopoulos. Wedding Photo Greece, 1892; 18 months old - 1st prize "Beautiful Baby Contest."; "Little Scholar," 1918; Harvard Graduation, 1936.*

Clockwise from top left: *Janus and Santayana, Rome, 1937; Cabinet meeting with Greek Prime Minister Plastires, 1943; With Hitler's car in Washington, D.C., 1948; In Cairo, 1944, with fellow writers John Hersey and Gerald Frank.*

Clockwise from top left: *"The Gold Mine" Muenacano Island, Amazon River, 1951;* The author and Adlai Stevenson; Lt. Christopher Janus with Danny Kay fund raising for Navy War Relief.

Top to bottom: *1936 Class Marshalls at Harvard 25th Reunion, 1961; General Alex Melas, Ed Weis and Janus - Greece, 1965; Greek Prime Minister George Papandreou and Kimon Friar celebrate 1st issue of Greek Heritage Quarterly, 1964.*

Clockwise from top left: *Janus and friend Aristotle Onassis in Greece, 1965; With King Constantine and Queen Anne Marie of Greece, 1961; With Supreme Court Justice William O. Douglas and Dr. Robert Hutchins in Greece, 1965.*

Clockwise from top left: *Mr. and Mrs. Christopher Janus with Acropolis in the background; With statue of "Peking Man," China, 1972; Janus visits and presents President Gerald Ford with "The Search for Peking Man," Oval Office, White House, 1975.*

Janus with Harvard Club awardees Marshall Field, IV and Herman Dunlop Smith.

The Janus Family, 1988.

"Janus Returns" - *Montgomery, West Virginia Centennial Parade, 1991, with daughter Niki and Melba Lou White, event organizer.*

Christopher Janus and Valerie Valentine, 1991.

Greek Heritage

I've lived in Chicago for over forty years now, and during that time I've become recognized as a good touch for help with fund-raising. Starting with the Navy and Greek relief campaigns, I've also raised money for numerous charities, including Harvard College, the Chicago Symphony Orchestra, the Friends of the Chicago Public Library, the Red Cross and the American Farm School in Greece. So in 1962, when Robert Maynard Hutchins, former chancellor of the University of Chicago and later head of the Fund for the Republic in Santa Barbara, needed help raising money for the Center for the Study of Democratic Institutions, his good friend Lou Bernat, a prominent entrepreneur and investment banker, recommended me.

Harry Ashmore, in his excellent book on Hutchins, wrote that Christopher Janus's "blandishments" convinced Hutchins to hold a symposium of studies of democracy in Athens, Greece, on "The Free Society."

Actually, it did not take much encouragement from me to persuade Dr. Hutchins that Athens, the birthplace of the democratic society, was the ideal place to hold such a symposium (the Greeks actually preferred the word *seminar*). In the first place, the Greek government was very much in favor of the idea, thought it good for tourism and such, and we were offered use of the Greek Parliament room, which was already set up with microphones, just like the United Nations, for translation. Frederika, who was queen of Greece at the time, was aware of Hutchins's great reputation as a scholar and communicator. She thought he was too much "to the left," but she nonetheless welcomed him, as did several members of the Greek Parliament, who had studied at the University of Chicago when Hutchins was chancellor.

Our first priority was to decide whom to invite. We wanted scholars and political leaders from all over the world. The second issue was how we were going to pay for the whole project. Hutchins, Harry Ashmore, and Hutchins's excellent staff at Santa Barbara took care of the first priority; my job was to raise the money. Here Valerie Valentine, an excellent money raiser and an experienced planner of trips, was invaluable.

In addition to a direct mailing campaign and personal solicitations from friends and foundations who could support the project, we offered a select group of individuals an opportunity to participate in the symposium. This offer included not only a trip to Greece, therefore, but an opportunity to mingle with our lecturers—no commonplace lot. They included such luminaries as Justice William O. Douglas of the Supreme Court, Denis Healy of Great Britain, Harry Ashmore, and a distinguished scholar from India whom I'll call Dr. P.

We limited our guests to 150 persons, including spouses, chartered an Air France plane through Georgina Gronner, an expert in the travel business,

Greek Heritage

which provided first-class transportation, and lodged them at the prestigious Grande Bretagne Hotel on Constitution Square. The program called for one week of lectures and discussions in the Parliament building and one week of cruising the Greek Islands. Queen Frederika gave a reception (not open to all members of the group, for reasons which would not be to Her Majesty's credit to mention), and the Greek government hosted various receptions and dinners throughout the whole of the first week.

Several important scholarly papers came out of the discussions, which were published at the Center for the Study of Democratic Institutions and in university journals. I think that symposium featured, as speakers and guests, one of the most impressive groups to visit Greece. Everyone had a fruitful and enjoyable time (several romances even blossomed), and we raised a handsome amount of money for the Center for the Study of Democratic Institutions.

There were, as ever, several small incidents that provided more human interest than scholarly, but they do give a little additional insight into the affair and the people involved.

On the day we arrived, I was about to have a little siesta, when there was a knock on my door. It was Dr. Hutchins. "Chris you'd better go see Dr. P., the delegate from India. He refuses to get out of bed until he sees you. He says you promised him several things, and he is waiting for them."

I went down the hall to Dr. P.'s room. The door was ajar. I knocked. A voice said, "Janus?"

"Yes."

"Come in." He was sitting up in the middle of the bed; arms akimbo, legs crossed. "Janus, you promised three things: one, to have my teeth fixed; some spending money for while I'm in Athens; and a woman companion. I will not leave this room until you keep your promises."

I remembered that when we invited Dr. P. to come to Athens, he had brought up these matters, and I had assured him that the dentists in Greece were excellent, which they are (more than I can say about the Greek medical profession in general), that delegates would be given a per diem allowance, and that I was sure he would meet some nice companion from our group. So now he wanted me to come through. We finally met all his demands, and I have to say that Dr. P. gave one of the best lectures of our symposium. He was a great wit, and a delightful person; everybody liked him. In fact, a romance developed between him and one of our prominent guests, a stunning blond who was also a fine writer and poet. After the symposium, they traveled to India and Ceylon together, and some months later Dr. P. came to Chicago to see this lovely woman.

A few days before he arrived she called me: "Chris you've got to help me. Dr. P. is arriving, and I'm not sure I can be seen with him. You know how it is in Chicago." The fact of the matter was that Dr. P. was a very dark man from India. The average person seeing him would take him for a Black, and my writer friend was one of the blondest blonds I've ever seen. Of course, this was 1962, and things have changed a bit now—or have they? Anyway, I agreed to join them. I was the "beard." For appearance's sake, Dr. P. was my guest and the writer my date, and I took them to the Pump Room, where we were seated at Booth One. I introduced him to the several people who came up to speak to me as my honored guest from India, a celebrity—and he certainly was much more of a celebrity than either of us—and a wonderful person. I don't think Dr. P. and my writer friend saw each other at their best in public, and after a week he returned to India with a broken heart.

A year later, however, Dr. P. was elected to the Indian Parliament, where he rose to head up his party. He married and now has three grown children, darker than dark. When I was in New Delhi a couple of years ago, Dr. P. met me at the airport and took me to his home, where he introduced me to his lovely young sister. He did not have to accompany us as a "beard" and we did not have to hide or be afraid to be seen in public places. Would that all the world could one day be this way.

But to return to the symposium, a couple of days after we arrived in Athens, the prime minister invited Justice Douglas, Robert Hutchins, and a few other guests to take part in a ceremony to place a wreath on the memorial honoring Greek soldiers who had died for their country. The memorial is right in front of the Parliament building, across the street from the Grand Bretagne. Those of our group who were not invited to the actual ceremony could watch from the sixth-floor balcony of our hotel, and most of our guests and lecturers chose to do so. The prime minister was ready to hand the wreath to Justice Douglas to place on the memorial when I spoke to him in Greek, suggesting that as Dr. Hutchins was the leader of our group, perhaps he should be the one to place the wreath. The prime minister and his aides replied that they thought a justice of the Supreme Court of the United States was surely more important than an ex-chancellor of a university. After some discussion, we settled on having Hutchins and Douglas jointly lay the wreath, which they did.

I don't think I've ever known a more charming,

sensitive, or witty intellectual than Hutchins, but he was also someone who was easily irked. Although I don't think he understood any of my Greek conversation with the prime minister, he sensed there was an issue here, and he didn't like it.

"Chris, what the hell was that all about? Can't Greeks ever agree on anything?"

"On the contrary," I tried to speak diplomatically, "the prime minister just wanted to make sure that you approved of Justice Douglas sharing this honor with you. After all, you're the boss." I believe he was appeased.

That evening, however, at a dinner party given by the government at the hotel for our whole group, Hutchins became quite upset. Before we left Chicago, Mayor Daley, knowing of our trip to Athens, had given me the "key" to Chicago to give to the mayor of Athens, at the same time inviting the mayor through me to visit Chicago. I told Hutchins about this and suggested that since the mayor of Athens (I don't remember his name now) spoke no English, I would be glad to translate for him (Hutchins) when he gave the key to the mayor on behalf of Mayor Daley. Hutchins replied rather testily: "Sure these guys don't speak English and you seem to be running the show, anyway, why don't you just give him the (expletive deleted) key."

I did present the key to the mayor, but I offered it on behalf of Hutchins and our group, and the mayor graciously replied, in Greek but looking at Hutchins: "Dr. Hutchins, we are honored to have such a renowned scholar and gentleman and your group visit Athens and we welcome you. But I do not have a key to give you because all the doors of Greece and all our hearts are already opened to you."

When I translated this Hutchins got up, gave a

bow, and said in his best Greek, "Sas eferisto" (thank you). From then the dinner went well. The food was delicious—lamb and artichokes, washed down with plenty of retsina, which Hutchins seemed to enjoy. The famous Strato group entertained us with Greek dances from the various Greek islands. Afterward Hutchins did thank me and congratulate me on a job well done.

Another evening the Greek Tourist Office gave us a party at a beautiful Greek taverna situated right at the foot of the Acropolis. It was a warm, lovely evening, and once more the wonderful food was accompanied by entertainment, this time including a belly dancer. I explained to the group that belly dancing is not really Greek at all but an import from Turkey dating back to their long occupation of Greece, but everyone liked the dancer very much. To show their appreciation in Greek style, they started throwing plates and money on the floor, and kept asking for more. By this time everybody had had quite a lot of retsina, which tastes innocent enough when you're drinking it, but can have quite surprising effects unless you're used to it. The wife of one of our very honored guests, perhaps the most honored guest, got up on the dance floor with the belly dancer, pulling her skirt up above her waist, and tried to do a belly dance as well. Our hosts were more shocked and embarrassed than entertained, and the incident (which the Greek press was too polite to report) is still talked about in Athens today.

Aside from this memorable evening, which our hosts of course forgave but didn't forget, our group also had some problems with our own embassy, and this despite the strong support from John Brademas, the congressman from Indiana who was also a participant in the symposium. To this day I've never been able to understand the lack of cooperation from our embassy in Greece. Toward the end of our stay, at yet another cocktail party given by the government in our honor, a senior official of our embassy, probably in his cups, came up to me and without so much as a hello said: "Are you another one of those Americans of Greek descent? And don't you know a leftist organization when you see it? And don't you know that you all are not welcome here?"

Well, I was shocked and felt like punching him in his flushed face, but sensing his probable condition I did nothing. Unfortunately, Norman Ross and Gigi Geyer, whom I had invited as representatives of the *Chicago Daily News* to accompany our group, overheard the remarks of the embassy official and reported them in the paper. I believe that the State Department in Washington issued some sort of apology to Justice Douglas and Hutchins. I never heard from them, but the incident marred an otherwise highly successful and important project for the Center for the Study of Democratic Institutions.

After the symposium the whole group was treated to a seven-day cruise of the Greek Islands, stopping at Crete, Santorini, Mykonos, Rhodes, Istanbul, and Delos. At each port a guide who was an expert on the history and art of the island was provided. Everyone seemed pleased with the lecturers and especially with meeting various Greeks on each of the islands. From all reports, it was a memorable cruise (having done this cruise a dozen or so times before, I didn't go): and aside from the educational pleasure of the trip, what made it so was that one of our most prominent lecturers was seen and heard at 3 o'clock in the morning having intercourse with one of the ship's hostesses on top of the grand piano in the salon! Apparently it was not just a one-night stand, for the couple later became engaged and from last reports are happily married, living in Greece with their two children. As they say, this is more of the magic of visiting Greece!

As I look back on my life and try to evaluate what projects I'm most proud of, that fund-raising trip ranks highly, but the founding of the *Greek Heritage Quarterly* (the American quarterly of Greek culture) brings me some of my greatest pleasure and satisfaction. Both were outgrowths of my increasing interest in, and appreciation of, my own Greek heritage.

I engaged Kimon Friar as editor, a fine scholar and translator of Katanzakis, (*Time* called his translation of "The Odyssey: a Modern Sequel" one of the greatest scholarly works of the century). We brought together a Board of Advisors that included some of the finest classical and humanities scholars then working: Sir Maurice Bowra from Oxford (Warden of my old college, Wadham), Mortimer J. Adler, Richard V. Benson, Huntington Cairns, J. R. Cominsky, Will Durant, Dudley Fitts, August Heckscherr, Harry Houghton, Denison B. Hull, Clark Kerr, Bernard Knox, Richmond Lattimore, Paul Manolis, Edward H. Weiss, Lawrence Durrell, Alexander Eliot, C. Kerenyi, Andre Mirabel, S. T. Papastavros, Pandelis Prevelakis, Mary Renault, and W. B. Stanford.

I modeled *Greek Heritage* after *American Heritage*—it was to be a hardcover book carrying no advertising. R. R. Donnelley and Son produced the first issues, and we spared no expense to make it an artistic work, featuring articles by some of the top classical scholars of the world. It was widely reviewed, and one critic in California called *Greek Heritage* the best publication of its kind ever done on Greek culture. It became an instant hit, and under the able direction of Valerie Valentine, our circulation director, we numbered at one time more than 25,000 subscribers.

I find it strange to think about and sadder to relate, however, that fewer than 2 percent of all our subscribers were Greeks or of Greek descent. We were supported rather by the Philhellenes and ordinary, educated readers in Great Britain and the United States. I pointed this out to George Papandreou, who at the time was prime minister of Greece and was himself a scholar, and he remarked that this was unfortunate. He tried to remedy the situation by subscribing to five thousand issues on behalf of the Greek government. Afterward, through Valerie's efforts, Aristotle Onassis bought one thousand subscriptions to distribute among friends and to first-class passengers of Olympic Airlines, which he founded and owned.

With this boost we thought we were on our way to producing a financially successful publication. But because of the support of the Greek government and other pressures, we decided to print *Greek Heritage* in Athens. The printer was Aspiota-Elka and they did a splendid job of art reproductions and printing. Printing in Greece meant that we had to ship the journal from Athens via ship, however, have it bound at Donnelley and Son, and mailed from Chicago. This caused us many delays, which we could handle in the beginning but not when an entire issue of the journal became waterlogged on the S.S. *Queen Frederika* during a severe storm, and the whole issue was lost. The delays and the loss of the issue wreaked havoc on our circulation. With rising costs for paper and limited financial resources (we were never able to collect full maritime insurance on the waterlogged issue), we had to abandon the project after two years. As of this writing, however, with potential help from the Onassis Foundation in Athens, an effort is underway to revive the publication.

One of the many things to come from *Greek Heritage*, however, was the formation of the Greek Heritage Foundation. We discovered that so many of our readers were interested in Greece and its culture that we decided to plan cultural symposiums in Greece, similar to the one Hutchins and I had organized earlier, where they could see the land that gave birth to Western civilization. We invited our subscribers to join our groups. We would arrange for the group to meet in the States, fly to Athens, and spend one week there for the cultural symposium and a week cruising the Greek Islands. The first several of these trips were a great success not only because of the expert lectures we offered but because the parties and festivities planned for the group were overwhelming. The king and queen invited us to the palace; there was always a reception given by the prime minister; and the Greek Tourist Office, Olympic Airlines, and my Greek friends, who included Kaity Argyropoulou, Leto Catacouzinou, Ian Vorres, Niki Goulandris, and Mary Caralou, lady-in-waiting to the queen, would all chip in to make the guests feel welcome. If Onassis happened to be in Athens during one of our symposia, there would be festivities on his yacht.

Our symposia grew year after year, and so many people came with us that they persuaded us to plan cultural symposia to other parts of the world. We traveled to Russia, South America, and other places, and eventually became the first cultural group to be admitted to the People's Republic of China in 1972. But that is a later story.

President Johnson Meets Prime Minister Papandreou

Greece and things Greek were now firmly entrenched in my life, even in Winnetka, Illinois, and I continued to be involved with the political and cultural life of the country—sometimes more involved than I wanted to be.

In the mid-sixties, there was one more crisis brewing between Greece and Turkey. Of course, as our State Department diplomat quipped, "Crises between these two countries are just normal," but this one was serious enough that the Greek prime minister, George Papandreou, was invited to come for talks with the president and the State Department. (It not only

President Johnson Meets
Prime Minister Papandreou

involved Cyprus but, as I recall, air rights between Chios and Turkey.) As is usual, a Head-of-State reception was planned for Papandreou, featuring various government officials, experts on Greece, big contributors to the Democratic Party—especially Greek donors—and apparently a few friends.

The prime minister suggested that I be invited. I had met him a few months earlier in Greece, when I was first publishing *Greek Heritage*, and he had become one of our best sponsors for the publication, as well as a warm friend. I'm not sure why he wanted me at the reception, but I believe it was because of my connection as publisher of *Greek Heritage*. Anyway, I was there, along with about fifty other guests.

It so happened that I got to the reception (held at Blair House, just across from the White House) just as Papandreou arrived, and he greeted me and we walked in together. A few minutes later, while I was talking to the prime minister, President Johnson arrived and came directly to meet Papandreou. They shook hands, but the president looked at me and said, "Please tell this nice old gentleman that we welcome him as a great friend, and tell him I have a man in Congress (I believe he was referring to Congressman McCormick) who is probably his age, and he's still a wonderful statesman!"

Papandreou laughed because he understood and spoke English perfectly, but instead of answering in English, he fell in with the scenario and made his answer to me, his "interpreter," in Greek. I told the president that the prime minister thanked him, but before I could bring myself to inform the president that the prime minister spoke English, Johnson interrupted me saying: "And tell him I'm sorry I can't stay now. I have to get back to the salt mines. But I'll see him for dinner and a talk tonight." And President Johnson walked out with his aides and secret service people.

I wasn't sure then whether Papandreou felt insulted, it all happened so quickly, but he sure was shocked, as was I and those who were within earshot of the conversation. I tried to tell Papandreou that was the Texas manner and nothing more, but I heard later that the prime minister was not just shocked, he was furious. As it turned out, they did have a fine dinner together, replete with drinks. The president had thoughtfully provided some retsina and 8-star Metaxa Greek brandy, and I was told that he congratulated Papandreou that Greece made such excellent brandy.

The following day the president and Papandreou met again, this time with State Department and Greek diplomatic officials. A crisis was averted; pressure on NATO was eased. Greece was promised more aid and, I believe, the prime minister went back to Greece not understanding the Texas manner but at least not angry. As usual, none of the Greek/Cyprus problems were settled then, anymore than they are now some twenty-five years later, but Papandreou told me later he and the president did agree on one thing: Greece makes good brandy!

Andreas Papandreou, son of George and also a former prime minister of Greece, blames the CIA and our State Department for the Papadopoulos dictatorship in Greece in 1967. There is considerable evidence to support his contentions. We know that the American Embassy in Athens did not like his father while he served as prime minister, suspecting him of leftist leanings, and they liked his son even less. Whatever the whole truth or value of Papandreou's evidence, Papadopoulos did establish a dictatorship in Greece, bringing the country seven years of some of the worst

President Johnson Meets Prime Minister Papandreou

tyranny and torture of innocent citizens in its long history.

Andreas Papandreou was put in jail by the dictators and remained in prison for nearly a year. I was honored to be one of his many supporters who finally helped persuade President Johnson to bring pressure on Papadopoulos to release him. Shortly after his release I met Andreas and his wife, Margaret, in Stockholm. We went to dinner at the Grand Hotel, and when Andreas sat down at the table he opened his coat and showed me that he was carrying a gun. "I'm out of prison, but my life is being threatened. The dictators and I are not through with each other," and indeed they weren't.

Meanwhile, I kept up my little anti-dictatorship campaign by writing articles in the *Chicago Sun-Times*, with great support from Jim Hoge, the editor, and Bill Braden, a political writer, and I worked with the underground in Greece, which was publishing a book about the dictators. As it turned out, eighteen well-known Greek authors risked their lives or imprisonment to defy censorship. I persuaded Willis Barnstone, my old friend who had married Elli, my former assistant at UNRRA, and was now a professor at Indiana University, to translate their articles from Greek into English. Harvard University Press, to their great credit, published the book. We called it *18 Texts*. (Now, although the fight against censorship in Greece could be called a deadly serious affair, it was not without its humorous moments. In 1972, when the fight had been going on for several years, someone published what purported to be a book of erotic verse. The writer was prosecuted, and in the trial it came out that the steamy poem was actually the Song of Songs.)

At this time my son Chris was serving in the Peace Corps in Tunis. He had been there nearly four years and was ready for a little vacation. He had never been to Greece and despite the dictatorship I recommended that he go there. He accepted my suggestion and full of enthusiasm to visit the country of his ancestors he arrived at the airport in Athens. I didn't realize that as a result of my press campaign in the *Chicago Sun-Times* against the dictatorship and my working with the underground in Greece, my name was on a political black list. When Chris showed his passport, bearing the same name as mine, they arrested him. The more polite word is *detained*, but there was a real possibility that he would be put in prison. He had the presence of mind to call the U. S. Embassy in Athens and they called me. The embassy personnel seemed hopeful that once the Greek authorities realized that Chris was not the person who was writing the anti-dictatorship articles they would release him, but knowing how the dictators do things and how slow the diplomatic process is, I decided not to wait.

Tom Pappas, of the Esso-Pappas enterprise in Greece, was one of the richest and most influential Americans in Athens and was a big financial contributor to the Papadopoulos dictatorship. I say *contributor*, but the better word is *briber*. He really had to pay to stay in business in Greece. Tom and I were friends from Greek War Relief days, although we did not share the same political views. His standard answer to me when we discussed the dictatorship was: "Chris, what are you? Aren't you a businessman? So long as you can make a buck, why should you care who runs this bloody country." Well I'd tell him I did care and so should he. We would agree to disagree and go

President Johnson Meets Prime Minister Papandreou

our separate ways. But on the question of my son's arrest in Greece, there was no disagreement.

When I phoned Tom and told him what had happened, he responded like a loyal friend. I heard the story of what he did from several mutual friends. The very morning I phoned him, he left the Grande Bretagne Hotel, where he lived, went directly across the street to Dictator Papadopoulos's office, and without so much as a "hello" he said, in effect: "George, you made a big mistake. If you don't release young Chris Janus, I myself will leave Greece and that will be the end to my support."

Chris was released that same day, but they would not let him stay in Greece. They did allow him to board the first plane leaving Athens, which took him to Nairobi in Africa.

Some weeks after this sad incident, the U. S. Embassy managed to bring about some results, in the form of an apology from the dictators. I received a cable from the foreign minister of Greece regretting the incident and explaining that the reason Chris was detained was not because of me but because Chris was a member of the Peace Corps. The Peace Corps was for underdeveloped countries and Greece was *not* an underdeveloped country. Therefore, he was not welcome. The cable ended in a conciliatory note saying, however, that I would be welcome!

Only the Greek mind could come up with such a bizarre explanation. On the day I received the cable, Roy Fisher, editor of the *Chicago Sun-Times*, and his wife, Ann, came for dinner. I showed him the cable and told him the whole story. He never used the story, and some weeks afterward he said to me, "Chris, I don't know why we didn't print that story." For a newspaper man who is one of the best in the profession (he later became department head at the School of Journalism at the University of Missouri), I wondered why too. Anyway, I'm glad to print the story for the first time now.

A year or so after this incident, I went to Greece, hoping that what the minister of foreign affairs had said in his cable was indeed true and that I would be welcome.

When I showed my passport to the authorities at the airport, I didn't exactly hear any shouts of welcome or bands playing, but I was not detained. Never before in my trips to Greece had my luggage been opened, but this time it was, and I was searched. I did not mind that, but what I did mind (and was also quite amused by) was that I was followed from the moment I got a taxi for the Grande Bretagne Hotel. Just like in the movies, my shadow (who looked like TV's Lieutenant Colombo) wore a trench coat and a turned-down hat, and, believe it or not, smoked a pipe and hid behind a newspaper. He was there when I checked into the hotel, and although I already knew about him, I was also warned by Mr. Doxiadis, the owner of the hotel. He called my room (Room 616, where I've always stayed when I'm at the Grand Bretagne), and warned me that I was being followed and to be careful. I really didn't mind having the little fellow on my trail.

I went to Zonars near the hotel for coffee—there he was sitting a few tables away. I took a walk in the Palace Gardens and he was not far behind. I returned to the hotel and went to the barber shop for a haircut, massage, and a pedicure—a wonderful way to relax after a long plane trip—and he lurked nearby. Much to the poor little fellow's embarrassment, I would say "Good morning" or "Good evening" to him, and he

President Johnson Meets Prime Minister Papandreou

pretended I was talking to someone else. But the most amusing incident happened a few days later.

When I arrived in Athens, I had a very bad cold. And before I left Winnetka, Maurice Wald, my doctor, had given me some special prescription for treating it. I had had the prescription filled at Phelan's drug store in Winnetka, but in my true careless fashion, owing to my hurrying when packing, I left the medicine behind. I discovered this in Athens when I wanted to take a dose and go to bed early. I tried calling Dr. Wald but couldn't reach him immediately. He called back in the middle of the night when I was half asleep. But I did try to write down the prescription.

The next morning, however, I could not read my scribbling, and I felt quite desperate. Then it occurred to me that Dr. Wald's overseas call to me had probably been taped. I got dressed, went down to the lobby, and to my relief, I saw my little shadow sitting there waiting for me. I went up to him. He seemed very uneasy and looked like he wanted to walk away, but I said in Greek: "My friend (palikari-mou), I know you're following me and you're doing your job and you're very good at it. But now you must do me a great favor. I have the flu, I don't feel well, and I want you to call the office that taps my phone and get the prescription that my doctor from Chicago gave me over the phone at about three o'clock this morning. I am sick. Take this (I gave him ten dollars) and do it right now!" He didn't say a word but inside of an hour I found Dr. Wald's prescription in my mailbox at the hotel. This is a true Greek to me.

I stayed in Greece about ten days, and while I was there I was able to help some fellow writers who were in prison. My aid was always made possible through bribes and with help from Tom Pappas. My little shadow never left me, and when I would go to a taverna at night, I'd make sure that he was sent a drink with my compliments.

Intervals in a Life

It may sound as if I spent most of my life traveling, mainly to Greece, but in fact the large part of it has been spent in Chicago. Beatrice and I lived in Winnetka for fifty years, raised our children there, and got very involved with local Chicago activities. One of the experiences that meant a good deal to me was the period during the mid-sixties when I was president of the Chicago Harvard Club, the oldest Harvard Club in the world.

William McKee Dunn, a director of the Chicago Harvard Club, called me at home one evening and said he had been directed to ask me if I would be willing to be nominated for president. I had attended several meetings of the club but had not been active in any of its affairs. I'm not sure why they asked me, but I was delighted to say to Bill Dunn that it would be an honor I would cherish.

A few weeks later at the Club's annual meeting, held at the Exmoor Country Club in Highland Park, I was unanimously elected president, and it was a job that I really put my heart into. I enjoyed it because I felt there was much to do to make the club a viable institution in the Chicago area. I felt that it had the capacity to do much within the community and that it deserved to be an important contributor, but for years it had seemed content just to exist as a money-raising and student recruitment agency of Harvard College.

With the prestige of Harvard, I felt our club could be a much more influential factor in Chicago's social, economic, and political affairs. I discussed my views with some of the past presidents of the club, including Fred Burnham, Robert Spindell, Joe Greeley, Lee Wendell, Larry Howe, and others and received their whole-hearted approval and support.

The first thing we did was to institute a series of "Dialogue Luncheons," which were open to the public. These were not merely lunches to which you would go, eat, and listen passively to some speaker. We urged the speakers to be moderators rather than speakers. Audience discussion and action were the goals. And the subjects were not abstract philosophical musings but topical concerns that were important to us all: "the Sexual Revolution," "the Feminist Movement," "the Soviet Threat" (and to this day I haven't found anyone—writers, Russian experts, the CIA, government officials—anyone in the world who predicted the collapse of the Soviet empire), "the Daley Machine," "Saving the Elephant," "the Planet Earth and the Environment," and a score of other such ideas. With the help of Marshall Field, who at the time was publisher of the *Chicago Sun-Times*, the Dialogue Luncheons were publicized and brought about a great deal of discussion in the community, and membership in the club increased about 25 percent over a two-year period.

My second innovation as president of the club was to establish the annual Harvard Club Service

Award, and to this day the award has been the main feature of the club's annual dinner. Unlike any other community service award that I know of, we like to think of the award as "a pure award." It is based on the Periclean principle of recognizing and encouraging action that serves the community over and above the service done through one's profession. You don't get the award for being an excellent doctor, educator, lawyer, or businessman—things that you are paid to do, however helpful they may be. This award recognizes excellence in service outside your chosen work.

The award itself is a bronze statue of John Harvard, enclosed in a velvet-lined box which Marshall Field and Valerie Valentine, members of our Award Committee, designed. So far the following Chicagoans have been honored with the Harvard Club Award:

1967 Herman Dunlop Smith and
    Mrs. J. V. Spachner
1968 William Hartman
1969 Daggett Harvey
1970 Mrs. J. Harris Ward and Daniel Walker
1971 William McCormick Blair
1972 Louis M. Sudler
1973 Harold F. Grumhaus
1974 Robert E. Brooker
1975 Mr. and Mrs. William Wood-Prince
1976 Mrs. Joseph Regenstein
1977 Edward F. Blettner
1978 Marshall Field, IV
1979 George E. Johnson
1980 Marion Despres
1981 William G. Swartchild, Jr.
1982 Marion M. Lloyd
1983 Daniel J. Terra

1984 Jerome H. Stone
1985 Arthur Rubloff
1986 Stanley M. Freehling
1987 Hammond E. Chaffetz
1988 James J. O'Connor
1989 Irving B. Harris
1990 James W. Compton
1991 Newton N. Minow
1992 Bernice Weissbourd

The award has become quite prestigious and most of us in the club feel that it has encouraged and improved the level of volunteer service to the community.

I believe that the third thing accomplished during my administration was bringing in more participation from the Radcliffe Club. In fact, for the first time in its history we had a woman as president of the Harvard Club, with great success. Also I should add in passing, we elected our first Jewish president, and although as I write this these changes may seem commonplace today, they were not fifteen years ago. In fact, when I was president of the club and held several meetings at the University Club, I was reminded that Blacks and Jews were not permitted to join. Mike Royko, then a reporter with the *Chicago Daily News*, called to ask why I would hold director meetings at such a place and how could a university club deny membership to Jews and Blacks. I dissuaded Royko from writing a column but did move our director meetings elsewhere and I resigned from the University Club. I am glad to report that today it is open to all. The world does change!

At the end of my two-year term as president, the Club honored me by issuing a special commendation which I very much treasure. The commendation reads:

> *"It is no unprofitable cause of life when a man shall at his private cost not only benefit himself but also the commonwealth."*
> —THUCYDIDES VI

JANUARY 1977
CHICAGO HARVARD CLUB AWARD
SPECIAL AWARD
CHRISTOPHER G. JANUS '36.

My daughter, Niki, who has been reading some of these memoirs as I am writing them, just told me: "Stop for a moment writing about things you've done in your life—write about some of the things you believe in."

If one could rate the various values and virtues to live by, I believe I would put loyalty at the top of the list. And I don't mean loyalty with conditions. "I'll be loyal to you so long as you are right." No, I mean loyalty in the primitive sense, and here I will say something that may sound strange: I mean loyalty in the Mafia sense—and that's the only good thing I can say about the Mafia. Or to put it on a philosophical level, I believe in what Professor Joyce calls the "loyalty to loyalty" concept. It means, "Right or wrong, I am with you. I may not agree with you—I may even think you're wrong, but my loyalty to you is unconditional."

I like to feel that I give such loyalty to my family and some of my friends. I would hope to get the same kind of loyalty in return, but it is not a condition of my loyalty; it may be an expectation, but it's not a requirement. I cannot think of a more beautiful virtue among people. Perhaps what I admire most about it is that it is not given to us by nature, like love, but is ours by individual choice.

The second virtue I like to live by is kindness. Santayana said, "Kindness is the last wall of human thought." I'm not sure exactly what that means. But how wonderful it is to see an act of pure kindness and to be able to give kindness to others—to everybody. And, here again, kindness is not natural, like the survival instinct. Kindness is a matter of choice, a choice that often goes against our natural instincts. That's why in our family, coming down from my grandparents, we have a motto: "Man helping man is God." I think the Elder Pliny first said this. It is not a natural instinct to think of another person before yourself, but when you do go beyond your instinct of survival and reach out—yes, to me, that is godlike.

And, of course, there is love. How many times have you heard, "What is life without love?" It's the greatest joy; the single greatest force in nature. But you can't buy it, or order it, or find it if it's not there. The facsimile of love may be all around, but I'm talking about love that is God given. And in this sense love is not a matter of choice; we really can't take credit for having it, or blame for not having it. And like faith, it can move mountains. Of course, it can also make the wisest businessmen look and act like fools. But it's the single most precious joy in our life and as the Psalms say, "none of the things we can desire are to be compared to it."

I won't keep bringing in the imaginary letters I wrote—after all, I've already published them—but I'd like to quote another one. This is the title piece of the book, *Only for Your Eyes*, and it is the letter Samson might have written to Delilah. And I think it expresses some of my own beliefs as well:

Intervals in a Life

From the prison house in Gaza Samson sends a message to Delilah telling her the secret of his true strength. Circa 1136 B.C. Samson exhorts Delilah to save herself by telling her the meaning of faith and the coming of a greater Judge.

To Delilah of Sorek, and only for her eyes:

I pray thee, Delilah, why didst thou come to the prison today? They did not have to tell me. I heard the rustle of thy cloak above the noise of the grind wheel; thy perfume still haunts the air. Was it to torture me further? Didst thou want to see a blind man turn the wheel? Or couldst thou not resist another look at these arms that held thee? Dost thou repent, Delilah? Hast thou spent all thy silver? Or art thou afraid?

HAVE no fear, Delilah! Alas, I am driven to love thee, just as I am consecrated to die. Therefore I send thee these last words—unless this scribe betrays me,—to forgive thee. And I give thee what thou askest. Thou canst no longer betray me, but heed my words, thou canst save thyself. Hence I freely tell thee wherein my strength doth truly lie.

FOOLISH girl, didst thou really believe my strength was in my seven locks? Hast thou heard of a symbol? There is no power, dear Delilah, in the beauty of one of thy red hairs. My strength to stop the mouth of lion, slay a thousand Philistines, or move a mountain is not found in any outward thing. My strength, O blind Girl, lies in my faith! And this thy people shall soon see.

THE faith of which I speak is not like a sword the lords of the Philistines took from me, or a secret thou canst sell for silver. Canst thou touch it? No. Canst thou see or hear it? No. It is not a thing of the senses in which thou are so expert. But it is a thousand times more real, though no evidence is unseen.

IN the beginning was the faith, and then God made the world. Faith is the essence of creation; the beyondness of our soul; the power of God within us to those who will take it. Take it, Delilah!

MAN, even a Philistine, is not the measure of all things. He is a speck upon a speck. But faith gives my strength beyond his strength; vision where his eye cannot see; it is his reach beyond his grasp.

BY faith man travels unafraid among strange ways finding new life and hopes. By faith man helps man, for the helping of man by man is God. Without faith he is at the end of the course. With faith, there is no limit to what man can become, yea, even thee Delilah, a woman.

BELIEVE, O Delilah, and be saved from the superstitions that shackle little men's minds. Believe in love and the voices of thy young heart though thou art hurt. Believe in a God that loves— though thou art forsaken. Believe in your mind without fears; your spirit without proofs; limit your destiny only by your dreams. Put all good things in thy faith, and cast out all evil. For we become like what we believe.

AND now, lest my words have not reached thy heart, I tell thee a secret for thy senses. There cometh today a great destruction. Therefore, I pray thee, leave not thy house; go not to thy pagan temple.

FOR thou canst live, Delilah; live for the morrow when a mightier Judge will come saying,—Thy faith hath saved thee; go in peace. He will bring a knowledge of love which today thou knowest only the counterfeit. Wilt thou believe? Or wilt thou die? O Lord, what is man that thou art mindful of him?

                                          Samson

Gaza
Arhn, Nissan

    Just as my life has not all been spent traveling, it has not all been full of big events. There have been many small occasions, incidental pleasures, that aren't often written about, but which make up the large part of any life, and a large part of its pleasures as well. The joys of spending time with family, playing foolish games, pursuing hobbies—these have all been important to me, and I'd like to touch on some here.

    When we travel as a family and also when we have dinner at a restaurant, we play some games which I've invented. I see them not only as sources of amusement but as a way of giving, especially my children, a little extra spending money.

    Our favorite game when we travel abroad is the recognition game. The first person who sees someone she or he knows well enough to greet by first name gets a dollar from everyone in the family. Offhand, it might seem that adults would have the advantage here, but actually my children have won most of the time. On vacation they see their classmates or friends traveling with their parents, just as we are. Niki, my daughter, has so far been the biggest winner, especially since she has been dean of women at two colleges (Wheaton and

Mills), and those college students seem to travel all over the globe!

One great exception was a few years ago when my son Chris married his wife, Thea, at Oxford. We all went over for the wedding, and we met a few days beforehand in London at Claridges Hotel for tea. I think our whole family was there: Niki, Dave, Lincoln, Myra, Beatrice, and me, along with an old friend, Pauline Vogelpoel Mann, and her husband, David. Beatrice and I arrived first and headed for the tea room. On the way I saw John Roosevelt, a friend and an associate of mine at Bache. But this didn't count, for we were not yet all together, so the game had not officially started. When we were all assembled, there were ten of us. The room was quite crowded and there were many Americans present, but after an hour or so none of us had yet recognized anybody, and we were ready to give up. Just as we were about to leave, a fine-looking gentleman, who was rather formally dressed but carrying a brief case, came up to me and tapped me on the shoulder: "I cannot leave without saying hello to an old friend. How are you, Chris?" It was King Constantine of Greece. I introduced him to everybody and everybody seemed quite impressed but when he left, there as a general howl, "Come on, that's not a king of anything. Kings don't carry briefcases. We are not paying." But I convinced them that it really was King Constantine, and everyone cheerfully paid up.

Another little game we play is guessing the dinner check. The person who can guess the amount within one dollar wins. Sometimes I offer $10 to the winner. Sometimes $100 depending on how flush I feel at the time. If the person guesses the exact amount—the bottom line, tax included—then I'm obligated to pay the winner an amount equal to the amount of the check. I reduce this amount to a "C" note ($100), however, if the check is too big. My wife once won the exact amount, and Niki, I believe, has won twice. Children (with some advice from their parents) have won numerous times, guessing within $1.00. But the all-time winner in Valerie, who has been with the family many times. It is uncanny the number of times she gets the answer. We accuse her of being able to read the bill upside down. Not really, she just studies the prices of food ahead of time!

I have two rather serious and very pleasurable hobbies:

Collecting copies of Omar Khayyam's *Rubáiyát* in foreign languages (the *Rubáiyát* has been translated into every written language), and collecting walking sticks from each country I visit.

"The walking stick serves the purpose of an advertisement that the bearer's hands are employed otherwise than in useful effort, and it therefore has utility as an evidence of leisure."—Thorstein Veblen

Getting a locally made cane from a foreign country is an easy and comparatively inexpensive way of remembering where you've been, and canes also make good presents to bring home. Even if the person you give it to doesn't use a walking stick, some of them are beautifully carved and very decorative and can be displayed as works of art, which, indeed, many walking sticks are.

According to my mother, the first walking stick I received was left to me by my father, who died in 1914, when I was just three years old. Actually, it's a Greek shepherd's stick made of olive wood from Delphi, circa 1820. The shaft is beautifully and delicately carved, and the handle is shaped like the head of a dolphin. My mother told me that my father carried it with him wherever he went. He considered carrying a walking stick to be not only a comfort but a mark of a gentleman, not necessarily in a fashionable sense but as a distinction between a Greek and a barbarian!

My father was about 5 feet 10 inches tall and I'm just over 6 feet, so the stick is a little short for me—not that I really want to go around carrying a shepherd's stick. Anyway, this stick is a prize in my collection, which numbers nearly three hundred. Of course, they are not all works of art, mostly they are simply mementos of my travels or gifts from friends who know of my hobby and have helped me add to it.

Another stick I value greatly is one that belonged to Beau Brummel (circa 1835). Beau Brummel, the reader may recall, was considered the most stylish gentleman during the modish Regency period in England (early nineteenth century). He invented the gentleman's tuxedo and was a close friend of the Prince Regent (later George IV). His cane is an elegant, formal stick, with a beautiful carved ivory handle and a gold and silver ferrule. (All walking sticks are made up of the same basic parts: the handle, the shaft, and the ferrule, which is the tip.) Brummel carried his stick with him at all formal parties at Buckingham Palace and elsewhere and helped promote the fashion that a walking stick was an indispensable part of a gentleman's wardrobe. I should add that I carry a walking stick only when, as Shakespeare said, "I'll fetch a turn about the garden," or when I take my usual morning walk along the lake. Thanks heaven I don't need it to walk, but it brings me comfort. I have to confess to a fear of dogs, and a walking stick does offer some measure of protection.

On a lighter side, a friend of mine at Disney

Studios, after they finished filming my *Goodbye, Miss 4th of July*, sent me a walking stick made from a great bull's penis. It's dark, strong, straight and upright—and when it's on exhibit, as it was recently when the Tavern Club in Chicago showed all my walking sticks, women especially seem drawn to it. They tend to touch it and ask, somewhat to my embarrassment, what it is. Depending on the woman, I either answer truthfully and we both have a good laugh, or I say (more often), "It looks like a branch of a black walnut tree." And, incidentally, my late friend and poker-playing buddy, Mel Boruszak, owned a forest of black walnut trees and did indeed give me a walking stick made from one of his trees.

Each stick in my collection has a story, but I must confine myself here to just a brief description of a few of the more interesting walking sticks:

There is a light, delicate walking stick with a carved silver handle, that was used by Queen Frederika of Greece and given to me by one of her lovely ladies-in-waiting; an American ebony and silver stick, circa 1856, that was later carried by Robert De Niro in the movie *The Untouchables*; one of New York city's famous "21" Club walking sticks—actually, I've been given several by various friends; several shillelaghs from Ireland (no collection would be complete without them, but, incidentally, Ireland is one of the few countries I've never visited). I have a "gentleman's stick," made in Paris and used by Aristotle Onassis, and I treasure a natural "Dog Face" stick from the Maine woods, given to me by Niki. A very naughty-looking stick is called "King Farouk's Diklek stick" and is from the Sphinx Club, back in 1935 Paris, which at the time was Paris's most exclusive whorehouse!

I bought a Dragoman's pointing stick (circa 1916)

from my guide in Cairo in 1943. Probably the most valuable (at least I paid the most for them!) are two (his and hers) beautifully carved, ivory walking sticks belonging to the family of Mogul Emperor Shah Jahan, who built the famous Taj Mahal in loving memory of his favorite wife. The Emperor's stick has the head of a ferocious looking lion carved in the handle; the handle of his wife's stick is simple, bearing lovely tracings in the ivory handle. Both sticks are made in three pieces which can be unscrewed, a convenience I discovered when I brought them through customs. (As antiques, it was not necessary to declare them.)

I have an elegant gold-topped walking stick that belonged to Heinrich Schliemann when he was excavating Troy (given to me in Greece by General Alex Melas, his grandson), and I expect to use it in the movie on Schliemann that we are trying to make.

From China Valerie brought me a handsome cane with a great owl for a handle. I've learned that the Chinese used the owl as a symbol of wisdom long before 2,000 B. C., when the Greeks first used it.

While in Brazil in 1952 working our little gold mine, I was given a piece of beautiful rosewood from the Amazon, which I had made into a cane with semi-precious Brazilian stones with some decoupage.

A friend from Zimbabwe sent me a heavy walking stick made from ebony, which he claims was used by Minister Mogobive in 1979 to clobber several of his enemies! The collection also includes a delicate "Grape and Snake" carved stick from Persia (Iran), and carried on occasion by the Shah of Iran when he was in power. I went to a metal shop in Wilmette and had them make me a brass and copper stick, to which I added a jade and gold ring to the ferrule engraved on the shaft by artist, R. Maki, with the beautiful verse from the *Rubáiyát* "Ah, Love! Could you and I with fate conspire/To grasp this sorry Scheme of Things Entire,/Would not we shatter it to bits—and then remould it nearer to the Heart's Desire." You might say that on this stick my two great hobbies combine.

While in Zaire, I found a stick with two heads (Janus-like) that I could not resist buying. After I brought Hitler's car to the United States, some sleazy guy (a member of the Nazi party in Skokie, Ill.) offered to sell me the cane he said Hitler used after the attempt on his life. It was a black walnut walking stick with a curved handle and a swastika on the shaft. He wanted $1,500 for it, which was cheap considering what collectors of Hitler's things are paying these days, but I could not bring myself to own it.

My friend and poker-playing buddy Louis Goldblatt gave me a cane with a cup for brandy (or whatever) in the handle; my Oxford classmate, now Lord Keith Joseph and a member of the House of Lords, added to my collection with a simple folding field-seat stick used at Ascot in 1950.

I designed a walking stick some years ago that I called "the Sans Souci Stick"—"massage its smooth, therapeutic knob and walk your troubles away." (Someone stole it from me while I was visiting friends in Bombay some years ago). And the collection includes several Swiss hiking sticks and many bamboo canes from Jamaica, Haiti, Hawaii, and the Philippines.

Cane makers seem to have a special propensity for making duck handle sticks, and I have at least ten of them! Some of the sticks I value the most are the ceremonial sticks that chiefs of various tribes used as their mark of authority; these include a chieftain's stick from Cuzco, Peru (circa 1880); one made of elephant wood from Burma; a very heavy, ten-foot mahogany chieftain's stick from the Amazon; and most recently a beautiful antique ceremonial stick from Sumatra made of ebony, given me by Valerie when she and I were visiting in Bali. The handle is a carving of a chief's head with real hair and a bandanna: below the handle head are twelve other delicately carved, proportionally smaller heads interspersed with carvings of real and mythical ferocious-looking animals. At the tip is a snake and a crocodile, which seem to be guarding ascent to the head of the ceremonial stick. We had a little trouble getting it on the plane and through customs, it looked so foreboding and strong: more like a mysterious weapon than an addition to my collection. The Tavern Club has asked me to share my collection again, and I plan to feature this last one. The owner of the antique shop where Valerie bought the stick said that the chief of the tribe in Sumatra also used the stick as his authority for marriage ceremonies, and it was supposed to bring the bride and groom great strength and good luck. I like that idea very much.

As I look back on my life and myself, what I am most proud of are not the various unusual things I've done, nor the celebrated people I've met, but my children, and the day-to-day living and loving we shared. And I have to give most of the credit for how well they have turned out to my remarkable wife, Beatrice. She didn't rear them under a code of strict discipline nor by talking to them of what was right and dignified and loyal and loving, she taught them by example.

During most of our children's early years, I seemed to be too busy traveling and trying to build a successful professional or business life to devote the amount of time a father should give his children. But despite this, I think our children always knew of my love and support. And they have developed into wonderful, generous, and successful human beings—not a small accomplishment at a time when our society and schools were being besieged by racial unrest, a lessening of some basic human values, drugs, and the highest record of street killings and other violence in our history.

Today, Lincoln, my youngest, is married to Myra, a wonderful mother and wife, and has three fine children, Alexander, Elizabeth, and Nicholas. He is a successful lawyer with Illinois Bell and well liked.

Chris, who got his doctorate at Oxford, which I was never able to do, teaches at the University of Chicago Lab School. He is married to Thea, a Phi Beta Kappa herself, and they have a lovely daughter, Olivia. Niki, named after my sister, Androniki, the heroine of *Miss 4th of July, Goodbye*, is a distinguished educator, former dean of women at Wheaton College in Massachusetts, and has had a longtime relation with both Harvard and Radcliffe. She is married to David W. Davis, the distinguished former head of Massport and now executive director of New Jersey's Garden State Parkway.

On this day, August 19, 1991, I am not writing remembrances but am really compelled to report (by candlelight) about Hurricane Bob, because here at Long Pond, Belgrade Lakes, Maine, we are practically in the middle of the hurricane. It started from the Bahamas early this morning, hit the eastern coast at 130 miles per hour, and early in the evening slammed into us here in Maine at about 7 p.m. Millions of people, including us, are without power, thousands of trees have been uprooted, hundreds of homes hurt, and untold damage has been done to boats. Miraculously, only a few deaths have so far been reported. I am pleased by how my children handle a situation such as this. Very calmly they decided to take the boats out of the water.

They didn't consult me on this or on any other matter about the storm. How quickly a grandfather is relieved of "command" or even influence! They removed all furniture from the various decks around the house and on the lake. They made sure we had plenty of drinking water (no electricity—no pump—no water!) Tape was at the ready to bind up the many and large glass windows, and they decided that when the storm hit us in full force, we would go beneath the house. My principal responsibility was to look after myself. They did not bypass me in an unloving way: they just assumed that they knew how to handle a possible crisis better than an 80-year-old grandfather. Who knows, maybe they did—-but I'm not quite ready yet to accept a secondary position in family affairs, even in a hurricane. Still, I must confess my pride in their calm handling of everything.

The winds increased in speed and fury, and the rain battered our house. Everybody remained calm and even cheerful: my granddaughter Elizabeth, age 9, read her book *On How To Be An Astronomer* by flashlight. Nicholas, age 4, and born on my birthday, March 25, played with building blocks. Alexander, age 11, was determined to take pictures but was depressed because his mother would not let him open a door to get an unblurred view of the storm. Their parents, Lincoln and Myra, tended the wood-burning fireplace and remained as calm and nonchalant as if they were back in their living room in Evanston watching television.

And Carol Kleinfelder, a good friend of Niki's and the family, checked all the upstairs doors and windows and advised us on the best and quickest way to get to the storeroom under the house in case we were struck.

I retired in the middle of all of this to write some notes. I found writing by candlelight not all that easy (my handwriting, Valerie tells me, is difficult to read under the best of light), so I returned to the living room and tried to get through by phone to the utility company to get some idea of when we could expect the return of electricity. Of course, thousands of other people were trying to do the same thing (I understand that power went out all over Maine) and it took me about an hour to get through. Meanwhile, I thought I'd play a little guessing game, with a ten-dollar prize (how easy it is to get the attention especially of children with a money offer) to be won by the person who guessed closest to the time the lights would go on again. I guessed midnight (at the time it was about 9 o'clock), and others guessed anywhere from six to eight hours away. Only Myra said: "You are all optimists. It will be at least twenty-four hours, and I guess forty-eight." As of the following morning Myra was the winner. The eye of Hurricane Bob passed us by just ten miles to the west. We were shaken up a bit, and three trees on the property were blown down, but we survived in good fashion, still without power, and with an experience I'm sure at least the children will never forget. Myra, however, had the best summation: "Yes, it's a great experience—but is this a vacation?"

Greatest Event
since Creation

On the morning of July 16, 1969, exactly on schedule, the giant Saturn V booster rocket carrying the Apollo 11 astronauts, Neil A. Armstrong, Edwin E. Aldrin, Jr., and Michael Collins, lifted off its launching pad at Cape Kennedy, starting the astronauts—and, as one reporter put it, all mankind—on an eight-day, five-hundred-thousand-mile round trip (with one first, historic stopover) to the moon.

I quote now from a calendar I have of famous events connected with space exploration: "Sea of Tranquillity, Moon, July 20, 1969—At 4:17 p.m., Eastern Daylight Time, *Apollo 11*'s tiny lunar module, *Eagle*, touched down on the moon. Six and a half hours later its hatch opened and two passengers emerged.

"Back on earth millions of people witnessed this moment, through a TV camera mounted on the module. The TV images were fuzzy, but their meaning was clear: for the first time in history, human beings were walking on the surface of a celestial body other than the earth.

Greatest Event since Creation

"It was a moment that most of the millions watching had thought they would never live to see. It was also a sight that they may not see again. Interest in moon travel, which had taken thousands of years to grow, would not last. A mere four years later, an Apollo mission left the moon for the last time."

Wernher Von Braun, one of the early geniuses responsible for this achievement, said that the importance of the event could only be compared with that moment in evolution when aquatic life came crawling up onto the land. President Nixon, aboard the aircraft carrier *Horner*, witnessed the fiery reentry of the Apollo 11 capsule as it splashed down in the Pacific, some 950 miles southwest of Hawaii, and claimed, "This is the greatest week in the history of the world since the creation." And Dr. Thomas Paine, NASA Administrator, said on the fifth anniversary of the mission: "The fundamental significance of Apollo was that for the first time mankind has been given a vision of the thin biosphere that surrounds our beautiful blue planet, Earth, which as we know, is the fragile home of all the life that so far has been detected in our solar system. And for the first time, terrestrial life that evolved here on this planet over billions of years has reached out to touch another world."

On the other hand, several of the scientists who worked on this great project modestly pointed out that putting a man on the moon was, from a scientific and technical point of view, not all that difficult. Once they had the scientific data, the rest was almost routine.

But thanks to Vice President Spiro Agnew, who invited me to the historic launching, it was the greatest single thrill of my life, and I'm sure others who were at the launching ceremony felt the same way. Following is the account I wrote at the time. I called it "Moonshot Trivia":

Two days before the moonshot, and the "great pilgrimage," as my lady taxi driver calls it, is well on its way. People, a million or more, from every country, every walk of life, and every possible interest, are converging on the five guest centers, all near Cape Kennedy, which have been opened to register and assist NASA guests. I'm at Melbourne, registered to stay at the Host of America Motel, and I arrive precisely at 12:09 a.m. on National Airlines, having left Chicago at 5:45 on Northwest Airlines and made a stop in Atlanta.

We are all here to see the beginning of the most expensive, the best-planned, the most daring adventure of all time, and it has just got to be successful. The Russians have just launched another lunar spaceship, and some think its purpose is to land on the moon, scoop up a bit of soil, and return to earth. Perhaps this isn't as sensational as putting men on the moon, but it is just as great a scientific accomplishment. So say some.

But to return to trivia . . . I arrive, and the moment I step off the plane three photographers come up ready to shoot but ask first if I'm "Mr. Campbell."

"Sorry, old boy. I'm Christopher Janus."

"Are you sure? You look just like Mr. Campbell. Important. Oh, there he is. Sorry."

I go in the terminal and some NASA "hospitality people" meet me, give me an envelope, and ask if there is anything they can do.

"Thank you, all I need is someone to help with my bag. I've strained my back and just shouldn't lift it. It's quite heavy."

"Oh, don't worry, one of the niggers" (this is still

the South) "will be here any minute and will help you."
It only takes a couple of dollars to persuade the taxi cab starter to get my bag and find me a car, and we're off, my lady cab driver and me, to the hotel.

"This your first visit here? You look warm in your coat and vest. This place is just packed with people. Are you sure you have a reservation at the Host of America? Only the most important guests are staying there."

One "yes" seems to take care of her questions, but she continues.

"Of course, we're glad to have so many people here, but then again you've helped boost prices everywhere. And when you leave and if the space program is cut down, where are we? Back in our own Appalachia!"

The five-minute ride from the airport to the Motel costs 90¢, and I know my driver is not going to get out of the cab to help me with the bag, so I give her a quarter tip and wait for some porter to show up before I get out. None comes, but fortunately the manager comes out, looking for a cab for another guest, and he takes my bag, registers me, and carries the bag up to my room for me.

"I understand," he says, "you are a friend of the vice president."

"Not really, I've only met him two or three times."

"Then you must be Greek. Like the Irish, you Greeks stick together, don't you? We have some fine Greeks here in Florida. Best sponge fishermen in the world—and good cooks, too. Well, just phone me if you need anything."

He puts my bag on one of the two beds and leaves. After a minute, there's a knock on the door.

"I'm really befuddled tonight. Here, I forgot to give you your key."

"And here," I said. "I forgot to give you this."

"Oh no, you mustn't do that. I'm the manager."

"And you mustn't deny me the pleasure of buying you a drink."

"Well, if you put it that way. All right. But now you just call me if you want anything, sir."

So I unpack my bag, make a few notes, and then turn on a gadget on the bed that for 25¢ sets up massaging vibrations. It's wonderful for my back, and I flatter myself that they installed this gadget just for me and my bad back. But by now I must already be dreaming!

Tuesday, the day before the great blast-off, is a little story all to itself. But right now I'm so full of excitement about the moonshot that I want to come to it right away. I'll move on to Wednesday, July 16.

It's 4 a.m. The phone rings. "Mr. Janus, this is Rod Phillips from NASA. I've been assigned to help look after you. It's necessary for us to get started—there may be a big traffic snarl. Will you have an astronaut's breakfast with some of us in half an hour? I'll be glad to come and pick you up."

I say that isn't necessary. I'm fully awake now and I tell him that I shall meet him in the dining room. Several other members of the NASA hospitality staff are present and Rod Phillips orders an astronaut's breakfast for me, explaining that it's going to be a very strenuous next six hours. The breakfast consists of a large orange juice, which he actually went to the kitchen to get himself, and a beautiful New York sirloin steak with two eggs, sunnyside-up, on top, and some sweet rolls and coffee. It's delicious. The only other time I'd ever had such a breakfast before was in 1936 in Paris, only then it was called a "Follies Bergères" breakfast. You ate it after the last show at the Follies, and usually some of the actors and actresses joined in.

Mr. Phillips explains to our group (we are about fifty people and include Jack Benny and Sargent Shriver, our ambassador to France) that so far all systems are "go": the weather is fine, and the only little problem with the moonshot, other than a leaky valve that was quickly repaired, is Dr. Ralph Abernathy's mule train, which could really slow up traffic. (Later I learned that Abernathy and some ten poor families were invited to leave their mules and join us in the VIP stands, which they did.) After a few further words of briefing, Phillips announces that we will not actually be leaving for Cape Kennedy—some thirty-five miles away—until 6 o'clock.

I promptly go back to bed until 5:30, when a Mrs. Rosemary Rowland phones to tell me what bus I'm to board. It turns out that I'm traveling with the NASA staff, who really have been up all night but don't look it. They say that they have been working almost continuously during the past thirty-six hours. Apparently some of the foreign delegations, including a large group from *Paris Match*, have been very demanding. Most special groups, however, are easy to get on with and are very generous in pushing the wares of their country. One man passes out "cigars especially made in honor of the moonshot," another, bottles of wine from his own vineyard. Of course, all the contractors and sub-contractors for NASA have been giving parties for all the delegates to the "shoot" and at the same time selling their companies. Actually this is a good thing, because I don't believe enough people appreciate what a great achievement this moonshot is, and equally, not enough of the public understands or appreciates the hundreds of great by-products that have been developed in medicine, industry, and engineering as a result of putting these men on the moon.

Well, we finally leave at six. It's light, and there is a bit of mist hanging over the countryside, but actually there is very little traffic. We have a police escort, and some of the roads are blocked off to give us priority in getting there, but still I don't think that anything like the reported million people came to Cape Kennedy for the event. I would estimate that there are perhaps five hundred thousand persons all along the Indian River (some had camped there all night) to witness the start of the trip to the moon.

Yesterday on our tour of Cape Kennedy we were taken to within a hundred yards of the Saturn. On about an acre of ground next to the VAB, they put up sections of bleachers: one for foreign diplomats, one for members of Congress, one for the press, another for the military, and another for all the other VIP guests. I sit now with the Percys, who hailed me as I walked by. I would say that ex-President Johnson and Lady Bird are the most popular VIPs present. Spiro Agnew comes in and sits with LBJ. Barry Goldwater is there in a red golf shirt; many people comment that that seems just too informal. I believe I am the only person there wearing a vest. Chuck Percy asks, "Aren't you hot?" and I give him my old story about the people of India being able to bear the heat because they dress warmly against the sun. I must admit that while I'm telling him the story, the perspiration is really streaming down my face. Percy is in shirt sleeves, and Loraine brought an umbrella which she shares with me. She also shares her coca cola with me, saying that there's enough for the three of us.

It is now about four minutes before blast-off. Johnny Carson and Hugh O'Brien stand up and people yell them down, and then everybody agrees that we should really all remain seated. Loraine asks if her umbrella is bothering anyone, but the people back of us don't answer.

Then come the final moments and the announcer starts counting "15, 14, 13," until "1," and there is the biggest fire I've ever seen. The ground shakes, and about 13 seconds after seeing the fire we hear the blast and feel its heat. Saturn rises unbelievably. It is one of the greatest sights I've ever seen, and the people around me whistle and cheer. Loraine kisses her husband, then me, and everybody acts as if they've just won a horse race and they had a big sum on the winner.

Well it was a horse race—possibly the greatest bet man has made in peacetime, and as of this writing, the bet is paying off.

A Birthday Party for Persepolis

My invitation to attend the Shah of Iran's party celebrating the 2,500th anniversary of the founding of Persia (some critics called it the most elaborate and expensive celebration ever given in the history of the world) came about, I think, because of my interest in the *Rubáiyát* of Omar Khayyam, the renowned poet of twelfth-century Persia. As I've mentioned, I'm a collector of the *Rubáiyát,* and to date I've been able to obtain copies of it in thirty-six different languages.

I got my first copy of the poem as a high-school graduation present from a cousin, Harry Stenis. I suppose I've read the *Rubáiyát* a hundred times, and my son Chris (for a Maple Leaf gold piece) has actually memorized all of Oxonian Edward Fitzgerald's first English edition. I've bribed all my children and my wife to memorize other great poems, and these have included Gray's Elegy—possibly the greatest poem ever written—T. S. Eliot's "Love Song of J. Alfred Prufrock," some psalms from the Bible, and parts of Plato's dialogues. The rule has always been: they get

A Birthday Party for Persepolis

only one chance to recite the poem in question and it has to be done perfectly the first time. And so far I'm proud to say every attempt has been successful. I withdrew the offer at some time—the children are all too busy with their jobs, and anyway I ran out of gold pieces!

Some months before the Shah's great party in October 1972 I was working on publishing a special edition of the *Rubáiyát* in four languages: English, French, German, and Greek, and I commissioned Ghika, the famous Greek artist, to do the illustrations. Kimon Friar, my editor of *Greek Heritage Quarterly*, helped me persuade Ghika to do them, and he made twelve beautiful watercolors for me plus a picture for the cover of the book.

In addition, and this is what led to my invitation to the party at Persepolis, I had invited the Shah of Iran through his consul general in Chicago, who was a friend, to write the introduction to this special deluxe edition. According to the consul general, the Shah agreed but suggested that perhaps either Kimon Friar or I should write the introduction for the Shah to sign.

Well, we did a little market survey to try to find out ahead of time how large a market there might be for a special edition of the *Rubáiyát* and we ran several full-page ads in the *New York Times* Book Review Section, advertising for possible buyers. The price for the book was to be $35, with a specially bound edition illustrated by Ghika and signed by the Shah for $150. We asked that no money be sent with the order. It didn't go. We did receive about twenty orders for the specially bound signed edition and, as I recall, forty orders for the regular. That was not enough to warrant publishing the book and to my regret we abandoned the project.

But through the consul general and the Shah, I was invited to attend the world's most expensive celebration. When the editor of the *Chicago Daily News* learned that I had been invited to the party (I believe that Bonnie Swearingen and Valerie Valentine were the only other persons from Chicago invited), I was asked to cable a two-thousand word story to the *News* on the event. (After some censorship from the authorities in Iran, it was received and featured in the paper.)

It was a great party. It was held at the ancient city of Persepolis, whose ruins in my estimation are as beautiful as those of the Acropolis in Athens, and you almost felt the presence of young Alexander the Great there.

All the leaders of the world, including the Pope, were invited and each leader was housed in a specially-constructed, beautiful tent. *Tent* is hardly the word to describe the accommodations. Each one had a cement floor, covered by beautiful Persian carpets. There were two or three bedrooms, each with its own bath, and some of the tents were decorated in the national style of the country housed there. Some of the furniture and most of the curtains were imported from France. The whole event was criticized a bit because although this was a party to celebrate ancient Persia and Iran, with the exception of the caviar, almost everything was imported. Even Farah Diba's dresses came from France or Italy.

But I must say, history and decorum aside, it was a great pleasure to enjoy the imports, especially the French cuisine. In my article to the *News* I wrote that we were served nightingale tongues. And when I returned the editor questioned this. I called up Chef Louis of the Bakery Restaurant to ask him to confirm

A Birthday Party for Persepolis

that nightingale tongues are delicacies in several countries, and he said, "Oh, sure," and referred me to an English and French cookbook telling how to prepare them. Though a great delicacy, and I had to try them, I found them too salty, at least as they were prepared in Iran.

The main theme of the festivities at the party was, of course, the celebration of 2,500 years of Persian history; the second theme was the entry of Iran into the twentieth century. This second idea was portrayed through the wonderful, and at the time quite advanced, telephone and communications systems, installed by Hughes Aircraft and established at least in the capital, Teheran, and on display at Persepolis. Each tent had at least five telephones that could connect you instantly with most any part of the world. There were big communication disks all around Persepolis.

There were also troops with machine guns encircling tent city, ostensibly to protect the hundred or so world leaders in attendance but also to thwart any attempted revolution against the shah. This was a time of great unrest in Iran. Though the enormous, very expensive party showed what kind of a show the shah could put on to impress the world with his taste and advanced ideas, there was starvation in other parts of the country, which had led to many riots.

Iran is one of the many blunders of our State Department and the CIA. We put the Shah into power in the first place, and with all his shortcomings as a world leader, he was nevertheless a staunch friend of the United States. I believe that experts concur today that the violence in Iran that ousted the Shah could have been prevented. Instead we failed to support him and even when he was dying of cancer gave him only limited asylum and medical help in the United States.

For a while he stayed in the Bahamas on Paradise Island in Jack Crosby's home next to the Ocean Club, which Huntington Hartford built. And I believe that Hunt had something to do with arranging the Shah's asylum in the Bahamas.

From there the Shah went to Italy and England, eventually ending up in Egypt, where he was welcomed on a permanent basis. He died there a broken and, he felt, betrayed man. Meanwhile, Iran under the tyrannical rule of the Ayatollah slid back in time to become one of the most barbarous countries in the world and we, the United States, are still hurt by the loss of Iran as an ally in that part of the world.

But back to the party. One afternoon there was Open House in Tent City, which meant that you could visit any tent and talk with the world leader staying there. Each tent displayed the flag of the ruler residing there. In fact, unless you recognized the ruler, it was the only way of distinguishing who was who. Tent number one was occupied by Emperor Haile Selassie, representing the oldest government of the world, that of Ethiopia. (The tents were numbered according to the age of the current system of government of each country.) Haile Selassie received us wearing his royal robe and holding in his arm his little Chihuahua dog. The dog had on such a heavy bejeweled collar he could hardly raise his head. Valerie asked the emperor if she could hold the dog herself, and he seemed very pleased for her to do so. He said something to the effect that she must like pets very much and that is a good sign of kindness. He even invited her to visit him in Ethiopia should she come that way. A few days later I heard that the little dog had wandered out of the tent and got lost. Haile Selassie was beside himself, for he knew that the area surrounding Tent City was mined. The Shah gave

A Birthday Party for Persepolis

orders to the army to find the pet, and it was really quite amusing to see some hundred armed soldiers searching under tents and even in the ruins of Persepolis for a pint-sized dog. He was found just a few yards away from his home, whimpering under an air-conditioning unit.

My next visit was to tent forty-nine, assigned to the United States and being forty-nine down the road really showed how young a country we are. President Nixon was unable to attend and sent Spiro Agnew, his vice president. I had met Agnew before in Palm Beach at the Everglades Club. And, of course, he had invited me to the moon launch. He greeted me warmly, and we spoke a few words in Greek, and I found his Greek to be almost as inadequate as mine. There were several reporters there also and the vice president turned to us and said, "Boys, the place is yours. Have a drink. Pick up a telephone and call anywhere in the world you want—courtesy of the Shah!" I picked up the phone, dialed ten digits, and the phone rang instantly in my home in Winnetka, Illinois. Unfortunately, I'd forgotten that it was Monday, when Beatrice played bridge at the Women's Athletic Club in Chicago. Our laundress answered the phone.

"Minnie," I asked, "Is that you?"

She replied, "Mr. Janus, that you? Huran! Where is that? How far away? Five thousand miles? Are you all right? Lord sakes, this is a miracle."

When I could get in a word, I asked, "How is Mrs. Janus? Please tell her I called, and will call again tomorrow. Everything okay, Minnie?"

"No, Mr. Janus, everything is not okay. The washing machine is broke and I can't fix it," etc., etc.

There were other people waiting to use the phone, and I thought I should end this less-than-urgent conversation about a washing machine. A little later I called Jim Hoge, and he was not a bit impressed that I was calling from Persepolis, Iran, on the first satellite telephone link in history. He simply said, "Where's the story for the *News*? They're waiting. And bring back some caviar!" and hung up.

An amusing story was making the rounds at Tent City as the delegates began to arrive. His Eminence, the Pope, could not make it, but he sent one of his chief high-ranking Cardinals to represent him. When the Cardinal arrived, the authorities could not find that he had been assigned to one of the tents. In fact, it looked as if all the tents had been taken. This was a real snafu, but the Cardinal himself was very composed and prepared to register in the hotel set up for visitors like me. One of the Cardinal's aides, however, was very mad, insulted and most verbal about what looked like a slight. He stormed that the Cardinal was not to register in a hotel; this was His Eminence's representative, and so on. Before things got much worse, however, the Pope's tent was located, and the Shah sent his special ambassador to apologize to the Cardinal. The ambassador approached the Cardinal and said something like, "Your Eminence, the Shah offers his deep apologies for this error. Will you please forgive us and forget?"

The Cardinal is supposed to have answered: "My son, of course, His Holiness will forgive you. But remember he has the oldest filing system in the world."

The parade was the most colorful and fantastic I had ever seen, with thousands of soldiers, floats filled with flowers—Cecil B. DeMille could have not planned a more spectacular event. The Shah and his wife, Farah Diba, each arrived by separate helicopter. It was amusing to us to see our friend King Constantine,

A Birthday Party for Persepolis

whom we had visited in Rome a few weeks earlier, film the parade with a camera we had presented to him from Chuck Percy and Bell & Howell. I did not stay for the entire celebration, which lasted for a week and ended up with a grand ball. Valerie did, however, and met the Shah and had pictures taken of herself with him and the queen.

They did load me up with caviar as I left. On the plane I sat next to Sally Quinn, who had not been given caviar. I shared mine with her but still had plenty left over for the boys at the *News*, for my wife, who loved it, and for Minnie, who was not sure that caviar was much of a present!

I've just uncovered the story that I wrote for the *News*, and I reprint it here because I think the reader may be as interested as I to see what seemed important and memorable about the party then, as compared with what I've been remembering as I look back on it twenty years later:

Chicago Daily News, *October 15, 1972*

Iran can't afford it, cry the critics, as heads of state gather here for 2,500th birthday party

The Big Bash at Persepolis
Christopher Janus is a Chicago investment banker and scholar on ancient cultures. He was invited to the Persian anniversary celebration by the Shah and wrote the following article for *The Daily News*.

PERSEPOLIS, IRAN. Everyone, at least once in his life, has his Persepolis, according to an ancient Persian proverb much quoted here Friday. What Persepolis will mean to his imperial majesty the

Shah of Iran remains to be seen.

He has ignored his critics and gambled by ordering probably the most expensive party ever planned by a monarch—the celebration of the 2,500th anniversary of the founding of the Persian empire by Cyrus the Great. It is primarily a weeklong festival to try to tell the world that Iran is discovering the industrial and communications revolution and slowly but surely is emerging from the status of an under-developed country.

Some of the Shah's critics say the party is 50 years too soon. All say $200 million, or even $20 million, is too much for any festival, especially when nearly half of the 30 million people of Iran are poor, underfed and illiterate.

But the Shah strongly defends his Persepolis festival.

At a reception he gave for us and a group of Iranian scholars Wednesday night, he pointed out that since 1962, when he inaugurated a 12-point program of social reforms, economic growth has been an amazing 9.2 percent, well over twice the rate of the developing world as a whole. In a little more than 10 years, the GNP has grown in Iran from $4.5 billion to $10.1 billion.

As for the over-all cost of the celebration, the Shah has reminded his critics that any figure of the true cost (which will remain a state secret) includes the building of a new highway to Persepolis—lighted by torches at 50-yard intervals—the building of a new telephone and communications system, at least four new hotels, two new airports, and scores of other permanent improvements.

This cost also includes the maintenance of the biggest security force ever assembled to protect chiefs of state in one place. It is estimated that there are more than 30,000 military and secret

A Birthday Party for Persepolis 231

service agents in and around Persepolis, though critics acknowledge that such a security force is probably a safe precaution.

It is very irksome to the correspondents covering the event as well as to the invited guests who have no diplomatic status. My car was stopped six times on the historic road to Persepolis. At one point I found myself facing a soldier aiming his rifle directly at me. We were also cautioned not to stray too far from the road. Some areas, including the satellite communications center, are mined.

There are at least three protective circles of defense around Persepolis—all manned by Iranian troops. They take their orders seriously but it seems many have different orders as to who is an intruder and who is a guest.

For one who has come to Persepolis armed only with what the guidebooks say, this military protection in the land of "perfect roses, sunshine, nightingales and peacocks" is a bit hard to take.

But little or none of this criticism has reached the chiefs of state that I've seen thus far. All seem in a mood for a party and to help the Shah honor the heritage and progress of his country.

Among the monarchs here is self-exiled King Constantine of Greece and his beautiful Danish wife, Queen Anne-Marie. This is the first time a king from Athens will have slept in Persepolis since Xerxes invaded Greece in 480 B.C. and Alexander the Great, 148 years later, in a vengeful and drunken orgy, burned Persepolis.

Spiro Agnew, who is of Greek descent, also slept in Persepolis Thursday night. But to the many Persians I've talked to this week, the most thought-provoking monarch here is the king of Greece. He did not arrive like Alexander, leading a fighting army. The only weapon he is carrying is a

Bell and Howell movie camera, a gift from Sen. Charles Percy (R-Ill.).

A Festive Mood:

Yet all is officially forgiven now and the party is on.

Fifty barrels of Iran's best wine, which Persians are said to have invented, is here to be consumed by the royal guests, scholars, and other distinguished visitors. Two thousand Iranian girls, many of them looking like ancient Persian miniatures, are serving as interpreters. There is enough caviar to feed an army and, as a matter of fact, many of the Iranian troops guarding us will, as a kind of booty, be given whatever is left of the caviar and other food when we are gone.

But, above all else, it is perhaps the living arrangements that contribute most to the spirit of conviviality and celebration. Each of the 50 chiefs of state lives in a luxurious tent, Persian rugs on the floor of some tents, all with hot and cold running water. Each tent has two bedrooms, a dressing room, small kitchenette, and telephones.

The tents are only a few feet apart, allowing for a living closeness and communication among these world rulers unique in history. I'm watching for Emperor Haile Selassie to walk over to Princess Grace's tent to borrow a cup of sugar.

I visited three of these tents. The first was Haile Selassie's, who as the oldest living monarch heads the protocol list. Second was King Constantine, who is three-quarters up the list. And, finally Vice President Agnew, who was not met by the Shah at the airport and because he is not a head of state is pretty far down on the protocol list. But his arrival, along with President Tito's, has caused the most general excitement among the weary village Iranians, mostly children, who have lined the streets waving their green and white and red

flags most of the afternoon and night.
In Agnew's Tent:
Agnew's round beige tent is like all others from the outside, but inside a special pastel green decor has been planned for him and Mrs. Agnew, with wall-to-wall carpeting, beautiful Persian rugs, and a little library which includes books on Iran, an autographed book on golf by Arnold Palmer, and a leather-bound copy of Omar Khayyam's *Rubáiyát*. Whether on purpose or by accident, the bookmark in the *Rubáiyát* is next to this verse:

> The worldly hope men set their hearts upon
> Turns ashes, or it prospers, and anon
> Like snow upon the desert's dusty face
> Lighting a little hour or two—is gone.

My young Persian interpreter asked me what this meant, and how it might apply to the honorable Vice President, but I let the question pass. Instead we talked about the clear and inspiring view from Agnew's tent.

Nearby is the actual road, my guide explained, on which Alexander the Great marched into Persepolis. You look up directly to the great platform and winged bull gates of the great palaces. I felt rather proud and less weary when my guide also explained to me that these excavations of Persepolis were done by the University of Chicago's Oriental Institute: "And it is among the best work in the world."

The Shah tried to reach out to Chicago a few years ago with a handsome gift to the University of Chicago for a school on Middle East studies. He still speaks of his disappointment that for various reasons the money was never returned.

"I was trying to bring the United States a

better understanding of Iran and the Middle East," he said. "I will still try, just as in Persepolis today we are letting the world know we are going forward. I do not mind the criticism about costs. I will not feed my guests just bread. It is all an investment to help solve the problems of our people.

"Persepolises are never easy and they are sometimes dangerous, but they are always challenging and they are necessary."

The Search
for Peking Man

My life for the most part, as the reader will see, has been lucky, blessed with a good family, loyal friends, and happiness. There is one experience, however, I wish I'd never had. The angel on my shoulder must have had more important things to look after. And that affair is what I will call the Peking Man episode.

It all started in what many people, especially world travelers and adventurers, would have called a fortunate way. Shortly after President Nixon went to China and the way was paved for China to be opened up to the West for commerce and travel, I received five visas to visit China. The only other group to be invited to China at this time (1972) was the so-called Ping Pong group. I was president of the Chicago Harvard Club then, and with the advice of Valerie Valentine, who had a great deal of experience in taking cultural groups to Greece, South America, and Russia, and had already been in touch with some officials in China through the Greek Heritage Foundation, I applied for visas to visit

China. We had a bit of an edge getting visas because many of the people in power in China, or close to that power, had attended Harvard. And then, of course, Henry Kissinger, who did most of the planning and diplomatic arrangements in opening up China to Westerners, is a friend, and he knew of our plans to try to be among the first American tourists to visit the People's Republic.

I'm not sure whether he actually intervened on my behalf, but one morning in May 1972, I received a telegram out of the blue, inviting me to visit the People's Republic and to bring four other guests, one of whom was to be Valerie. I chose Willis Barnstone, my friend from *Greek Heritage* days and a professor of Romance languages at Indiana University, who had just published a translation of Chairman Mao's poetry. We planned to give Mao a leather-bound copy of his poems in English. I also invited Everett Hollis, a Harvard man and distinguished lawyer in Chicago, and Gabe Joseph, who at the time was advertising director of the *Chicago Sun-Times*. Gabe was one of the first friends to urge me to try to get into China, and I promised him an exclusive on any stories I reported. Shortly before we were scheduled to leave, however, Gabe had to go to London on some urgent business for the newspaper and could not join us. I then invited Frank Voysey, a prominent Chicago investment banker, who I knew was also a good traveler and would be a good companion.

For the Chinese, the greatest visual attraction we brought was Valerie, a lovely, dashing blond. It must be remembered that China had been closed to most of the world, especially the United States, since 1949, when Chiang Kai-shek was overthrown, and it was a rarity for the Chinese to see an American woman, especially a blond. Wherever she went she drew a large crowd, and once when she visited a silk shop in Hang Chow, the shop immediately filled up with people, who wanted not so much to buy silk as to see the blond American woman, fashionably dressed in something other than the drab Mao outfits most Chinese women wore. The proprietor of the silk shop finally had to close the door and not let in any more people.

We were in China for nearly two weeks and were given VIP treatment. We had three cars with drivers at our disposal, and there were three young interpreters. We were not expected to go anywhere unescorted, and everywhere we went we were objects of great curiosity. I felt that people who did talk to us were careful not to appear too friendly or inquisitive for fear of being identified with the "decadent West." In particular it seemed as if some of the older guard avoided Frank Voysey, the most genial of our group, because he looked so much like the typical English landlord!

An important part of my mission to China was to meet Chairman Mao and present Willis Barnstone's excellent translation of Mao's poetry to him, and every day we waited for the expected invitation. Finally, on the tenth day of our visit, I was given word that we had an important appointment the following morning and to be sure to have the group ready early. "At last," I thought, "it's come, and I'll be able to report to our State Department (they were keenly aware of our trip) and perhaps get an exclusive story for the *Sun-Times*," which I had promised both Marshall Field and Gabe Joseph.

The morning arrived, we were in our cars, and then our guides announced that we had been invited to visit the museum and caves of the Peking Man, some thirty miles south of Peking. What a disappointment!

Quite honestly, I was not sure just who or what the Peking Man was, and no one in our group had requested such a visit. En route we had to be cleared through two military checkposts. Everett Hollis, our learned lawyer (it gave me great comfort to have him in our group), had forgotten his passport, and that presented a bit of a problem, but our interpreter apparently exclaimed with considerable authority that we were very important Americans on a special mission and we were to be allowed to pass.

We arrived at the small museum of Peking Man about 11 o'clock. After a brief tour of the caves, of course, we were given tea and a briefing. The Peking Man, as we probably already knew, the director explained, had lived some five hundred thousand years ago, maybe much earlier, and his fossils (actually the remains of some forty-seven different individuals) were discovered in 1926. It is still one of the most important anthropological discoveries ever made. Then we were shown various drawings, photographs, and artifacts, including tools and objects indicating that Peking Man was a hunter, who knew about fire and cooked with it. We were also shown a statue reconstruction of Peking Man, and Valerie and one of our Chinese hosts took a picture of me beside it. At the end of the briefing, we all expected to be shown the fossils themselves. When they weren't forthcoming, I finally asked the director of the museum: "And where do you keep the fossils?"

"Mr. Janus," shot back the director, "that is the question I must ask you. Where are our fossils? We have the receipts from your Marines, from when we turned our fossils over to them just after Pearl Harbor. You have never returned them and you don't even acknowledge that you have them! But they belong to us—they are part of our heritage." The director was visibly upset and spoke in an impolite tone that we had never heard from anyone else in China.

Before answering, I looked for some support from our attorney, but he just remained calm and said nothing. I finally replied: "Mr. Director, I don't have your fossils, but I'm sure our State Department can help with the matter."

The director then spoke quietly: "I'm sorry Mr. Janus, I did not mean to be rude and imply that you have the fossils, but you are the first American to come here since the war, and we have been told you are very important. Will you help us find our fossils? I'm sure they are in your country somewhere."

During our briefing before our group came to China, we had been requested: "Just be good ambassadors." So, more out of politeness and diplomacy than any great interest in the matter, I simply said: "Yes, I will help you find the fossils." The director thanked me profusely and said he was going to report our conversation to the authorities in Peking. I was not sure what he meant by that, and I never dreamed what my promise to help find the fossils would involve me in. But my involvement with the Peking Man fossils came about as simply as that. What the State Department may have told the Chinese authorities about me and my group before we went to China, I never have known.

During the next few days, however, I didn't think about the Peking Man. My main interest was in our proposed meeting with Chairman Mao. Finally we were told that the Chairman was unwell and we would probably not be able to see him on this trip. But they appreciated our bringing a translation of his poetry. As a result of his efforts, Willis Barnstone was invited to prolong his stay and visit other parts of China, which he did.

When I promised the director of the Peking Man Museum that I would help find the Peking Man fossils and have them returned to China, my plan was simply to write a report to the State Department explaining how strongly the Chinese felt about the fossils and their suspicion that our country was deliberately hanging on to them. Certainly, I felt, it would improve our relations with China, and build on the Nixon-Kissinger agreements, to show the Chinese that we wanted to help find the fossils.

The Chinese, at least at the time of our first visit, considered these fossils to be equivalent to crown jewels. They hoped that now that scientific testing methods had advanced so much since the war that with the fossils they might prove that man had first developed in China. They believed that the fossils might prove to be two or three million years old, not just the estimated five hundred thousand. Knowing the Chinese tradition of ancestor worship, their great interest in the fossils was understandable.

When we left China and returned by train to Hong Kong, however, my simple and limited intention in helping them out was drastically changed. We were met at the railroad station by at least a dozen photographers and reporters. I had not been in contact with the press in China, although Willis Barnstone, Everett Hollis, and Frank Voysey had given interviews to the *New York Times*, which appeared shortly after our return. But they told me they had not discussed Peking Man with the *Times* or any other media people. So I've always assumed that it was the Chinese themselves who gave out the story about my promise to help find the fossils. Anyway, the moment I got off the train the reporters' questions came flying at me: "Why did they pick you to find the fossils?"

"I don't know and why do you assume they picked me?"

"How are you going about it? Will you offer a reward?"

"I haven't developed a plan, but as a matter of fact, I will offer a $5,000 reward for any information leading to their recovery."

That was a mistake on my part—in fact, the whole meeting with the press was bad judgment, because now I really was becoming directly involved in the search for Peking Man. I should add here that when the Peking Man fossils were first discovered in 1926 the story was reported throughout the world. Now it would be starting all over again. The interviews with me were indeed reported worldwide, and shortly after I arrived back in the United States the story, together with that picture of me beside the statue of Peking Man, was on the front page of the Sunday *New York Times*. That's how it all started.

And here I don't have any intention of telling the three-years' search for the Peking Man that ensued with the help of our State Department, the CIA, and the FBI. Macmillan asked me to write a book about my search, published under the title *Search for Peking Man*, and the Canadian Broadcasting Corporation made a documentary on it, narrated by Christopher Plummer. Hundreds of other stories and features have appeared, including a book by Professor Harry Shapiro of the Museum of Science, New York, who is an expert on the Peking Man fossils but who hasn't welcomed competition or help in the search.

It was inevitable that the movie people would become interested in the search. Otto Preminger and I appeared one night on Tom Snyder's TV show. Afterward, Preminger invited me to lunch with him the following day at New York's "21" Club to discuss the possibility of making a movie together. After that lunch he introduced me to a writer who could do a script, and we were on our way to making a movie. Preminger at that time was agreeing in principle to put up half the money. Shortly thereafter I brought Preminger to Chicago to meet with Irv Kupcinet, star columnist for the *Chicago Sun-Times* and a vice-president of the American National Bank, who had expressed an interest in helping to finance the movie.

When I opened this chapter, I said that I regretted ever becoming involved in the Peking Man matter. That regret is not for the search—I enjoyed it, and it was a wonderful experience in many ways. Rather, I deplore the movie part, which brought a blemish to my life. Basically, a business project went sour, but that's not the way it all appeared in the press. To continue the search and to raise money for the screenplay and other expenses, I had obtained the best legal advice I could get and formed a limited partnership. At that time, this was a great tax write-off. The monies raised from investors were not sufficient to make the movie, however, so I took out bank loans in my own name to cover the expenses. (Interestingly, some prospective investors said: "Chris, I'll give you all the money you need if you don't make the movie." Movies like *The Graduate* had offered investors huge tax write-offs, and the possibility still existed for doing that here. But I refused—I was hooked.) I wanted to make that movie, and I was so obsessed that I risked my money and my reputation.

The project began to fail when Preminger demanded that he be paid back his money after the movie was made before the bank got theirs, and after a two-year delay (which is not unusual in making a movie) the movie still hadn't been made, and the banks demanded to be repaid. As the general partner in our limited partnership I was responsible for the bulk of our loans, at the time about $650,000 net. This was not a great sum, and with time I could have handled it—in fact, I did repay 50 percent of the debts. The rest of the story, unfortunately, is told in litigation, which was settled by plea bargaining.

What I remember most about the whole matter, in addition to the grief and sorrow it caused my wife and family is this: Judge Prentiss Marshall said in court that the banks would have loaned me the money, even if I hadn't wanted it for a movie purpose. A friend in the Attorney General's office told me that "the case did not have a life of its own." The lawyer made it a case. And finally, a vice president of one of the lending banks which brought the suit against me said: "The lending officer who handled your loan had a personal vendetta against you." When I protested that I hadn't known the man, the reply was: "Yes, I know—he just didn't like your lifestyle." The lending officer, who was a department head at the bank, was eventually fired and has since died.

I'll end this chapter with a report on the most important lead I've had in the search, one which I've never written about before:

Although I'm no longer actively searching for the Peking Man fossils (a five-year effort was quite enough!), I still get letters and calls from persons who think they know where the long-lost fossils might be or who want to know what the status of the search (and the reward) are. The reward has been withdrawn.

The most important call came from a Marine. He

identified himself as George Inness and said that he was terminally ill in a Dallas hospital and wanted to get something "off my chest." Inness said that he was a member of Company D—the Marine group responsible for guarding our legation in Peking up to the time of Pearl Harbor, when President Roosevelt shut down the legation and ordered our Marines to return to the States. Our legation was located in a squarish compound, half of which was occupied by Marines and the other half by the legation. There was a wall between the Marine quarters and the legation grounds with a gate in between.

Marine Inness claims that he was on guard at the gate at midnight just before Pearl Harbor when he was approached by two marine officers carrying a footlocker, who ordered him to open the gate into the legation section where they buried the footlocker "about 25 feet away." Inness did not know what the footlocker contained, but it is known that the Chinese packed the Peking Man fossils in a Marine footlocker when they turned them over to the Marines to take them to the States for safekeeping.

At the time I got this, which seemed to be a very promising and exciting lead, I did some checking and then phoned our State Department with the information. (Both the FBI and the State Department worked with me when I was active in the search for the fossils.)

The State Department suggested that I write directly to our ambassador in Beijing, Leonard Woodcock, and get his advice on how best to proceed. We would have to get permission from the Chinese to do any searching in the area. The Chinese, especially at the time, were very suspicious of U. S. actions and aims.

After a couple of weeks I got a letter from Ambassador Woodcock saying they had looked into the matter and unfortunately there was nothing much that could be done, because some time ago the Chinese had taken over the old legation and Marine area and had built a large apartment building complex on it. Well, that seemed to be the end of yet another lead.

However, when in 1980 I was invited by the Peking Museum of Natural History to visit (and, incidentally, receive a commendation for my efforts in connection with the search for Peking Man), I told them the whole story and regretted what bad luck it was that we couldn't have done some digging in the old legation grounds to see if indeed there was a Marine footlocker buried there.

They exclaimed, "What apartment building on the old legation ground? There is no apartment structure there. The whole compound is pretty much the same as the Marines left it, except that now some of the offices are occupied by the Bechtel Corporation."

I was astonished and a bit embarrassed to hear this and suggested we go immediately to the compound and see for ourselves. My hosts said that they would be glad to take me there but would not meet with the people at Bechtel themselves, since the Chinese government might misinterpret their motives in dealing with a U.S. corporation. This is not the time nor the place to go into the phobias the Chinese had in dealing with Americans then, but I don't believe things have improved very much today.

My hosts dropped me at the old legation grounds— there certainly was no apartment complex there!—and I was able to meet with one of the officers of Bechtel, who, incidentally, was an Oxford man. I told him the whole story and he was surprised (since he knew the U.S. ambassador) that such erroneous information had been passed on. "Some careless bureaucratic underling got his facts screwed up," he said and then agreed to let us "look around and do some digging."

The following morning I went back to the museum, told them the story, and suggested that we get a metal detector and start exploring.

They agreed (but to my surprise not very enthusiastically that it was a good idea. Then they asked if I could provide them with a metal detector. I suggested that the Chinese army must certainly have metal detectors, and why not ask them for one. For reasons that I still can't comprehend, they did not take to this idea. When I suggested that we try to buy one in Peking, they thought they would have to get a special permit.

Somehow the idea was beginning to get through to me that they had been in touch with their government officials, who perhaps did not want an American to be the one to find the fossils. (It is not always easy for a Westerner, as they say, to fathom the Eastern mind!)

Anyway, it was finally decided that I would somehow provide the museum personnel with a metal detector. I shipped them one from Hong Kong but have never heard from them again.

But I like to believe that they did indeed search for the fossils in the old legation ground and were unsuccessful in their search. The fossils are still out there somewhere, waiting to be found.

Poets at the White House

During the Peking Man affair, I remember having coffee with President Gerald Ford in the Oval Room one Sunday morning. I don't, of course, often have coffee with the president of the United States, but Don Rumsfeld, one of the ablest and most dedicated men in government I've ever met, was Ford's chief of staff at the time, and he set up the private meeting for me. It had nothing to do with politics.

One of the things I wanted to do was present the president with a small statue of two football players comforting each other on their loss of a championship game. It so happened that a few weeks earlier, Michigan (Gerald Ford's alma mater, at which he played football) had lost to Wisconsin, and it had been a sad occasion for the president, who watched the game on television. His reactions to the loss were widely reported in the press. Sculptress Mani Duffy, daughter of my friends George and Kay Duffy, was inspired to do the statue. I was visiting in Florida with the Duffys just at the time when Mani finished the little statue and, without being told of her inspiration, I was nonetheless moved by the sadness it portrayed. I told George I thought it was a fine work of art and George replied, "Yes, I'm proud of Mani for doing it; it's one of her best works. I wish Jerry Ford could see it. I think he would really appreciate it." Apparently George had gone to college with the president and watched him play football. He understood how important the game was to him, especially the annual game between the University of Michigan and Wisconsin.

One thing led to another and I said, "Well, why don't we offer it to the president? Would Mani agree?"

George answered: "I was hoping you would suggest that, and if anybody can do it—since you know Don Rumsfeld—you can. Will you?

We all went to the White House that Sunday morning—Beatrice and I and George Duffy, with Kay, Mani, and their son, George, Jr., who had been in a terrible automobile accident and lost the use of his legs. At the White House George, Jr., was in a wheelchair and was helped by an aide to the president who had also helped President Roosevelt and was expert in maneuvering the wheelchair. We were given a mini-tour of the White House and then taken to the Oval Room. The president was sitting at his desk when we came in. He got up, came over and greeted me by my first name, and then recognized George and embraced him. We were invited over by the sofa where we had coffee and cookies.

As the president and George reminisced, it occurred to me that this was no momentous event in history, but it was a great pleasure and a thrill to be visiting with the president of the United States, the single most powerful man in the world, having coffee and cookies on a peaceful Sunday morning.

George had asked me beforehand to present the statue to the president on behalf of Mani and the Duffy family. I took it out of the box and we all went over to the president's desk for the presentation and a picture, which the President suggested. I made a little speech, and President Ford received the statue and turning to Mani said: "It is beautiful; you've caught the sadness of how it feels to lose." I thought that was just the right remark, and it certainly pleased Mani.

As we made motions to leave, the president turned to me and said, "Chris, I understand you've been to China. How was it and what's all this business about the missing Peking Man?" Obviously, Don Rumsfeld had briefed the president about my trip. I briefly told the President that one small way of improving our relations with China (and they needed a lot of improvement!) would be to assure the Chinese that our country did not have the missing fossils but that we would do all we could to help find them.

President Ford responded: "Go to it, Chris. I understand our State Department is helping you—and if there is anything I can do let me or Don know."

I thanked him and before leaving asked if I could present him with a copy of *The Search for Peking Man*. He thanked me for the book, asking me to sign it, and then asked the photographer to take a picture of us together, with the president holding the book. It turned out to be a great picture, and Macmillan used it in the foreign editions of my book. It was also circulated in a press release to China and worldwide. And this small gesture on the part of the president did I think let the Chinese know of our good will regarding the fossils, and in a small way, perhaps, improved our relations with them. All of us left the White House feeling wonderful and saying among ourselves that Gerald Ford was one of the warmest human beings and presidents we had ever met and probably the most underestimated, as history will show, ever to occupy the White House.

Well, as I've said, I don't make a habit of visiting presidents, but I have in fact met several. The first time I saw a president was when I was a sophomore in Montclair High School. I was invited (I really don't remember why) to join a group of foreign students to meet Herbert Hoover in the White House. There were about twenty-five of us, and we were all lined up waiting our turn to shake hands with the president of the United States. This was in the middle of the Great Depression. The president looked rather grim, and as I stood in line I was wondering what words of wisdom to say to him. When my turn came, Hoover smiled, shook my hand very strongly, and before I could say anything, said cheerfully, "Welcome young man, and how are things in Greece?"

My answer was, "Mr. President, I've never been there." That handshake became even stronger and quickly pulled me ahead. With everything else the president had to think about that day, I'm not sure whether the thought came to his mind, "Then what are you doing here?" but it was a little rebuke I think I might have deserved! But then again why was everyone making me out to be a Greek? I never really thought of myself that way until much later in life.

Perhaps the most meaningful trip I ever made to the White House, however, was the one I made in 1980, when I became involved in a special affair.

"Why not a reception at the White House to honor the poets of the world?" This idea occurred to me while watching Channel 11 one evening, where First Lady Rosalyn Carter was introducing Ella Fitzgerald, who had been invited to sing for the president and a few guests. Then Mrs. Carter announced that the White

House would be sponsoring other cultural events, featuring members of the Bolshoi Ballet, a pianist, a choral group, a magician, and even an acrobatic group.

So far as I could determine, no president had ever given a reception at the White House exclusively for poets. I knew that Robert Frost had been honored individually, and that Carl Sandburg had once been invited but couldn't come, but I wanted a ceremony to honor poets worldwide. Odysseus Elytis, the Greek poet, had just won the Nobel Prize for poetry and that, of course, also prompted me to try to bring more attention and honor to poets.

I presented the idea to *Poetry Magazine*, on whose board I had served for a number of years. For the past several decades, I and J. Patrick Lannan, a highly successful businessman and patron of the arts, had organized and co-chaired some rare-book auctions and dinner parties at which we raised money for the poetry association that published *Poetry Magazine*. We had also honored some distinguished poets over the years. The first poet was Robert Frost, and the last to be honored while I was on the board was T. S. Eliot. We also recognized Carl Sandburg and Richard Wilbur. I once tried to get Ernest Hemingway to come to one of our receptions, at which we hoped to raise money while honoring him. At the time he was living in Cuba. He turned me down, however, even though Pat Lannan offered to send a plane to get him, and we invited him to bring his wife Mary, his dogs, and anyone he chose. His refusal took the form of a three-page, handwritten letter, complaining that I, or we at *Poetry Magazine*, did not understand or appreciate the privacy that writers and poets needed in order to live and write. "This money raising business is a lot of garbage that should not be imposed on the artist." It was a good, strong, very nasty letter. I did not bother to answer since, in fact, I agreed with a lot of what he wrote. We did, however, auction off his letter, and it brought a tidy sum for *Poetry Magazine*!

When I presented my suggestion in 1980 to the board of *Poetry Magazine* for a White House party for poets, however, they did not receive it with any great enthusiasm. This was partly due to the fact that President Carter was a Democrat—and many of the members of the board were Republicans, some of them good John Birchers! Politics, sad to say, was raising its ugly head even among poets and supporters of poetry. I told the board (I was gradually losing my popularity with them) that I was going ahead with my idea with or without their support or sponsorship.

I had meanwhile discussed the proposal with Rosalyn Carter, and she agreed wholeheartedly with the idea. Eventually even the board concurred with the soundness of my scheme and wished me luck. Only a few members attended the White House reception, however—one that the president later told me was the best party given while he was in the White House. And, indeed, it was a grand affair.

We first had to decide on the list of poets to be invited, and for this I sought the cooperation of other poetry organizations around the world. The most helpful suggestions came from the New York Poetry Center, which had done an excellent job providing audiences and support for poets everywhere. All in all we submitted a list of about fifty poets to the White House—and I have to confess that I had never heard the names of most of the writers submitted.

I did, however, concentrate on securing one poet, and that was Odysseus Elytis, who, as I mentioned, had just been selected as the Nobel laureate for literature. He was the second Greek to win the prize. (Poet George Seferis was the first.) I had great difficulty in reaching Elytis but finally did so through Kimon Friar, translator of Kazantzakis and, of course, excellent editor of my *Greek Heritage Quarterly*. I had a good conversation with Elytis, and although my Greek is not all that strong, I understood enough of what he was saying to realize that here I had another Hemingway explaining to me how important privacy is to a writer. In addition, Elytis pointed out that it was a long, time-consuming journey from Greece to Washington. With all the patience I could muster, I emphasized that I was extending an invitation from the president of the United States to a party honoring him, and that his presence would be a great help and inspiration to other poets, especially young poets, who needed all the inspiration and help they could get.

Despite my persistence the best he would agree to was that he would think it over and let me know. I took this to mean a polite "No." A week or so later I received a call from one of Elytis's friends, who suggested that perhaps if the president himself wrote Elytis direct, he might change his mind! This really infuriated me, and I asked her whether she was just giving her own opinion or was repeating Elytis's wish. She said this had been her idea. I did not ask President Carter to write the personal invitation, and Elytis did not attend. Nevertheless, the affair with Elytis confirms my opinion (although I hope I am wrong) that many poets, like many artistic people, are the vainest of creatures and often the most selfish. This saddens me, for I think that artists should be the most sensitive and giving of all civilized creatures.

Well, after we agreed on the poets to be invited, our next step was to prepare an international guest list.

Valerie Valentine was put in charge of the list from our end and Rosalyn Carter invited us to meet with members of her staff at the White House to work out the list with them. I think we settled on about five hundred people, and nearly all those invited accepted with great enthusiasm. We also started getting pressure from scores of others wanting an invitation. This reception suddenly became the hottest invitation of the year, and this is where my dear friend and associate from the *Poetry Magazine* board J. Patrick Lannan tried to horn in.

    I think this is a good place to say that Pat Lannan was a great financial supporter of poetry (more than once he came up with the money to pay the printer's bill for the magazine), and he collected paintings and other works of art, especially those of young artists in need of help all over the world. At times he was financially generous to a fault, although his detractors would say he could afford to be and ought to be generous, considering that he had made his millions as the "velvet-glove raider." He was a financial genius and an unqualifiedly ruthless one. What I write here Pat and I often discussed directly face to face. In all the years that I knew Pat I saw him embarrassed only once, and this was in connection with the White House party.

    On the day of the party, Pat invited one of the chief reporters of the *New York Times* to fly to Washington in his private plane. On the way Pat apparently dictated a story for the reporter. The reporter, it so happened, was a friend of mine, who knew that I once wrote for the *Times*, and he asked me to check out some of the details Pat had given him. It was indeed a good, complete story: there were the names of the poets who were to be honored, the list of the celebrity guests, and acknowledgment of how gracious and thoughtful President and Mrs. Carter were to give such an event. There was only one incorrect piece of information. The article claimed that the whole idea of the party had been Pat Lannan's—that he had used his influence from the Kennedy family with the president to arrange it—and try as I could, I could not find my name anywhere in the story, not even among those attending the party. I told the reporter that it was an excellent story except that he had gotten one of the names wrong. The reporter asked which one, and I said, "Just tell Pat you discussed the story with me and ask him about the name."

Within an hour Pat called me and said there had been a misunderstanding on the part of the reporter; they had both had a bit too much to drink on the plane. "And, of course," Pat said, "when he used my name, he should have used yours." I told Pat he was a lowdown liar but that we ought to get on with the party. We did, and I enjoyed it immensely.

The *Times* article called the event a festive and meaningful affair, giving credit to both Pat Lannan and me, and also mentioning Valerie Valentine, Martin Janis (whose firm handled the public relations for the party), and Anthony Angelos, who had been a great supporter of Jimmy Carter during his presidential campaign, and who had funded a special black-tie dinner party at the prestigious "F" Street club the night before. In that party before the party, some fifty special guests, including the president, Senator Charles Percy, and Congressman John Brademas, had offered a special toast to Rosalyn Carter for giving the White House reception. The First Lady was given credit not just for having a reception for poets but for turning the affair into a kind of seminar featuring poets and poetry reading.

For at the party itself, writers like Gwendolyn Brooks, Poet Laureate of Illinois and Pulitzer Prize winner, Nobel Prize winner Saul Bellow, and John Nims, editor of *Poetry Magazine*, were assigned special rooms in the White House at which guests could visit them and where they gave readings. In addition, a light buffet was served, and a string quartet played gently and unobtrusively in the background.

Among the Chicagoans attending the event, which turned into a festive party once the brief readings concluded, were the Henry Bartholomays, Nick and Evangeline Gouletas, the Ben Gingisses, Gardner Stern, Beverly Dowis, the Leonard Weislows, Sugar Rautbord, June Friedlob, Faye Schwimmer, Charlene Cooperman, the Howard Brandsteins, Arlynne Simon, Mausy Sayle, Eve Heffer, Bernice Pink, the Harry Arslans, Fred Chamanara, and A. Bradley Eben. Valerie quipped: "There were more backgammon players than poets!"

President Carter took a break from a briefing on the brewing Iranian and Afghanistan crises and joined Joan Mondale, wife of the vice president, the First Lady, and Amy in the receiving line. He shook hands and spoke with everyone, saying he hoped there would be many more such parties and receptions for artists of the world in the White House. And it was refreshing to hear the President of the United States speak so forthrightly.

Ann Gerber wrote an excellent report of the party for Chicagoans and gave an account of a charming interview she had with the First Lady, whom she quoted as saying: "Poetry holds our hopes, our dreams, our emotions. It gives comfort, encouragement, joy. When Amy was small, Jimmy would read poetry in front of the fire, and we would discuss its meaning." Those words rang true with a lot of us, I think, and help explain why we need to acknowledge poets' work publicly every so often.

No Sale at the Taj Mahal

Of my many travels throughout the world during my lifetime, I'll never forget my visit to India. It's said that once you visit India, and especially Kashmir, you'll never be the same again!

Following are some observations I made on the spot in Kashmir. (Larry Townsend at the *Chicago Tribune* asked me to consider doing a piece for him, but I think I'll let them stand as I wrote them, especially my encounter in the bazaar with one of the cleverest natural salesmen I've ever met, either in a bazaar or on Wall Street!)

People who speak of being different after a visit to Kashmir mean it in a happy spiritual or mystic sense; they aren't referring to the shock of seeing outdoor cremations or bodies floating down the Ganges River or hearing the widely held opinion that the cash value of a sacred cow is more than that of a child. And although this claim may have been the brainchild of some clever ad man, the Indian Tourist Bureau, or one of the many holy men you meet in India, this much is true: India is a complex country that stirs you emotionally, stimulates you intellectually, and inevitably

No Sale at the Taj Mahal

makes an onslaught on all your senses.

A visit here is a great adventure. From the moment you arrive in India you see and feel the size, beauty, and sheer power of the mountains. Kashmir, which is the size of Great Britain, is a valley eighty-four miles long and twenty-five miles wide, surrounded by the challenging snow-capped Himalayas. It is permeated by the cool, clean air, which, if you breathe too much, too quickly, makes you light-headed. Some people say it gives you a "high." And always exotic fragrances come from the several nearby seventeenth-century gardens built by the Mogul maharajahs.

On a more mundane level, many of the things you can do in Kashmir seem easier: on the golf course at Gulmarg, 8,700 ft. high (the highest course in the world), your swing is easier, the ball goes higher and farther, and when you come to putt, the ball seems to overcome obstacles all on its own to drop into the hole. I am not an expert trout fisherman, but I've never caught bigger and more accommodating trout anywhere in the world than in Kashmir's placid, spring-fed lakes: they are quick to strike, seem almost eager to have you reel them in, and are most delicious to eat. I have never been in Kashmir during the winter season—Kashmir is now a year-round resort—but I'm told that the crisp, powderlike snow of the Himalayas offers some of the best and most challenging skiing and tobogganing in the world.

Most visitors to Kashmir arrive first in Srinagar, the capital of the state. It's a half-hour taxi or bus ride from the airport to Dal [Or Nagin] Lakes, where the houseboats are, and these houseboats by force of tradition are the region's main attraction. They were developed by the British at the close of the last century in consequence of an edict by the presiding maharajah prohibiting the ownership of land by Europeans. So the British built houseboats instead, and these and other houseboats are now available for rent to tourists—some for as little as a hundred dollars a week, with meals and servants included. Some of the houseboats are quite elaborate, with canopied beds, mirrors on the ceilings, and piped-in music. One is called *Las Vegas.* Never mind that the plumbing doesn't always work—there are silk rugs on the bathroom floors.

Every houseboat has its Shikaru, a punt or gondola, that helps give Srinagar the designation "the Venice of Asia." The Shikaru can comfortably take up to four passengers and the gondolier. You sit on silken cushions under a canopy of plaited straws and flowers hung round by lace curtains. Your gondolier may insist on singing an Indian song or two, but despite this cacophony it is quite wonderful to be transported this way. After a long journey (and India is an eighteen-hour plane trip from the United States), riding in a Shikaru offers an ideal and welcome time for rest and reverie. Unfortunately, your peace is frequently broken by other Shikarus run by small tradesmen, who are always on the lookout for tourists. During one of my scenic journeys, I was accosted by at least twelve aquatic peddlers, who offered me everything from some rather beautiful antique brass ornaments to toothpaste, toilet paper, and honey made from lotus blossoms.

Your experience with aquatic peddlers, however, is quite tame compared to what awaits you when you enter the city bazaar in Srinager. If you enjoy shopping and matching wits with tradesmen, as I do, the bazaar is an Arabian Nights experience not to be missed.

Hookah-smoking old men tend the stalls in the narrow, shop-lined streets of the bazaar, and here you will find the best of Kashmir's artistry and handicrafts: papier mach objects (for which Kashmir is famous), delicately carved woodwork, embroidered wool shawls, hammered silver and semi-precious jewels of every kind, and, of course, the famous silk Kashmir carpets.

My most notable encounter in the bazaar was with an old rug peddler:

Peddler: "Ah, Sir, welcome to Srinagar. How do you like our happy valley?"

"Yes, it is beautiful."

"You must be sure to see our silk rugs while you are here. You will appreciate Kashmir all the more."

"Thank you, but I'm not interested in buying a rug."

"Oh, no Sir—not to buy, just to see."

"Thank you, but some other time."

"Please, Sir, I want to learn from you. Just tell me which you like the best. Just look."

"Okay, but I'm not interested in buying."

"Just please tell me which do you like the best?"

"Well, this one is quite beautiful."

"Ah, Sir, what taste! You have picked the most beautiful rug in my shop."

"Well, thank you for showing me your rugs. Goodbye."

"Oh, Sir, just one thing more. I want to learn. If you bought this rug, what would you pay?"

"I'm telling you, I'm not buying a rug."

"Not to buy, not to buy. Just what you think it is worth. I want to learn."

"I'd say two hundred dollars."

"You are amazing Sir. You are a good businessman. You have missed the price of the rug by only fifty dollars, but you may have it for just two hundred dollars."

"I told you I'm not interested in buying."

"Sir, you are a tough bargainer. Okay, you can take it for $150 and never mind that it took a poor artist six months to make it."

"But I told you . . ."

"Never mind, Sir, you will remember Kashmir for this rug long after you have forgotten the Himalayas. I'll wrap it in a small bundle."

I bought the rug!

The attraction of Kashmir, of course, is more than Srinagar, spectacular scenery, and cunning, amusing tradespeople. The problems of India, especially the almost daily conflicts of the different religious factions and the even more alarming overpopulation problem, do not seem as critical here as in the other states of India. On the population problem, the familiar Western nursery rhyme has been rewritten as follows: "There was a young woman who lived in a shoe. She didn't have many children, she knew what to do!"

The men, women, and especially the children of Kashmir are, it is said, the most healthy and attractive among India's 800 million population. Parents who still arrange the marriages of their children regard candidates from Kashmir as the most desirable.

For additional sightseeing there are many resorts, archaeological ruins to explore, and places of interest short distances by bus or rented car from Srinagar. Gulmarg, twenty-eight miles away, offers a magnificent view of the entire Kashmir valley from its height of 8,700 feet, and has good and reasonably priced tourist accommodations. Further north is Pahalgam, 7,200 feet above sea level. Here is the habitat of the famous brown bears of India, and other animals as well. They cannot be hunted, only photographed. Sonamarq at 9,000 feet and just fifty-one miles from Srinagar, offers excellent camping grounds and skiing, and is the approach to a number of glaciers. Treks are made from here east to Tibet. On a clear day, with some luck, you can get a glimpse of Mount Everest—and this, many travelers contend, is in itself reason enough to visit Kashmir, as I am doing, even if I may never be the same again.

But my trip to India included more than the breathtaking beauty of Kashmir. For, as I have mentioned, the beautiful and terrible exist side-by-side in India, and nowhere was this more vividly brought home to me than when I traveled south, to Agra, to see the Taj Mahal, one of the wonders of the world.

Visitors to the Taj Mahal are advised to return at different times of the day to get the full impact of its beauty, for the Taj is one of the most beautiful structures in the world and a romantic symbol of a man's love and devotion to a woman. Anyway, that is how my guide Hamid talked to me about the Taj, and I was determined to spend an extra day or two at Agra to see it as he suggested.

He got me up at sunrise to see it; it was indeed beautiful, with the rising sun bathing it in a soft light. And I saw it exactly at noon, with the scorching sun overhead. And finally I visited the Taj in the moonlight, which, according to Hamid, was the best time of all to contemplate its exquisite beauty. But I have to confess at no time was I as moved by the sight of this magnificent structure as I felt I should have been, and the reason was that no matter what time of day or night I visited the Taj, it was literally mobbed with tourists like myself.

Being a guest of the Indian government (they

often invite writers to visit), I did have a few extra privileges when I visited the Taj; I was permitted to see several of its chambers not ordinarily open to the public. But this did not really make much of a difference.

On one of my visits, I stopped, and saw that across the river running parallel to the Taj there was a bit of a wasteland, without people milling about. I asked my guide whether we might go over there to get what I felt would be quite a different and more private view of this beautiful edifice. He immediately deterred, saying that the land was indeed deserted; that some of the villagers used the area to bury their animals; that there were villains about; and that, anyway, it was a long, bumpy ride, and we would have to go through a very poor village. He said it would not be a good experience. Of course, this made me all the more interested in going, and since I was a guest and insistent, he finally agreed to take me. I'm glad we went, not so much for the different view of the Taj Mahal but for the view of India I got en route to the little village.

It was early in the morning, but already it was quite hot; some of the villagers were sleeping outside down near the road. The sacred cattle were everywhere, but what caught my eye most were three little girls, not more than ten or twelve years old—the age of my grandchildren. One of the girls was carrying a nanny goat. I immediately asked the driver to stop, as I thought the children would make a good picture. My guide, who was always supposed to be looking after my welfare, suggested that it was not a good idea to stop. We would be besieged by some of the villagers begging for alms or trying to sell us something. But I wanted a picture of the girls. The three children immediately came over to our car, but they seemed to be more interested in the car itself than in me or my guide and driver.

Through my guide I asked if I might take their picture. I especially wanted a shot of the little girl and her nanny goat, and I offered them some rupees, which the guide took from me and gave to them. There was some conversation between them and the guide. They were perfectly willing to have their picture taken, but they wanted a ride in our car. Apparently not many cars passed through their village. I had all three of them with the goat pile in the back seat with me and we had a merry, bumpy ride to the outskirts of the village, where we left them off.

I then proceeded a mile or two farther to get my view of the Taj Mahal from across the river. It offered a fine view, but there were villagers about and a stench that certainly detracted me from what I thought might be a romantic and spiritual impression of the Taj.

On the way back, we found the three little girls waiting for us, apparently expecting another ride. I took their names and the name of the goat and promised I would send them copies of the pictures. It was really a wonderful experience meeting these children. Of course, they reminded me of my own grandchildren, and they were so happy and appreciative of the ride in an automobile. Then it happened.

When we arrived back in the village, we were met by the father of the girls. At first he seemed a bit apprehensive, as if he wondered whether we had kidnapped his children, but when the guide told him what happened and that I had given them some money (apparently I had given them the equivalent of about one dollar, which was a lot), the father seemed pleased. A spirited conversation ensued between the father and my guide.

Apparently the father asked whether I was interested in the girls. I gathered that my guide correctly reported that, No, I was just interested in taking some pictures of them. Then, according to my guide, the father said that he had four girls, the youngest of whom was back at the house, and that he would be willing to sell one of his children if I was interested. I was really shocked to hear this, but before I instructed my guide to tell the father how I felt, I thought it would be interesting to pursue the subject a little further. For example, how much was he asking for one of his children?

The father asked, Which one of the girls would I be interested in? I replied that I really was not interested in a purchase but if I were it would be the little girl holding the nanny goat.

"Oh," said the father, according to the guide, "She is my favorite, and she is a good and obedient worker. How much was I willing to offer?"

I said that I was not offering anything, but what did the father think she was worth? The guide carried on the "bargaining," and he said that the father was asking the equivalent of about forty-five dollars, but then he added: "If you really want this girl, I'm sure the father will let her go for twenty-five."

That was my second shock—twenty-five dollars to buy a human being! I turned to the little girl with the nanny goat and said, "Would you like to come with me and be one of my children?"

The guide smiled as he gave me her answer. She said, No, she would rather stay here and look after her goat.

And with that I gave the father a ten-dollar bill, and we drove away. I still can't believe the father was serious, but the guide assured me that he was. The rest of the day I thought no more about the Taj Mahal—only about the little girl with the nanny goat. And I think they are right—I shall never be the same.

An Irresistible Prank in Bali

I've always wanted to go to Indonesia, particularly to the island of Bali, and in 1991, thanks to Continental Airlines and the Grand Hyatt Hotel in Bali, I made it, as their guest. It was a memorable, two-week experience, and while there I made some observations that I'm including in a book on travel Valerie and I are planning.

Picture a lush tropical island about the size of Delaware, shaped like a stubby sunfish with a volcano for an eye, swimming west to east: that's the beautiful island of Bali, in the Indonesian archipelago about six hundred miles south of the equator. Add to this image every conceivable tropical bird: parrots, cockatoos, Mynah birds, and canaries, all wild and flying about in the trees and bushes (and even on your hotel terrace), and then populate the island with deeply religious, gentle, and courteous olive-skinned people, who don't seem to have a word for "No" in their language, or at least never use it, and you have what the Balinese themselves call a paradise on earth—and also an island where gods have chosen to dwell.

This is the way Bali stuck me on my first visit, even before I read the travel brochures. To fully understand and appreciate Bali it's important, however, first to recognize how essential their religion, their gods, and their deeply ingrained superstitions are to the Balinese.

My excellent guide, Mr. I. G. N. Beratha of Pacto Ltd. Tours and Travel, told me there seem to be more temples and places of worship in Bali than there are homes. More than 90 percent of the Balinese are Hindu, and they practice their religion in their conduct with each other as well as in their worship of their numerous gods. The Balinese worship the same trinity of gods, Brahma, Shiva, and Vishnu, as the Indians. But they also have a supreme god, Sanghyang Widi Wasa, who lives at the summit of Mount Agung, the 10,308-foot volcano (the eye of the sun fish) that physically and spiritually dominates Bali. That volcano has erupted several times during the past fifty years. But life goes on as usual and lovely homes, hotels, and farms have been rebuilt right at its base, which overlooks one of Bali's most beautiful lakes.

The Balinese take their gods seriously but with joy, and they don't worship out of fear of punishment but out of love of earthly life and each other. The worst punishment for the Balinese is not death, which they consider simply a release from the senses. What is of supreme importance is what form they will come back in reincarnation. Their greatest reward is to come back as another, perhaps more beautiful person; their worst fear is to be reincarnated as an animal. My guide, however, remarked: "I wouldn't mind coming back as a great tiger, or a beautiful bird flying over the sea—or a lap dog in Beverly Hills!"

I felt it was important to try to attend some of the more private ceremonies of the Balinese. Being present at a cremation, however, is not something for everyone to witness. But in Bali, cremations are not sad affairs; they are rather festivals celebrating the release of the body from its senses to an exchange place at which it will enter another, perhaps higher, phase of life. The burning of the body itself, however, usually enclosed in a replica of an animal like a bull, is a frightening, sobering, and unforgettable sight.

It's a special privilege to witness a tooth-filing ceremony—something that every Balinese must go through in some fashion. The ceremony is an initiation into adulthood. A priest files down the canine teeth and incisors of the young man or woman so that the teeth will be even across. It's important to the Balinese when he or she enters the spirit world to eliminate any resemblance in themselves to fanged demons or other animals that can never get in to the spirit world.

Equally interesting and inspiring is a visit to the Tanah Lot Temple, about a two-hour drive from Depensar, built on an ocean rock that gives you one of the most magnificent views of Bali's west coast. This and the Royal Temple of Taman Ayun, surrounded by its lovely moat, are favorite sites for marriages of Western couples. A visit to these temples offers not only their beauty of structure but the inspiring sight of them, surrounded by palm trees and exotic flowers against the azure sky, giving lessons without sermons!

I found the Holy Monkey Forest interesting. Here you can buy food, which the monkeys will eat from your hands. If you're lucky, they'll even do a little dance for you. This forest is not like a zoo in any way. The monkeys are not caged but live in the trees and are very tame. Some of the older monkeys, however, are also a bit bold and aggressive. Women are advised to hold on to their purses. We were told that since they are well fed they are happy to remain in the forest though occasionally you may find one on your hotel terrace.

The Balinese are a gentle, hospitable people, but they are strict in observing certain customs, which the visitor should be careful to respect, especially in the small villages. Here are some rules our guide advised us to abide by: wear a sash around the waist when visiting temples; don't sit or climb on temple architecture; never touch someone's head, for the head is considered sacred; never draw attention to feet, which are considered base. Don't stare at people who are bathing in the open; bring gifts on visits, as the Balinese do; use only the right hand to offer or receive, since the left is considered unclean.

Attire is generally informal in Bali and you may find it wise to bring only some summer wear and shop locally for additional things. The batik shirts or dresses, locally made, are very economical. They also make good presents to bring home. No visa is necessary for a short visit, and there are no inoculation requirements, although you may want to ask your doctor's advice for travel in this part of the world.

Shopping for the local crafts (and Bali is a center for beautiful artwork, wood carvings, and silver jewelry) in the hotel boutiques is frequently cheaper than buying in the village stores, but bargaining is usually not done in the hotel shops, certainly not as vigorously as you are expected to do in the village shops. The rule of thumb is to try to buy the items at half the offering price. Then you have a fair bargain.

Ubud, about a thirty-minute car ride from Depensar, is considered the island's cultural center. Here are the best shops for purchasing batiks, original art works, superb wood carvings, and antiques. The buyer should, however, be aware that many antiques in Bali are not necessarily older than one hundred years, the legal age for avoiding customs.

In Celuk, their jewelry center, we visited Wayan's Art Gallery where we obtained silver jewelry, dolls, leather fans, and the famous Wayang leather puppets, all at incredibly low prices. At the many roadside stands, we found delightful wind chimes, wooden monkeys, and interesting kites.

Swimming can be a bit of a bother since the visitor is accosted by scores of Balinese selling their goods. They include sports shirts, swimming trunks, sandals, and sarongs, along with the latest copies of Gucci, Tiffany, or Cartier watches (selling for ten dollars, whereas the original goes for three hundred in New York). These salespeople will beg you to stop at their shops, all different, and follow you until you enter the hotel grounds.

On a more practical side, modern Bali offers the visitor all the amenities at a reasonable price—perhaps one of the best economical vacations in the South Pacific. Several of the hotels, like the Hyatt Hotels where we stayed, have golf courses. Tennis courts are plentiful; there is deep sea fishing, and you can have the chef in your hotel cook to your order the salmon or mackerel you just caught in the morning. Meals are generally not included in the price of your hotel room, but the entertainment offered in the way of Balinese dance lessons, puppet shows, fruit carving, weaving, scuba, and tennis lessons are free.

Bali offers excellent restaurants, especially in the hotel. There are Asian as well as Western dishes. As a visitor I was urged to try the Balinesian dishes,

An Irresistible Prank in Bali

especially satay, with its delicious spicy peanut sauce. And treat yourself to room service, especially breakfast. They make a special ceremony of serving you, starting either with a gentle knock on the door or with ringing chimes. Then the waiter greets you while balancing the tray with one hand and removes his shoes with the other. The attention shown to you is really wonderful, and it lasts until the waiter leaves and brings you back to your own world when he says: "Have a nice food" or at night, "Have a nice bed." But that's Bali, the modern and the quaint of it. In the beauty shop in the Bali Hyatt you can get a first-class haircut for five dollars, a pedicure for six, and a massage for fifteen. And it was there that I couldn't resist playing a little prank.

Whenever I travel in a plane for more than five hours or so, especially to a foreign country, the first thing I inquire about at the hotel is the availability of a good massage. And if the plane trip lasts more than six hours, I also often go to the barber shop, get a shampoo and haircut, and usually end up getting a pedicure, manicure, and facial as well—the works. It's a good way of relaxing, and it helps with the jet lag.

The thirty-hour trip to Bali (with stopovers in Los Angeles, Honolulu, and Guam), was a long, long haul, and I was glad when I arrived at the new hotel to find their excellent health and beauty club. You had your choice of a male or female masseur, and they were so good that it became my fixed practice after a game of tennis and a swim in the sea to get a massage every morning. And I became very friendly with the entire staff of the massage office.

This in no way implies that these masseurs ever offered or were willing to offer any of the services one usually associates with "massage parlors." They were strictly professional, and the massage was something I looked forward to every day.

The day before I left Bali, after my tennis game in the morning, I went to the massage office dressed as usual in my white tennis shorts and shirt with a Bali Hyatt insignia on it, a gift of the management. I had finished just before noon, when the staff all went out for lunch, but I remembered that I had some business to attend to with the public-relations office and asked if I could use their phone. Hamid, the manager, said of course, and invited me to use the phone at the massage reception desk saying, "Make yourself at home, and when you finish, please put up the sign that we are out to lunch returning at 2 o'clock."

As I was phoning, before I had a chance to put up the sign, a lovely young woman walked in. She looked Swedish—tall, blond, and with a great figure that immediately reminded me of the Petty Girl posters. (During World War II, it seemed to me that every GI had a poster of either Rita Hayworth, Betty Grable, or a Petty Girl on his bunk.) Anyway, that's how attractive this girl facing me was.

She indeed turned out to be Swedish, her first name was Kristen, and she was from Stockholm. She wanted to know whether she could change her 2 o'clock massage appointment for an earlier one, since there was a tour she wanted to take. Before I could tell her that I was just there using the phone, she said: "I don't mind if Hamid doesn't take me—anyone will do. I'm having some soreness in my right hip, and I'd like a massage before I go on the tour."

Is there any normal man who wouldn't be tempted to do what I was tempted to do? I fell into the role of masseur and asked her whether she wanted a strong, medium, or soft massage (usually the first question a masseur asks his customer). She immediately responded she wanted a strong massage and gestured by clenching her fists. I still hesitated a bit but then asked how long she had this soreness in her hip. She explained that she had hurt her hip two days ago climbing into a boat after swimming, and it was very painful and bruised, as I would see.

Finally I said, "Okay, you can go into room number one. Get yourself ready, and I'll see what I can do."

I put the "Back at 2 p.m." sign on the office door, braced myself, and went into room number one. There she was, stark naked, sprawled on the massage table. She was on her stomach. Obviously she had been here several times and knew what to expect. But she said, "If you don't mind, forget about the feet (the usual starting point) and do my right hip."

I immediately struck up a professional pose: "Please, I'm the masseur, let me do my job as I know best, and I'm sure I can help you." Then I started with her feet. Having had so many massages myself I felt I knew the technique.

I massaged her toes, one by one, rubbed her feet and ankles. "Oh, yes," she said, "that feels good." Then as I rubbed her legs and hips, I began to feel a bit guilty about the whole thing, though I'm sure she was really enjoying it.

"Kristen, I hope you won't be mad, I just couldn't help it. But I'm really not a masseur. I was just using the phone when you walked in."

I was not at all sure how Kristen would take this, but she turned her head, looked up at me, smiled, and said: "Don't you think I knew that!"

Cricket's Love Song

What was a little cricket doing 1,000 miles out in the Pacific on the promenade deck of a 28,000-ton world cruise ship, singing its heart away? How did it get there? How long could it survive away from forest dwellings, trees, or gardens, or perhaps just the loving care of humans?

Since the publication of my book *Miss 4th of July, Goodbye* and the appearance of the Disney movie based on it, I've often been invited to give lectures. I talk about the book and other subjects, sometimes telling stories connected with those I've published in *What They Always Wanted*.

I've given lectures at Oxford, Wells College, Harvard, and various literary and social clubs throughout the country, and most recently I gave lectures on several cruise ships under the flag of the Royal Caribbean Line, owned by Jay Pritzker, who is a good friend and one of the most prominent, generous, and creative businessmen in the world. On these cruises I'm billed as a "storyteller," and my stories are based on my travel experiences throughout the world. My talks have been very well attended. But if there's a bingo game, I'm lucky to have twenty-five passengers show up. Such are the interests and attention span of cruise passengers!

Anyway, it was on one of these cruises that I found myself asking the above question.

Every evening just before midnight, I would walk the deck of the ship, usually abandoned at that time of night. It gave me a chance to exercise just before retiring and also an opportunity to review quietly what I was going to say in one of the four lectures I was scheduled to give the following morning. This was an ideal time for contemplation. On this clear night the stars seemed unusually bright, reflecting on the wine-dark sea (as Homer would have put it); the wind was a whisper; and I was alone. At least I thought I was alone. Just as I was rounding the bow of the ship I heard a cricket's chirp. A cricket's chirp a thousand miles out at sea?

I was particularly fascinated by the cricket because as a child we had lived in a mountainous area of West Virginia, near a rustling brook. Every night we would sit on the porch and watch the fireflies and listen to the crickets—hundreds of them. As I now recall, my first lesson about "the facts of life," was not with "birds and bees" as examples, but crickets. The most commonly heard of all the cricket's songs, my mother told us, was that made only by males, which attracts the female "if she is in the mood." The cricket chirps by rubbing the upturned scrape on one forewing along a row of some two hundred teeth on the underside of its other forewing. The mating song serves a two-fold purpose: it induces the female to copulate, and the fighting chirps that are interspersed with the mating song repel other males.

But who or what was my cricket, hidden somewhere on the promenade deck uttering its clear and urgent song, singing to? It seemed highly unlikely that there was a female cricket aboard or a male to repel. Was it singing just for the sake of its song, out of loneliness or desperation? Was it calling for help? Crickets are known to be among the smartest of chirping insects, and have clear, driving instincts for everything they do. I have seen cricket fighting in Shanghai, a favorite Chinese gambling sport for thousands of years. Owners and people who sponsor these unique fights claim the cricket can be trained to stun or knock out its opponent. In one famous match, enthusiasts claim that a cricket with both its forelegs bitten off played dead, and when its opponent came close enough, the prostrate cricket grabbed it by the throat for a kill and victory. At one time this champion cricket was on display in a glass case in the famous bar at the Raffles Hotel in Singapore and was the subject of many stories. More important for this story, in the Orient the male cricket is kept as a pet because it is good joss (luck). My questions and curiosity were at least partly satisfied the following morning by a notice which appeared in the ship's daily newspaper:

> *Young couple would greatly appreciate any information leading to the recovery of two pet crickets which are missing from their bamboo cage. They are each about 2 inches long, delicate, greenish in color with transparent wings. They sing a merry, clear song and are harmless to humans. Please contact cabin 39.*

After breakfast I could hardly wait to call on the couple and give them what I hoped would be good news about their crickets, or at least about one of them. I knocked on the door of cabin 39 and a lovely young Chinese girl appeared.

"Good morning," I said. "I think I heard your cricket on the promenade deck last night."

"Do come in, please. This is my husband Lu Chang. I am Mai Lee. You heard our crickets?"

They were a young Chinese couple, just married, and this was their honeymoon. "Oh, please show us where our crickets could be. We are most grateful because they are also our most favorite wedding present from our best friends. It is the custom in China to give a cricket as a wedding present for good luck and long life." Then Lu Chang added, smiling, "They also insure fertility," and they both laughed and blushed a bit.

Mai Lee got her little bamboo cage and Lu Chang brought a net. I also learned that the cricket would not sing in the cage. "That is as it should be, isn't it?" Mai Lee said. (Apparently they would let the crickets out of the cage at night for a little freedom, exercise, and song.)

I took them to the bow of the ship where the night before I had heard the cricket's song. We examined the various fixtures and the railings and looked all over the front deck, but nowhere did we see the crickets. I also told the couple that I had heard only one cricket, or at least the chirp came from only one point on the deck. I had no knowledge of a second cricket.

Mai Lee explained, "That is understandable because only the male cricket sings. The female listens and, if she is interested, responds by flying to the male."

"Just like a female," responded Lu Chang. Then he added, "I think we have to wait until this evening. Will you come with us?"

"Of course," I said. "I am utterly fascinated by your story and also by your optimism that we will indeed find your little pets. How long can they live without food or water?"

"Oh, we will find them," said Mai Lee hopefully. "They are hardy creatures and they also know we love them. If they see us, they will come back—and I will sing to them, too."

That evening just before midnight, Mai Lee, Lu Chang, and I went up to the promenade deck and resumed our search for their good luck and, as Lu Chang reminded me again, their fertility pets.

There was a warm, gentle breeze and by good fortune a full moon to give us light. The sky was clear and there was the special silence that you feel when looking at the stars from the deck of a ship in the middle of an ocean. We stood very still but did not hear or see the cricket and I feared the little pets were forever lost.

Suddenly Mai Lee began to sing a very soft, plaintive song in Chinese. Lu Chang looked at me and said: "Mai Lee always sings to the crickets. I doubt if they really respond to her but whether or not she is the cause, they do seem to chirp away at her songs."

I asked her to translate her song. It went like this:

> *"Oh, little ones, come to us.*
> *We have a warm hearth and sweet roots*
> *   for you.*
> *Come to us and sing a song*
> *   And gladden our hearts."*

The first time Mai Lee sang, nothing happened. Just the soft whisper of the wind. She sang again, this time it seemed to me at a higher pitch, and sure enough, we heard the sounds *"re-re-"* *"re-treat, re-treat, re-treat."*

"He's up there," cried Mai Lee pointing to a spot right under a small search light. "He's right there. I see him. But don't move. I think they'll come down."

Then came the cricket's song again, but this time there was a variation in the pitch and the rhythm of the song.

"He is saying something else," said Mai Lee. "Let's wait awhile."

"I think," said her husband, "you are a little overly romantic. I should climb up and try to net them while we see them."

Just then one of the crickets did jump down but on the ship's railing.

"Oh, no," cried Mai Lee, "he'll be blown off the rail into the sea."

Suddenly the second cricket jumped down right next to its mate. Lu Chang came forward with his net. "Not now, please not now," implored Mai Lee. "You will scare them and they'll fall into the sea."

It was too late. The first cricket did jump, not into the sea, fortunately, but on the deck next to Mai Lee's feet. Then the second cricket followed.

"Don't move," Mai Lee told her husband. "The poor creatures are just exhausted, weak, and hungry."

Then she knelt down slowly and gently cupped her hand over the pets. There was no resistance, no movement. They seemed happy to be rescued into such tender hands. Lu Chang gave her the net in which they were to be taken, and we all went happily back to their cabin.

Mai Lee put her pets back into their little bamboo cage, made sure the door was firmly closed, and then gave them some special roots, lettuce, and sweetened water. Within a few minutes one of the crickets started singing, as if in gratitude. Lu Chang reminded us that this was the first time they had heard the crickets sing while they were in their little cage.

Mai Lee and Lu Chang thanked me profusely, although I really did nothing except point out where, by chance, I heard the cricket sing the previous night.

One evening about a week later, I got a call from Mai Lee asking if I would come to their cabin. She said they had a little surprise for me. I could not imagine what it could be.

Mai Lee met me at the door of their cabin and said, "Please come in, but close your eyes. Now look." What was the surprise? There were now four crickets, not two. "We are blessed with twins," laughed Mai Lee. "You will do us a great honor if you will accept one of these twins as a token of our appreciation and gratitude. I hope it will bring you luck in whatever you do." They had found a bamboo cage in the ship's oriental gift shop similar to the one they had brought with them and presented it to me with the little cricket inside.

I thanked them, wished them good luck, and made them promise they would write to give me news of themselves and their special pets.

All this happened in March and I didn't hear from Mai Lee and Lu Chang again until the following January, when I received a Christmas card from them postmarked Shanghai. Inside the card was a special announcement with a picture.

> *Mai Lee and Lu Chang are happy to announce they are the proud parents of twins—2 boys: Zhou, weighing 4 1/2 pounds, and Christopher, 5 pounds—born on Christmas Eve 1988.*

Mai Lee attached a little note saying that Lu Chang insisted, and she agreed, to name the second son Christopher, and they both hoped I would be pleased.

She also asked how my cricket was. I was too happy with their news to spoil it by writing that shortly after my arrival in Chicago, my cricket had also escaped. Unfortunately, I could not sing Mai Lee's plaintive calling song, and though I searched high and low in my ground-floor apartment and around the building on Lake Shore Drive where I lived, I never heard or saw my little cricket again.

Beatrice

Mai Lee and Lu Chang's love story had ended happily, with the birth of their twins, but soon after that my own love story, after fifty long, wonderful years, was to end in its own way. Beatrice died on November 16, 1989.

On the second anniversary of her death, we spread her ashes under the copper beech tree that the village of Wilmette had planted in her memory. It grew in the little park within view of our condominium on Sheridan Road. It is difficult for me to write about her now. It says enough to write she was a perfect wife. I was an imperfect husband, but we had a wonderful and loving life together and brought forth three fine children.

On the day of her death I was very angry. I was angry at the well-intended but blundering doctors; I was angry at myself for agreeing to the fatal heart operation and not asking more questions; I was angry at the unfairness of life; and finally I was angry at God. On the day of her death, however, I vented my anger and wrote a few things, and I've been urged to include the little essay in these memoirs. Here it is:

WITH A LOVING FAITH, RESPECT (AND A FEW QUESTIONS) TO THE *GREAT ALMIGHTY ONE* UPSTAIRS

Greetings:
    In case your divine computer doesn't yet have all the data, this is the story with personal comment:
    It was a bright warm Saturday morning (10/28 planet Earth). Beatrice looked out our window and remarked how wonderfully the lake glistened—just like the Mediterranean Sea and wouldn't it be lovely if we went to Greece in April, especially to Corfu. I agreed.
    This day we were having breakfast a little earlier than usual because Beatrice had a special appointment with Gunilla, her devoted hair dresser and friend.
    I offered to drive her but as usual she wanted to walk—walking was part of her disciplined and daily exercise program.
    Half hour later, just as I had finished reading the *New York Times*, the phone rang: "Mr. Janus? This is Sam at the Beauty Shop. I was having a cigarette outside and I saw an ambulance at this Union Oil station at the corner. I'm sure it's your wife, Mr. Janus. She collapsed on the street."
    The ambulance was still at the gas station when I arrived. At first they wouldn't let me see her. I told the paramedics that all she probably needed was some clear insulin. They said no. It was a heart attack.
    They finally let me talk to her. She was conscious and said she really felt alright. The expert paramedics (one doctor later said they saved her life) said she was far from alright and suggested I follow the ambulance (but not at their

speed!) to the Emergency Center at Evanston Hospital.

When I arrived at the hospital, a nurse was administering oxygen. A young doctor came and said, "Lady you nearly died."

Beatrice said, "Don't be so dramatic. I'm not dying. How soon can I leave here? My husband and I are going on a cruise Tuesday. He has to give some lectures."

"Mrs. Janus, that's a decision your doctor will have to make."

She was taken to the Intensive Care Unit. After a week of tests and wonderful care by the nurses and doctors, the doctors decided on heart surgery. There was a crisis after the surgery, but then it seemed she was making normal progress. On Thursday morning (November 16) at 10 o'clock, one of the doctors called me to say he was "guardedly optimistic." Two hours later she was dead.

My wonderful wife was such a private person. I'm not sure she would approve my writing this even to share with friends. But somehow, for myself and for our friends, I must.

Everyone who knew Beatrice remarked how lovely she was. And perfect strangers, too, would stop her on the street and say how beautiful she wore her hair. She had great style.

More important, she was a remarkably warm human being of great—but not forbidding dignity. She was always reaching out to people, especially people she considered less fortunate. She considered possessions a responsibility that had to be shared to make a better world for everybody. She spoke little about herself: she lived as an example of what she believed. Her sense of justice and tolerance was evident to all who knew her. Her unconditional loyalty to me—was clear, strong, and loving. And I feel she passed on these strong virtues to our children. In this often sorry and unfair world she was indeed—and there is no better way of saying it—a good person.

So, Oh Lord, where were You? What went wrong? What's the big idea? Dare we talk of love and justice? I haven't been a daily praying person. But our children prayed and I prayed and cried, "Oh Lord, take me instead."

Yes, I know: mystery is a part of faith and there are things we cannot know. As Santayana said, perhaps the spiritual should always be enigmatical to protect it against the intrusion of uncongenial minds.

Anyway, this is not the time to be angry—which I cannot help but be, or to talk of death or be cynical—but to think of the Nativity, good tidings, and going forward.

Beatrice and I had more than 50 years of a wonderful, happy and loving life—blessed with three great children—and supported by a legion of loyal and warm friends. Thank you, dear Lord, take care of your new Angel, and a Merry Christmas to all.

Big Bash at Eighty

I've always loved little celebrations, birthday parties, anniversaries, Greek Independence Day (March 25—also my birthday), the Fourth of July, Thanksgiving, and, of course, Christmas and New Year's. Celebrations, properly observed, with imagination and a sense of festivity, raise the human spirit. They can remind us what's it all about: our goals, past and present, and our victories, and by reminding us of the past can perhaps better our efforts to improve the future. But, above all, a celebration has to be festive, and that's what the party that was given to me on my eightieth birthday excelled at.

My children, Niki and Dave, Chris and Thea, Lincoln and Myra, and their children, together with Valerie Valentine and Don Dadas and his lovely wife Demmi planned my eightieth birthday party, which was held in their sumptous penthouse party room on Lake Shore Drive, on March 25, 1991.

Niki came in from Boston the night before. When Lincoln picked her up at the airport in his new van, he was surprised at the amount of boxes and luggage she brought. She had gone to the Boston flower market and

Big Bash at Eighty

brought at least eighty beautiful plants—tuberoses, begonias, and carnations, along with two honey-baked hams. The day of the party she fixed my breakfast, cooked numerous dishes, and then jogged for four miles, before she left to help decorate the party room at 11 a.m. What energy, vitality and spirit my beautiful daughter has.

The penthouse room was decorated under the supervision of my granddaughters, Olivia and Lizzie. There were hundreds of balloons and streamers, with pictures on the walls illustrating many of the important events of my life.

About 250 of the 300 people invited were able to come, and all arrived laden with presents. The invitation urged friends to bring a little present or a reminder of some special event of our lives together. Dorsey Connors (Mrs. John Forbes), an old friend, acted as a kind of master of ceremonies. Valerie arranged for the music—Don Yonkers, a miraculous one-man band, whom she had seen perform at the Tavern Club. There was dancing, and so much food! Every kind of cheese imaginable, two roasted baby lambs, honey-baked ham, moussaka, dolmades, fasolata, potatoes, vegetables, an enormous fruit basket, six different Greek desserts (which the Dadases made), and finally, the beautiful birthday cake, planned by Myra, which had the two faces of Janus on it. Minnie and Jimmy, who have worked for us for many years, were there to help serve.

The owner of the new and wonderful Pegasus restaurant sent over two cases of wine and there were champagne, retsina, B & B, Jack Daniels, and someone even brought a case of 8-Star Metaxa brandy, which apparently was overlooked and was untouched. George Kapotas, a wonderful Greek sculptor, presented me with a beautiful carved marble statue of the god Janus, and he also brought a statue of an eagle and dove in celebration of the Persian Gulf victory, which we plan to present to President Bush. Senator Paul Simon is helping us with the White House arrangements. And George wrote a wonderful poem about my being a very young man of eighty, which was delightful.

This is not the place to thank my friends again for coming to the grand party or to acknowledge their gifts, but many of those gifts showed an imagination that tells a lot about the giver—and the recipient. And since my editor advised me to "write about anything that will tell the reader something about yourself," I'll describe some of the more idiosyncratic presents.

Probably the most unusual—but it's for real—is naming a star after me! The document reads: "Know ye herewith that the International Star Registry doth hereby redesignate star number Monocros RA 7h19M24sol-8042 to the name of Christopher G. Janus. This star will henceforth be known by this name. This name is permanently filed in the Registry's vault in Switzerland and recorded with the Copyright Office of the United States of America." Enclosed with the document is a map of the heavens where I can find my star.

I still have a certificate from NASA entitling me to go on a civilian trip to outer space (I wonder if that will happen in my lifetime!) and maybe then I can get a closer look at the Janus star. If I can't go I hope that one of my grandchildren—Alex, Elizabeth, Nicholas, or Olivia—will have the fun and excitement of seeing the star closer up.

On a much lighter side, one of the gifts received was a life-size, inflatable Barbie-like doll. She came fully clothed, wearing a low-cut blouse and a skirt above the knees. Her hair was long and blond, and she had big brown eyes, and a mouth slightly open, as if ready to speak. I had my picture taken with her, and she looked so real that when I showed the picture to a friend a few days later his remark was, "Say, who's the broad?"

On another level entirely, I received a gift that also looks "real"—a beautiful, ten-inch sailing ship made of pure crystal. I'm looking at it as I write, and it seems ready to move with the slightest breeze.

Tiffany boxes can be deceiving, however; I opened one and found in it, wrapped in white tissue paper, a real shrunken head, from an Amazonian tribesman. I think this was arranged by some of my poker buddies.

Some of the gifts I cherish the most are letters, poems, and music that remind me of time spent with the giver, doing various things in many parts of the world. Gifts remind me of spending Carnival in Rio; of traveling on a submarine in the Pacific; of nights spent in Machu Picchu in Peru, in a geisha house in Tokyo, playing blackjack in Las Vegas; of partying on Onassis's yacht on the Hudson or sleeping in Eva Braun's stateroom in Hitler's yacht in the port of New York; of walking on the Great Wall in China while Valerie played backgammon with the Chinese; or visiting the purported prison near the Acropolis in Athens where Socrates drank the hemlock. One of the letters reminded me that I took a short siesta on Marcos's bed in Manila. I stood long and pondered in one of the caves where the Peking Man fossils were discovered, rode a hot air balloon at 4 o'clock in the morning during the international balloon races in Santa Fe, New Mexico. I put a flower on Omar Khayyam's grave near Teheran during the 2,500th anniversary party given by the Shah of Iran. I wrote a poem sitting on the site of the foundation of Plato's Academy in Athens (excavated by my eccentric uncle Pan Aristophron). I swam the Hellespont, even though my crewman, Nana Karopame, would not go in the dirty Turkish water. I played poker in a Cairo hospital with King Farouk in 1943. I saw the Duke and Duchess of Windsor walk out of El Morocco in New York because Angelo, the maitre d', could not immediately give them the head table. I drafted a book review of Samuel Pepys's diaries for the *Chicago Sun-Times*, writing on a desk used by Pepys in the Pepys Library in Cambridge University. One of the letters reminded me of the time the writer and I visited the Sphinx Club, the most notorious whorehouse in Paris, in 1937. I heard Hitler speak in Berlin in 1936, and although I didn't understand a word of German I was moved to the point of saluting him myself. After a bull fight in Madrid, the matador offered the ear of the bull he had killed to a lovely senorita sitting next to me, but the ear fell first in my lap. One of the letters reminded me that Telly Savalas, his brother George, and I spent an evening in the Polo Lounge with California's Miss Teenager, and a little after midnight her father, wearing a sweatshirt, came and got her, swearing at us for keeping his daughter out so late. There were a dozen other letters reminding me of things long forgotten, including a smiling picture of Phyllis Diller and me.

And there were several short speeches given at the party, including remarks by my friends Art Nielsen, Dorsey Connors, Don Dadas, and Paul Allen, the minister of my church. He spoke beautifully about me, telling our guests that I had brought a fresh and liberal spirit to the church, which he welcomed in our staid Winnetka.

As I'm going over the letters and gifts, I see an

offer of two first-class round-trip tickets to any destination Midway flies. Unfortunately, as of this writing, Midway Airlines may not be flying anywhere—but what a thoughtful and generous present.

Telegrams and messages came from friends in many parts of the world including Greece, Australia, and England (from my classmate at Oxford, now Lord Keith Joseph). I see telegrams from Loraine and Chuck Percy, King Constantine of Greece, Jay Rockefeller, President Bush, Disney Studios, and my friends Ian Vorres and Niki Goulandris in Athens. Maria Pappas gave me a hundred bookmarks her mother had made from West Virginia flowers.

I was especially happy to share this occasion with my cousins from Texas, the Tom Stenis family and Vaughan and Arista Stenis, who just celebrated her own 92nd birthday. George and Jean Biggs (George is the son of my original patrons back in Montclair, N.J.) also came from Texas, and brought with them music in cassette form and sheet music arranged and composed by George.

One of my favorite poems, "What Is Success" by Ralph Waldo Emerson, was given to me beautifully framed. I want to make the poem part of this book because it so strongly reflects some of my own philosophy of life. Here it is:

> *To Laugh Often and Much*
> *To Win the Respect of Intelligent People*
> *And the Affection of Children*
> *To Earn the Appreciation of Honest Critics*
> *And Endure the Betrayal of False Friends*
> *To Appreciate Beauty*
> *To find the Best in Others*
> *To Leave the World a Bit Better Whether*
> *By a Healthy Child, a Garden Patch*

Or a Redeemed Social Condition
To Know Even One Life Has Breathed
Easier Because You Have Lived
This Is to Have Succeeded.

Finally, one of the mementos given to me was in the form of a long, colorful report on some of the important happenings in the world on the day I was born. (Incidentally, according to this report I was born during what the Chinese consider the year of the pig, and people born under this sign are "endearing and gallant, gentle, yet strong of will. They are the vanguard of purity and good." The paragraph continues: "Nothing is too much to ask of a pig," and this makes me laugh.) But here are some of the important events that took place on March 25, 1911:

Roald Amundsen, Norwegian Explorer, is first to reach the South Pole . . . President William Howard Taft congratulates him . . . Heavyweight champion of the world is Jack Johnson . . . World Series Phil. A's over N.Y. Giants . . . Tunes of the times include "Alexander's Ragtime Band," "Oh, You Beautiful Doll," "The Whiffenpoof Song," and "Little Grey House in the West" . . . the Chevrolet Motor Company founded . . . First coast-to-coast plane flight finished—took 45 days . . . First Indianapolis 500 auto race . . . 10,000 troops sent to the Mexican border as revolt spreads . . . books in March 1911 include *Ethan Frome* by Wharton and *Mother Carey's Chicken* by Wiggin . . . Population in the U.S.A. 93,803,000 (now it is 252,502,000) . . . the average annual income $521 (now it's $34,213) . . . a dozen eggs cost 32 cents (as against over a dollar today) . . . a one pound loaf of bread costs 5 cents (over a dollar today). People who share my birthday include James Lovell, Jr., astronaut, and

Elton John, singer, and people my own age include Mitch Miller, Claire Trevor, Ronald Reagan, and lovely Ginger Rogers.

At the end of the party, Don Dadas surprised me by giving me the Eclecteon Fine Arts Society's 1991 award for distinguished contributions to the literary arts. It was beautifully presented in a silver frame given by Nina and Rouben Terzian of Cristofle.

How could I not have had a wonderful time on my birthday with such friends and family, such imaginative gifts, and the wealth of information and reminders that were given to me? I'm sure the reader will understand my enthusiasm in sharing these gifts with them.

Well, I mentioned that my friend George Kapotas gave me a poem talking about being a young man of eighty, and I still feel like a young man. I find it very boring to listen to some of my contemporaries—most younger than I—tell how they fell in the shower, stumbled going up the stairs, tripped on a curb, or slipped on the pavement. It's not that I'm unsympathetic—rather my friends sometimes just seem almost boastful describing their accidents or to be calling a little attention to themselves: "Hey, age has finally caught up with me, but I'll make it."

Well, I don't feel old, either physically or mentally, and I can't take pride or credit for something inevitable. Sometimes my loving children treat me as if I'm over the hill, but for the most part I'm told that I don't look my age, and my doctor reports that I have the cholesterol level of an eighteen year old. And when I'm with younger people, especially my ten-year-old granddaughter, I feel and act very young indeed!

I say all this as a little preface to a confession. Yes, it also just happened to me. I've had my first fall—but I haven't told anyone about it, not even my poker-playing buddies, who would commiserate with me. Perhaps I'm doing something a little worse. I'm writing about it.

It was my first stumble as a senior citizen, and it was really a lulu! Of all places it happened on LaSalle Street, where for over twenty-five years I've walked and worked without stumbling (at least physically stumbling). It was during lunch hour, when all the bankers and traders and secretaries are out on the street. It was not raining or snowing, and I don't know how I stumbled. I was wearing a new pair of shoes. Maybe that had something to do with it, but I believe it was because I was dreaming a bit of days when I worked on the street as an investment banker, and I fell right in front of the Board of Trade, where I had my first office. It was in the middle of the sidewalk. Nobody pushed me, I didn't dodge anybody or make a quick move. I just fell, one foot stumbling over another. I fell on my knee, cut my trousers, and also hurt my elbow. But no one seemed to mind or notice, and I was glad for that. A young girl picked up my glasses, said, "These must be yours," and went on her way. And I got up, feeling a bit sheepish, and went on my way, too. So I have had my first fall.

I've come pretty much up to the present in these memoirs, and now I'd like to end my remembering by looking at two tiny incidents in the past, neither particularly important, but both important to me because they involved the two great loves of my life.

I cannot imagine any man writing an honest autobiography without discussing the subject of the women in his life, and "women in his life" should not necessarily imply that they were anything more than good friends.

I do not hold with the popular belief that it is impossible for a man and woman to be friends without having slept with each other or, if married, violated any of the marriage vows. I've always enjoyed the company of women and of the scores I've known over some sixty years, I can't recall (with perhaps two exceptions) the name of a woman I've hurt or regretted knowing or who has, to my knowledge, regretted knowing me. Nor have I ever tried to hide my friendships or meet in secret, out-of-the-way places.

I must confess that overall I've always preferred the company of women to that of men. The only exception is when I play poker—I do not enjoy women in a poker game. I've always found women to be more sensitive, stimulating, understanding, and enjoyable as friends than men. And is there anything in the world more beautiful than a beautiful woman? I think not. But beauty in a woman is sometimes the least of her attractiveness. For example, I don't care how beautiful a prostitute is. Prostitutes turn me off. Even during wartime, I could not be with a hooker. Someone, I think it was Henry Kissinger, said that power in a man is the greatest aphrodisiac to a woman. For me, goodness in a woman makes the greatest aphrodisiac. A good and kind woman, no matter what her age or looks or nationality, can always attract me. Is this strange or abnormal? Am I exaggerating? I hope not.

I must admit at times I have been shocked at the advances made by some women, and although I am attentive and even a bit of a flirt, I do not believe in casual sex. As Valerie puts it, "You talk to a telephone operator you've never seen like you're in love with her, and you're so charming, women think you're mad about them."

In the preface to these remembrances, I mentioned that my publisher asked me to tell the whole truth. I do not intend to say more about this subject nor do I think it is necessary to remember all the women in my life in whom I have been interested or who have been kind, good, and, in their own ways, beautiful. Rather, I shall end with two vignettes about two of the most beautiful I have known.

On Valerie's birthday, December 12, I took her to the Ocean Club on Paradise Island in Nassau, my favorite vacation place in the world. I first became acquainted with the Bahamas and the Ocean Club when I was active as a financial consultant to Huntington Hartford. Valerie and I flew from Miami to the Ocean Club on the airline Merv Griffin bought when he took over the Paradise Island Resorts, and, as we disembarked at the airport, there were six or seven Bahamian service and maintenance crew at the airplane. One of the older members of the crew saw Valerie as she got off the plane. His greeting (exclamation really) was: "Lady, where was you when I was young?" Some of the other crew whistled, and Valerie just smiled and waved. And that set the tone and theme of our joyous stay at the Ocean Club celebrating her birthday.

At the same time I could not help remembering a much earlier time when I was at the Ocean Club with Beatrice, and we were playing tennis. As we finished the game, a man from the adjoining court came over to Beatrice and said: "I have to tell you, I have never seen a more beautiful woman in the world." The man turned out to be John Forsythe, the actor. I believe Beatrice said a formal "Thank you," and kept on playing without missing a stroke!

How lucky I am to have been blessed in my life with two such wonderful women.

In the Offing

This ends my remembrances. Here are a few of my projects and plans for the future:

Even before I wrote *Miss 4th of July, Goodbye*, and saw it transformed into a Disney movie, I wanted to make a feature film on the life and adventures of Heinrich Schliemann, the highly successful German entrepreneur who against all advice from professional archaeologists, located and excavated the ancient city of Troy and took possession of its fabulous gold treasures. A screen treatment by John Jopson, based on Lynn and Gray Poole's book on Schliemann, *One Passion: Two Loves*, which I had written some years ago in Greece, has been submitted to Disney and other producers for a movie tentatively budgeted at $25,000,000. We are trying to sell the project on the basis that this could be an adventure movie (with Harrison Ford, perhaps?) as exciting as successful as *Raiders of the Lost Ark*.

As of this writing the eminent anthropologist Mary Leakey and I are in the midst of planning an indepth series of safaris to Kenya and Tanzania. One of the purposes of the safaris is to help raise funds for the preservation of the rock drawings in Tanzania and Kenya that Mary and her late husband Louis discovered over the past decade. These rock drawings (written about and reproduced by Mary in her book *The Vanishing Art of Africa*), are estimated to be over 40,000 years old, much older than the famous cave drawings in France. Mary is in Kenya working out the details of the safaris and I along with Stephanie Kuna, head of the Preservation Trust in the United States, from this end are organizing and getting the participants for them. We are seeking monetary support for the preservation of the rock drawings and we are working with the United Nations, but we are limiting the guests on each of these safaris to just ten people. This will allow the staff, Mary and me time to give each participant individual attention and facilitate conversation and lectures not workable in larger groups.

Meanwhile, I have been working on a project dear to me over the years: getting Omar Khayyam's famous *Rubáiyát* translated into every language. Right now, we are preparing to translate it into Swahili, the language of over seventy million people. Other than the Bible and some of Shakespeare's plays, very little important literature has been translated into this language. The *Rubáiyát*, it seems to me, will be an excellent, enlightening and beautiful literary addition to the library of works in Swahili.

Frederic J. Glazer, the prominent Director of the Library Commission in Charleston, West Virginia, is one of the most creative, enterprising and able administrators I have ever met. With his excellent board of directors, he has made the Charleston Library and Cultural Center a much talked about model for libraries all over the world. Fred is always a pleasure to be with, and I must give him credit for helping to bring me and my work back to West Virginia. Every time we meet or talk over the phone, Fred has a new idea to enrich libraries and promote education throughout the States. But his interests also go far beyond West Virginia, to libraries all over the world.

The most recent project he introduced me to is the great UNESCO campaign to support Bibliotheca Alexandrina. This is the a project to revive the ancient Library of Alexandria which in its time (3 B.C.) was the largest and most noted library of the ancient world. Historians are not agreed on why it was intentionally destroyed by fire, but that blaze represented one of the great cultural tragedies of ancient times. And now, through UNESCO and with the cooperation of the Egyptian Government and some 40 other countries, more than $70 million has been pledged toward a goal of $160 million dollars to reconstruct this wonder of the Ancient World. Construction is scheduled to begin in late 1992, with a three year goal to finish the library.

On a personal note, one of the stories my father was fond of telling me when I was a boy in West Virginia was how Ptolemy the III built the library intending to have a copy of every book or manuscript in the world there. Ptolemy sent emissaries to every country to obtain such copies or the original works. One of these emissaries about whom my father talked with great pride, was named Xenopoulos, our family name in Greece. This particular Xenopoulos was also one of the three principal Greek advisers to Ptolemy and, according to my father, had great influence in literary and political affairs. I've never been able to find Xenopoulos in any history of the ancient library of Alexandria, and I suspect that my father, always the romanticist, might have just indulged in a bit of poetic license for my benefit and heritage. On the other hand, history tells us that Greeks, of course including Alexander, exerted much power in Egypt at the time, unfortunately they were unable to prevent the burning of the library, for which some historians blame Julius Caesar, who was dallying in Alexandria with Cleopatra at the time.

Ever since NASA put a man on the moon in 1969, I have wanted to experience going into outer space. Before the very tragic 1986 Challenger space disaster NASA invited some civilians to sign up for a trip to outer space. There was a $500 registration fee with no fixed date for departure! As I remember, Walter Cronkite was one of the first prominent civilians to sign up. I booked as well, and I am hoping that NASA will revive the project on one or more of its planned space flights. Why do I want to do this? I'm not sure. But it seems to me that the perspective one would get from seeing our earth from a distance would add enormously to our understanding of ourselves and our meaning in the universe.

I'm very much interested in a project regarding Greece and Roosevelt University in Chicago. Ted Gross, president of the university, recently invited me for lunch to discuss establishing a branch in Athens. I was pleased and surprised to learn from Mr. Gross that there are more Greek students at Roosevelt than students of any other foreign nationality and that the Greek government encourages students to do graduate work at Roosevelt. At the same time, we will be seeking financial help from the Onassis Foundation and other foundations in getting scholarships for these students and also in establishing an Onassis Chair of Art at Roosevelt. Incidentally, Greece is one of the countries contributing to the campaign to support Bibliotheca Alexandrina.

Finally, in the offing on a very personal note: I would like to marry lovely Valerie Valentine, a loyal friend and associate for many years and a good friend of my children, but she feels that marriage may change the beautiful romantic relationship which we have. However, one day she may change her mind and I'll be waiting.

Epilogue:

Great Grandfather George

My cousin, Mimi Iatropoulos, died recently in Athens and named me his sole heir and "executor of my manuscripts and ambitions." The only manuscripts that have been found among his modest possessions, however, are 180 pages of faded notes neatly sewn together written by my great grandfather George Xenopoulos, which he kept in an antique sandalwood box. The latest date on the notes is July 14, 1899, four months before he died. Outside of the box in large Greek letters is printed: "Private: Personal Notes and Observations: George Xenopoulos."

George Xenopoulos was my great grandfather on my father's side. I never met him, although I remember stories that my father, mother, and uncles used to tell about him. He became a family legend and hero.

When Great Grandfather George was born in 1811 in Kifissia, then a small village outside of Athens, Greece was still under the occupation of the Turks. At the age of nine, he took part in a raid with his father on a Turkish Treasury Office. There was some trouble, and young George distinguished himself by shooting a Turkish guard.

Greece's War of Independence began in 1821, and shortly after that George signed up as a cabin boy on a Greek freighter, the *Eleftheria*, and sailed around the world. He was gone two years and spent some time in Alexandria, Bangkok, Persepolis ("my favorite site"), Shanghai, San Francisco, New Orleans, London, and Naples. When he returned to Greece, his family had moved to Pella, the birthplace of Alexander the Great.

Young George attended the Gymnasium at Salonica, where he graduated with high honors. From then on, he was mostly self-educated. He acquired a reading knowledge of English and was proficient in French, Turkish, and German. Later he became a schoolmaster in Pella and eventually he was elected superintendent of schools for the district of Salonica, which was the second largest educational district in Greece.

At this time, the Greek educational system was in chaos. As superintendent of schools, George distinguished himself by working for the complete separation of the school system from the Greek Orthodox Church. He became known for his insistence on free, Socratic discussion in the classrooms, and since there was a great shortage of teachers, he helped introduce a monitorial system in which learning by rote was discouraged and pupils taught themselves and each other in the classrooms.

Meanwhile, his father decided it was time that George took a wife. Following the Greek custom, his father chose a bride for him, Olympia Trindafellidis, a sixteen-year-old girl from the island of Lemnos. He negotiated and approved a dowry from the bride's family: three hundred thousand drachmae and a large house in Salonica, facing the sea. The marriage contract also specified that all children should be raised according to "classic tradition." What that meant was not exactly clear, but two stories that may have some bearing on it stay in my mind. When my great grandfather was just seven days old, his father took him from his mother, much against her wishes, and left him overnight on a mountaintop to determine whether, Spartan-like, he was physically fit to live. Fortunately for young George, this happened in the middle of the summer when there was no danger of freezing to death. "But what about the wolves?" his mother cried. Anyway, I suspect that his father did sneak out to see George several times during the night and apparently he was not any worse off because of the ritual, for he lived to be nearly ninety years old and was always in excellent health.

The other story concerns George's eldest sister, Athena. (There were four children in the family: George, his younger brother, Alexander, and two sisters, Athena and Androniki). When Athena, at the age of fifteen, was given in marriage to a Greek general, Apostolos Melas, the usual dowry was arranged with the precondition that the bride be a virgin. After their wedding night, the sheet from their bed was placed in the window so that all passersby could also see that she was indeed a virgin.

Many Greek families of the time objected to this tradition, but, nevertheless, to make sure the requirement was met, they would take their daughter to a doctor before the wedding so that he could do what was necessary (and there is a way) to make the bride appear a virgin on her wedding night.

I don't know what, if anything, Great Grandfather George intended to do with these personal notes. It is quite possible he wrote them in preparation for an autobiography. But as you read the comments about himself, it is also easy to conclude that he was making some of the notes simply as a kind of self-analysis for his own satisfaction and trying to understand himself better. He tells us his favorite maxim was Socrates' "Know Thyself." I include them here for two reasons: they tell something about my ancestors and their life in Greece, and, more important, they describe a man who was much like me. Great Grandfather George's philosophy, ambitions, tastes, and motives—indeed, his whole life—speak strongly to me today, and these notes, transferred to a twentieth century context, could practically be my own.

The notes are written in clear and neat longhand in Katharevousa Greek, interspersed with expressions in German, French, and Turkish. A total of 82 different subjects are discussed in the 180 pages of manuscript. There are several references to Sigmund Freud, with whom he had studied and whom he very much admired. His library contained many of Freud's early lectures, papers, and books, dating to the publication of *Interpretation of Dreams* in 1900. There are also 12 small rough ink sketches of persons and places to illustrate the chapters "Recurrent Dreams," "Favorite Possessions," and "My First Dog." Only a few of the pages are dated; the earliest date shown is March 25, 1861.

Today some of the comments may appear eccentric and strange; others are modern in thought and phraseology, and a few are contradictory, but most reveal a unique, wise, and gentle man, who was not much of a product of his time or his ancestry. He lived in a century that was an important turning point in Greek history.

The fifteen chapters I've selected here are among my favorites. I think they help portray the kind of man Great Grandfather George was—or perhaps the kind of man he wanted to be. All the notes are translated and edited by my cousin, Mimi Iatropoulos. A few of the sentences, particularly under the categories "Turks, Women, and Sex," "Early Recollections," and "Fears," are in a kind of secret shorthand which have not been deciphered.

Note: A Codicil dated March 25, 1975, at the end of Mimi Iatropoulos' Will reads:

To Christopher G. Janus, My Beloved Cousin:

When and if you accept the responsibility of editing and publishing these private notes of our great grandfather for our family, you are instructed to take before March 25, 1990, the finished manuscript to the main office of the Union Bank of Switzerland, Zurich— and present it to any one of the officers in the Trust Department with this number (deleted here for obvious reasons) and with these identifying words:

"I have come for the Turkish Surprise."

George Xenopoulos
Personal Notes 1811-1899

PHYSICAL
Tall, slender, olive skin, long fingers. Thin wrists. Long, straight nose. Feet like the Charioteer's. Brown eyes, weak left eye. I have a long mustache and thick eyebrows. Strong brow. Full hair, grey, cut short. Good, strong voice; good teeth, excellent health. (My mother told me that when I was 7 days old, my father left me overnight on a mountain-top to test my stamina).

MY FEARS
Harsh words from anybody, even a child.

Threats. Dogs. Turks. Owing money. Tax collectors. Legal actions. Noise in the dark. Sound of bullets. Fighting. Fear of floods. Though I consider myself a brave man and have proven it in battle, I am always conscious of what must be a yellow streak in my genes. I am brave only because I will myself to be brave.

OBSERVATION

As a young boy walking on Hymettus, I was attacked by an alien, large dog. My father said it was a wolf. Ever since then, the sight of a strange dog sends chills through me. But I have found something very interesting: if I have a walking stick with me, I am never afraid of a dog—or any animal.

I have a theory, and perhaps this Professor Freud will help prove that there is a "stick" for every fear—and one day we will discover what these "sticks" are and free ourselves of fears.

MT STRENGTHS

Unconditional loyalty to my friends and country. Can think abstractly. (Plato says that is the first mark of an educated man.) Would give my life for a cause or for a friend. Good sense of humor, and never take myself too seriously. A leader among my peers. I have enthusiasm for life and am determined to stay active and always go forward regardless of obstacles.

MY WEAKNESSES

I frequently lie to be kind. Find it difficult to say no. Have a bad sense of direction. (I can get lost a short distance from my village.) Cannot read or play music. Am easily imposed upon. Can't teach grammar or chemistry. At times, very impulsive, very impatient.

THINGS I DON'T LIKE TO DO

Kiss my godfather's ring. Kiss the Archbishop's ring. Genuflect or cross myself in church.

Wait in line for anything; fill out registration forms. Watch my parents quarrel. Leave my house in the morning. Make noise in the W. C. that can be heard outside, or be in the W. C. with anybody else. Lock doors or carry keys. Carry bags or packages. Carry money.
MY SPIRITUAL BELIEFS
Do not believe that there is an after-life. Not afraid of God or death. Don't want to be rewarded for doing good. Though I believe in a greater power beyond us, I don't believe that God knows every sparrow that falters. Love is the theme and inspiration of what religion I am capable of. I believe what the elder Pliny said: "Man helping man is God."
RECURRENT DREAMS
I am clinging to an angel which has only one wing; I am falling from an olive tree. I am drowning in the sea. A sabre is run through my dog. My hair is full of honey. I want to run but I can't. There's a terrible fire in the forest.
BOYHOOD DREAMS
I am Patroon on an island with 1,000 acres and I have many slaves; they are free to go. I am a philosopher like Socrates. I win the Charioteer Race at Olympia. I build a world university on the ancient foundations of Plato's Academy. I am a good orator. I am a leader of the underground against the Turks and return to Athens as a hero, showered with flowers in the parade. I am a Prime Minister of Greece and Turkey. (We have conquered Turkey.) My great wealth is in gold coins.
EARLY RECOLLECTIONS
My father was a leader of the underground fighting the Turks. When he would disobey the curfew at night to go to a meeting or on a special dynamiting mission, we never knew if he would return. One night when I was 9 years old, he took

me with him. I carried sticks of dynamite hidden under my pants legs. We blew up a local Turkish payroll office. There was trouble but it was a successful mission. I had to shoot a Turkish guard when he stopped my father on our way home to search him. After that I was a "Palikari" and became a regular member of the underground.

As a boy I was always too shy to kiss or embrace my mother. My father embarrassed me by talking about sex and making lewd gestures and laughing. He tried to make me smoke cigars. "Be a man," he would say. One night the village bully, together with some of my school friends, tried to force me to bugger a sheep; I didn't like it.

MY FIRST DOG

What I liked best about the stories my father used to tell me of the wanderings of Ulysses was the scene of his return home to Ithaca after an absence of nearly 20 years. His wife, Penelope, had warded off all suitors and temptations and was faithfully waiting for her husband. At this point in the story, my father would always add: "And that is the way it should be."

More interesting and impressive to my young mind, however, was the devotion and loyalty of his dog, Argos. Tears would come to my eyes when my father told about Argos.

"Yes, he waited and waited and waited, and he grew very old and weak, but he was determined to live until the return of his master. It was faithful Argos who first recognized Ulysses and came to him. He licked his master's hand, looked up lovingly at him, whimpered a bit and then laid down to a long and forever sleep." Not exactly Homer, but I always loved my father's version of the story. Then here again he would add his little lecture. "There is no greater virtue for man or beast than loyalty. If you have to be known for only one good quality, then let it be loyalty." The story, despite the homily, had only one immediate effect on me: I wanted my own dog!

Greeks are not known for their love or care of pets. Aside from the sheepdogs which are bred for commercial purposes, none of my friends have dogs for pets. One woman down the road has a beautiful Abyssinian cat with specked eyes that looks just like cats in ancient Egyptian drawings. But I believe she keeps her cat for conversational purposes rather than for any friendship the animal brings her.

There is also a former colleague on the Salonica school committee who has two monkeys for pets. He has trained them to do many tricks; they turn somersaults! One swings the other like an acrobat in the circus; he has taught them to pick olives from his orchard; they scream and alert him when visitors approach; they bring his slippers in the evening in exchange for a fig or banana. But I cannot imagine monkeys, however clever, as loving pets. Furthermore, they do not keep themselves clean like a dog.

One day just before my 8th namesday, my father gave me the greatest surprise and the best present I've ever received. He presented me with a six-week-old Mastiff puppy. The moment I picked him up, he licked my face and I kissed him back. But before my father gave me the puppy, I had to hear the conditions and the lecture: First, the puppy must be my complete responsibility. I was to feed him (soon he ate as much as I did), walk him, train him to obey. He was my dog; he was devoted to me alone and I was responsible for him. Then came the lecture: I was always to remember this was a noble dog from a most ancient, royal breed. The Emperor Caesar himself had 12 great mastiffs for protection and he also used them on

Great Grandfather George

his lion hunts. If I treated and raised my puppy properly, he would become my friend and be loyal to me forever and without any exceptions. My father stressed that the "without any exceptions" part of the oath was the only kind of loyalty that mattered. Anything less would not be loyalty in the noble Greek sense. My father ended his little sermon by saying he hoped I would always have that Greek sense of loyalty inside me—for my family, my country, and for certain friends and comrades.

I once tried to pass on this concept of loyalty to my only son, Christos, but he is really of another generation—a generation that thinks only of the new world, especially America. "Of course, Papa," said my son, "I will always be loyal to you—so long as you are right." I felt sad, first because I failed to make him understand what I was really talking about, and, second— even if he knew my meaning, I believe his answer would, in the new world philosophy, still be the same: "So long as you are right."

Inside of a year, my puppy, whom I named Ulysses, grew to be a beautiful and noble dog—the most talked-about animal in the community. He was almost as high as a young lion and weighed over 125 pounds. He was very gentle, seldom barked, but scared many people because of his size. He was my constant companion, walked to school with me, returned home on his own, and then instinctively knew what time to come back to get me when school was out. And he helped me make friends because many people who would ordinarily not greet me would stop and ask me about my rare dog and, after some hesitation, ask to pet him.

Unfortunately, we soon had to part. After the raid on the Turkish Treasury and the shooting of

the guard, there were reprisals. None of us who took part in the raid were ever identified, but the local Pasha personally ordered that Ulysses be taken from us and be used as a watchdog in the Turkish barracks. The Turks would not allow me to see him. Out of cruel treatment, or perhaps loneliness, or, I prefer to think, loyalty, Ulysses died within a month after we were separated.
PERSONS

Lord Byron, whom I met briefly as a boy before the Siege of Missolonghi, has remained my favorite poet and hero for all the Greeks. I heard the German, Heinrich Schliemann, speak to a small gathering of businessmen and professors from the Academy about his excavations at Troy. (He never removed his top hat during the meeting.) I am fascinated by this man's exploits in archaeology and schemes in business. It is said he mastered Greek in less than 6 weeks and could recite whole pages from Homer. He married Sophie Kastromenas, a local girl of 15, poor but from a good family, whom our Archbishop of Athens picked for him. Part of the marriage agreement was that she recite perfectly a page from Homer.

My favorite reading at present are Freud's papers, and I am glad to be able to read them in German. Freud is an original and most remarkable young genius. He is opening up for us the mysteries of the subconscious. This is fascinating, but it can be dangerous.
PLACES

Of all the places I have visited in the world outside of Athens, I believe I like the beauty of Persepolis best; and, of course, I associate our own great Alexander with it. Is it possible a 30-year-old warrior conquered the world? Yes, if he is Greek! Other places I visited include Alexandria, Shanghai, Bangkok, San Francisco, New Orleans, London, and Naples. But I prefer my own dear Athens. How bright and pure is the light. There is one place near Oxford, however, that I visited when I went to London, which stunned me with its beauty and order, Blenheim Castle. The English may not know how to cook, but they do build beautiful castles and, like the Germans, breed many monarchs.

BOOKS

My favorite books, which I always keep at my bedside, don't vary: *Plato's Early Dialogues*; *The Book of Job*; *Ecclesiastes*; *Plutarch's Lives*; *Rubáiyát* of Omar Khayyam, which as a boy I knew by heart; and a great favorite of mine, *The Diary of Samuel Pepys*, a most unique and valuable writing. His first-hand account of the great fire of London in 1666 is a classic. I was fascinated that Pepys, to keep his diary secret, wrote in his own special shorthand. Lord Byron's poems are also with me, and there is a volume of Turkish erotica: short stories which are delightful, exciting, and beyond anything, I am sorry to say, that any Greek or even French writer has done on the subject.

FOOD

I take great pleasure in food and have tasted dishes all over the world. The best, most original food I have ever had was in Bangkok. (And I must also say that Bangkok has the most graceful and lovely women I've ever met.) But here in Greece, I love our yogurt made from goat's milk, honey from Hymettus, figs from Turkey, and our own lamb; sweet fish from the sea and octopus, which cooked well is delicious! Occasionally, I have a rabbit stew. My favorite wine is Pallini, a white wine from Marathon. After dinner I have recently tried to become accustomed to smoking a hookah, a habit of my father's, but I really don't like it or any kind of smoking, and I can't forget that like belly dancers, which I abhor, the hookah is a Turkish custom.

MY MOTIVATIONS—MY MOTHER

I am so unlike any member of my family. My father, Alexander, had no intellectual ambitions. He was a down-to-earth survivor; no frills; no illusions. He did distinguish himself as a leader of the underground against the Turks. My brother and two sisters were content to remain what they were born into. My brother was a sheep farmer most of his life. My two sisters married early and were happy in being good and obedient wives, bearers of children.

So what made me what I am? My environment up to the age of 11 was the same as my family. Professor Freud from Vienna might say however, "But there was a difference, your mother."

According to my sisters, I was the indisputable favorite of my mother—and my mother didn't mind other members of the family knowing it. She believed that I, and I alone, was destined to be something special—and no doubt her belief in me gave me a confidence in myself which has supported me all my life.

What I remember most about my mother was her gentleness and her drive to do everything well. "Who can do the most, can do the least," she would say. She was immaculate in her appearance and she always smelled as if she had just bathed.

(The favorite recreation of the women in our village is the sulphur baths. The baths themselves are marble and are beautifully maintained. Here the women gather in the afternoon—three or four times a week. They bring with them fruit, wine, and cheese; they bathe, gossip, and relax in complete privacy and away from their husbands and children.)

Our house was orderly and clean. My mother's cooking was simple and tasty. I was always chosen to pick the most tender vine leaves from our orchard to make the dolmades. Her fasolata was delicious. We still make our own feta.

My mother always dressed me rather formally. Even in the summer, I seem to remember wearing a coat. I can't recall being without one. One day at school, my classmates pounced on me and took my coat off.

But what I remember most vividly about my mother was my shyness towards her. I seemed never to have kissed her, or she me. And she never disciplined me nor did my father. In many ways, this was beneficial to me since I had good motives and a strong sense of responsibility. Nevertheless, this lack of discipline from my parents gave me a feeling of insecurity. At times, I would pretend to my school friends that I was strictly forbidden to do such and such a thing so as to have my friends believe my parents were strict with me and really cared.

TURKS, WOMEN, AND SEX

The Turks occupied Greece for nearly 400 years. History will be the final judge, but I believe that during these 400 years (1421-1821) the Greeks influenced their Turkish conquerors far more than the Turks influenced us.

They did leave us their Turkish coffee, which I, and all the Greeks, drink, and the bazouki, and the belly dancers. Many Greeks, including myself, still wear the Fez, which I like.

But more important, they brought to many Greeks the philosophy that sex with a woman was just a function—a highly pleasurable one—but sex was not a symbol of something more meaningful and important. The Turks never succeeded in introducing the Harem into Greece because of the opposition of the Greek Orthodox Church, but they did contribute to further reducing the status of women to objects of pleasure, a necessity for children. I've never known a Turk, even in these days, to have a woman just as a friend on an equal basis, but we Greeks are careful of and value our friendships with women. I must note, however, that the philosophy of the Turks regarding women somehow never influenced me—much to the amusement and sometimes ridicule of my father and many of my friends. As a young man, and even much later in life, I was never able to indulge in sexual intercourse just as a matter of pleasure or relief—though I have to admit there are few greater pleasures.

I have never been to a brothel (though my father offered to take me to one on my 12th namesday) even when I was a seaman and had many opportunities when we put in at many of the great ports of the world.

I did, however, once visit a friend in Turkey whose father had a harem of more than 200 concubines. After dinner, I was offered, as a hospitable gesture, any of his concubines (except four of his special favorites) to spend the night. Two came to my room, bathed and massaged my body with oil and perfumes, but I just couldn't function. For their sake (because they would lose face) and my own privacy, we agreed that this would be our secret!

I have regarded intimacy with a woman one of the greatest experiences two people can have. It is kind of a mystical experience. I'm not sure that the women I've known share this view. It is quite possible I am only fooling myself in making sexual intercourse a symbol of something more than it is, or is intended to be. Women are much more matter-of-fact about sex except when they fall in love, then it becomes quite different and an all-engulfing matter.

Great Grandfather George

I don't wish to dwell more on this subject since I am now writing more from memory than recent experiences. Still I have to note:

I've rarely been able to enjoy sex with a woman I didn't know.

I've never quarreled with a woman and I don't have any enemies who are women.

I've never made love to a virgin, except my wife, nor have I ever wanted to.

I've never knowingly taken another man's wife nor made love to a friend's sister.

I do not believe that I have acted this way out of conscience, religion, or morals, but rather out of my own preference, style, and simple good manners.

MY POEM—MY AIMS

I have written only one poem in my life and that was on my 21st birthday. It is not a poem in the traditional style; it is more like lines wanting to become a poem. But the words reveal how I felt at 21—and I believe now at 88, I haven't changed much in these views:

Cynic's Choice

> *What is important—including the asking of the question? Being alive is important—or else the question itself is absurd. So you're alive—now what? So add purpose to the importance of being alive. Art alone is a good answer.*

> *Now what? So add freedom to do what you want. And then what? To Live with dignity. So what now? Do something creative: build a road, teach, make a fortune. So far, so good. You are alive—you have a purpose—you live in freedom with dignity—and you create something.*

Anything more? Yes, share with someone. More than that—love someone. Why? For no reason—just for itself. Maybe to feel God. Just to reach out. Is that enough? It's a start. Everything else is equally uncertain. At least do these things. Why?

ON PROLONGING LIFE

I like what the Russian scientist, the elder Mitchnikoff, wrote about living a long life. He said in effect that it is erroneous to consider old age as a physiological phenomenon. We should not accept old age as a normal phenomenon—just because everybody ages!

Aging is a disease—a disease for which one day a cure will be found—I hope it is soon.

It is too early to predict that it will be possible for man to live forever; it is not too early to affirm, however, that life as we know it now can be greatly, very greatly prolonged.

And, why shouldn't man live longer? So many other things in nature do: the turtle can live for 500 years; it is not unheard of for a swan, a crow, and a falcon to live more than 100 years. We are told that the olive tree of Plato, which I pass frequently on my way to bathe in the sea, is more than 2,000 years old. It is commonly asserted that the baobab (an African tree) lives to an age of five to six thousand years.

As a young seaman when I visited San Francisco, I was taken to a grove of Redwood trees, some of which are scientifically certified to be at least 2,000 years old. I brought back some seeds of the redwood which I still have. Some Americans, I'm told, eat these seeds.

Of course, none of these examples give us reason to consider any one of them potentially immortal. But a few thousand years is not too bad for the existence of a living organism even if it is just a plant.

It is possible that the secret of this longevity, when discovered by science, may prove useful in the studies for the prolongation of human life.

Meanwhile, my friend and neighbor, our own Dr. Papanikalaou, stops by frequently for a game of tavli and expounds on his philosophy for living longer. He is a great believer in drinking at least a gallon of pure spring water everyday. He wants me to eat daily two dishes of yogurt made from goat's milk. Dr. Papanikalaou personally recently visited a village in the Georgian section of Russia where the average age of the inhabitants is 92! There are men and women in this village who work each day in the fields who are over 100 years old. An indispensable part of their diet is yogurt eaten with honey or mixed with figs. Dr. Papanikalaou and other scientists believe that yogurt may hold many of the secrets the body needs for extending its life span.

Dr. Papanikalaou emphasizes the importance of laughter in our daily lives. "Good belly laughter," he says. Also, optimism and thinking positively about life. We must remember that even as we are today, many men and women live to be over 100. We should live believing that we can do the same.

There is a document, I'm told, which verifies that a certain P. Kizarten in 1724 in Austria was 185 years old when he died. The founder of the Episcopacy of Glasgow, a G. Kentigerim, lived also to the age of 185. And there are some people of faith who believe that Methuselah was indeed 969 years old when the Lord took him. And Dr. Papanikalaou talks much about the deadly power of fears—real or imaginary. "Our stresses and fears can kill us even more quickly than some of our diseases."

Last night, Dr. Papanikalaou came over and was much annoyed with himself because he spent most of the day with older people. "Older people," he says, "should not keep each other company. You will bore yourself to death. The older you are, the younger your friends should be!" (I seem to be an exception since I am older than he is).

Other advice he gives as follows:

For Your Body: The best form of exercise is games. Swimming and soaking in salt water two or three times a week is an excellent way to condition yourself for a long life. My friends do not believe it, but last week I swam from a friend's boat in the Aegean. While I was swimming, a little dolphin swam alongside of me for several minutes, gently nudged me, and I could swear he tried to speak to me as he swam away.

For Your Mind: Keep active. Do something creative. Paint, sculpt, write a poem, work with your hands building something. Work in your garden. Care for a pet.

For Your Soul: Lose yourself in doing something good for someone else.

Finally, I place a great importance on sexual activity for older persons. (I wonder if the Professor Freud agrees!) I urge every man to have a young mistress to play with, or to "breathe with" once a week.

As I am nearing 90, perhaps this is wishful thinking on my part. But I do have a fervor for the idea and as it is now nearing Spring again, I will examine it further.

SOME FAVORITE POSSESSIONS

A small but beautiful marble head of Athena from the Cyclades. I will give it to the National Museum in Athens. (There is no record the gift was received.—CGJ, 1992)

An antique rosewood walking stick with an ivory head made in Paris and dated 1776.

A first edition of Fitzgerald's *Rubáiyát* of Omar Khayyam. (I paid only 2 shillings for it in London, but I would not part with this utterly beautiful work for 1,000 drachmae).

An antique silver drinking vessel from my colleagues in Salonica. Professor Mariotis tells me it is copied from a silver cup Alexander designed himself and always used when he drank water in Egypt. (Silver is supposed to purify water.) I drink water and wine from my silver cup everyday. I like the feel of the cup, and it is beautiful. Our water in Athens comes from Marathon and is clear and pure.

A Kokolareko (raw silk) jacket from Macedonia with gold buttons. I have worn it for 10 years and it gets softer and more comfortable with every wearing.

A hollow gold signet ring (it could be 5,000 years old) which Heinrich Schliemann is said to have found at Mycenae and gave as a bribe to the Mayor of Athens, who sold it to a local antique dealer.

A small, exquisitely made pistol with an ivory handle from Germany which my father always carried with him during meetings of the underground committee.

An Ikon from Mt. Athos, which belonged to my mother. On the back, she wrote the date of my birth and "To My Little Palikari." A gold Patek pocket watch with a long gold chain made in Geneva, with an ingenious alarm mechanism, left to me by my father.

An antique sandalwood box with a fine lock and brass hinges made in Venice, circa 1760, given to me by my generous and thoughtful wife on my 50th birthday. Here I keep my private papers and notes.

July 14, 1889

When last year, in accordance with the Codicil, I presented this manuscript to the Union Bank, as instructed, the official said "What Turkish surprise?"

I said, "I don't know."

The official then handed me a heavy, solid brass box, somewhat larger than an average shoe box, and said: "Well now you know!"

In the box were 158 English gold sovereigns, all dated before 1875, 212 Alexandria gold pieces, which, if authentic, were made around 323 B.C., and some 400 assorted Turkish gold coins.

Thank you, Mimi! Thank you Great Grandfather George!